TRANSIT CULTURE
AND
POSTCOLONIAL TRAUMA

Ukrainian Studies Series
Editor: Vitaly Chernetsky (University of Kansas)

OTHER TITLES IN THIS SERIES:

Ukrainian Sunrise
Stories of the Donetsk and Luhansk Regions from the Early 2000s
Kateryna Zarembo

The Tears and Smiles of Things: Stories, Sketches, Meditation
Andriy Sodomora
Translated by Roman Ivashkiv & Sabrina Jaszi

"In the Tight Triangle of the Night":
The Early Poetry of Yuriy Tarnawsky (1956–1971),
between Modernism and Postmodernism
Maria Grazia Bartolini
Translated by Stanley Luczkiw

Cosmopolitan Spaces in Odesa: A Case Study of an Urban Context
Edited by Mirja Lecke & Efraim Sicher

Dnipro: An Entangled History of a European City
Andrii Portnov

TRANSIT CULTURE AND POSTCOLONIAL TRAUMA

Tamara Hundorova

*Translated from the Ukrainian
by Tanya Savchynska*

Boston
2025

This book has been published with the support of the Translate Ukraine Program

UKRAINIAN ⁄⁄⁄⁄BOOK INSTITUTE

Library of Congress Control Number: 2025950743

Copyright © 2025, Academic Studies Press, English Translation

ISBN 9798897831166 (hardback)
ISBN 9798897831340 (paperback)
ISBN 9798897831173 (adobe pdf)
ISBN 9798897831180 (epub)

Literary Editing by Teresa Pearce
Editorial Assistance by Hlib Olhovsky
Cover design by Mari Kinovych
Book design by PHi Business Solutions

Published by Academic Studies Press
1007 Chestnut Street
Newton, MA, 02464, USA
press@academicstudiespress.com
www.academicstudiespress.com

Contents

Preface — vii

Chapter 1 Postcolonial Transit — 1
  Maidan: Revolution and Performance — 2
      Maidan as an Intellectual Challenge — 3
      Sociocultural Codes of the Maidan — 5
      Carnival and Revolution — 8
      Performance as Socialization — 12
      Maidan as a Cornucopia of Possibilities — 14
  "Internal Colonization" and Re-colonization — 18
      "Internal" and "External" Colonization — 21
      "Internal Orientalism" — 24
      The Symbolic Place of the Author: Who Is Writing? — 26

Chapter 2 Postcolonial *Ressentiment* — 31
  Ressentiment: Resentment and Colonial Resistance — 32
  Eastern European (Res)sentiment: *Biography and Geography* — 40
      The Ideal Geography — 41
      Europe as the "East-Central Part of the Body" — 43
      Galicia: A Collection of "Alternative History" — 45
      The Ideal Autobiography — 47
      Looking from the Center and the Periphery — 50

Chapter 3 Post-Memory and Transgenerational Trauma — 52
  The Return of History — 53
      Archive, Museum, and the Female Body:
      Metaphors of Memory — 58

Chapter 4 Post-Soviet Transit — 68
  Farewell to the USSR: Donbas Transit and the Last Soviet
      Generation — 69
      Voroshilovgrad Transit — 69
      Memory as a Palimpsest — 76
      Donbas and Global Migration — 83

Chapter 5 Biopolitics and The Post-Totalitarian Generation	90
The Phenomenon of the "Sick Body"	91
The Loser Phenomenon	104
The Symptom of Matricide	111
Chapter 6 After The Trauma: Chornobyl and Catastrophism	124
Chornobyl as a Catastrophe	125
The Nuclear Sublime	137
The Chornobyl Apocalyptic Discourse	140
The Chornobyl Witness: From Madman to Stalker and Archaeologist	143
Lina Kostenko: "Ukrainian Madman"	146
Markiyan Kamysh: "Stalker"	156
Chornobyldorf: "Archeologist"	159
Chapter 7 Verka Serduchka: Kitsch Therapy in Transit	164
Serduchka as a Doll	169
Serduchka as Lady Surzhyk	172
Instead of an Epilogue	178
From Inside the Transit	178
Bibliography	182

Preface

I have been asked on numerous occasions to write a *Post-Maidan Library*, by analogy with my *Post-Chornobyl Library*. *Transit Culture*, which first came out in 2013, was in fact a continuation of *The Post-Chornobyl Library*. In the book, I analyzed the cultural and literary phenomena that unfolded in the early twenty-first century. At the time, the word "trauma" sounded somewhat abstract, but less than a year later, the Revolution of Dignity (later referred to as Euromaidan) began in 2014, and the concept of trauma became firmly embedded in our consciousness. In this new edition of the book, I continue to archive our post-totalitarian cultural experience.

Certain periods of modern history gain significance only in the light of the events that bring them to a close. These events, like a magic lamp, shed light on the previous era. Such was the Maidan protest of 2014, which marked the beginning of Ukraine's most recent history and ended its post-Soviet era. It also laid bare past historical traumas and narratives. The Orange Revolution, or the first Maidan, of 2004 had marked the beginning of a re-evaluation and a "parting with yesterday." The period of the early twenty-first century, including the two Maidans - the two Ukrainian revolutions - is what I refer to as the transition leading to the demice of the post-Soviet memory. I am particularly interested in the phenomenon of *transit culture*. The defining feature of *transit culture* is that not only does it signify a historical era or period of time, while also being influenced by historical, social, and political realities: *transit culture* is a type of culture that manifests a situation of transition and change and programs a new consciousness that is oriented not toward the past, but toward the future. At the same time, the narratives that defined the past era are being rewritten, and the traumas of the past which permeate and deform the body of the present become more pronounced.

This, therefore, is a book about the situation of transition, about the rejection of and rupture with the post-totalitarian past. Centered around cultural consciousness at the beginning of the new millennium in Ukraine, this book explores three main issues: *postcolonial traumas*, which in the early twenty-first century manifest themselves in association with past empires and old historiographical narratives; *post-totalitarian consciousness*, which emerges in sociocultural ruptures, postcolonial resentment, and generational crises; and *generational post-memory*, which serves as a means of overcoming the fissures and traumas of sociocultural and family history. I analyze postcolonial narratives and the phenomenon of *ressentiment*, and I discuss the intergenerational trauma that hovers over the present like a shadow, and the phenomenon of post-memory that echoes in the magical realism of family sagas and dramatic tales. The Chornobyl catastrophe here becomes the backdrop for a meeting of the Sixtiers and the 1990s generation in a discussion about the right to bear witness, while the clown doll Verka Serduchka serves as a mediator between various poles of transit—Soviet past and post-Soviet future, center and periphery, "Sovok" and "showbiz."

The main agents in this book are memory, generations, and the body. It is in them that I believe the traumas of the past—both distant and recent—are most clearly manifested. I examine these in the course of my analysis of the major novels of the 2010s: Oksana Zabuzhko's *The Museum of Abandoned Secrets* (2009), Serhiy Zhadan's *Voroshilovgrad* (2010), and Lina Kostenko's *Diary of a Ukrainian Madman* (2010). All these works deal with a search for the pivotal moment in national history that connects the past and the present and unites different generations with mystical ties. The theme of the "last Soviet generation" assumes a special resonance as it fights for the right to its history and biography and roots itself in "home territory." I also explore the post-totalitarian phenomenon of the "sick body" and the "loser" as an archetype of the 2000s generation, which manifests important non-conformist ideas and represents postcolonial homelessness.

The symbolic space examined in the book is culture *between the two Maidans*. I see it as a convolution that projects a whole range of significant cultural concepts and ideas onto our mental map while also exposing past historical traumas. *Transit culture* is a phenomenon of the new millennium, a time when, as Marianne Hirsch has noted, the number of genocides and catastrophes is increasing at such a rate that the traditional historical archive is no longer able to contain and explain the "bodily, psychic, and affective impact of trauma and its aftermath," or "the ways in which one trauma can recall, or reactivate, the effects of another."[1] *Transit culture* is similar to *post-memory* in the sense that it does not conform to linear chronology or the logic of progression. It can also be called post-postmodern, since it reveals the construction of the new identities and testifies to a return to the grand narratives of family, nation, and responsibility. It allows us not to dwell on trauma, and it addresses the symptoms of trauma. Ultimately, this book is about talking through *trauma*.

---

[1] Marianne Hirsch, *The Generation of Postmemory: Writing and Visual Culture After the Holocaust* (New York: Columbia University Press, 2012), 2.

The transgenerational effect of trauma is that it is delayed, revealing itself after the event or situation that caused it; it recurs in the memory of subsequent generations and has a cumulative effect. The subject thus becomes an archive of loss, a site wherein the memory of the trauma is stored. Moreover, trauma continues to exist within the subject as *other*, influencing their self-perception, sense of their place in the world, and ethical and cultural values. As Jacques Derrida figuratively noted, "Not having been taken back inside the self, digested, assimilated as in all 'normal' mourning, *the dead object* remains like *a living dead*, abscessed in a specific spot in the ego. It has its place, just like a crypt in a cemetery or temple, surrounded by walls and all the rest. The dead object is *incorporated* in this crypt—the term 'incorporated' signaling precisely that one has failed to digest or assimilate it totally, so that it remains there, forming a pocket in the mourning body."² [italics mine—T. H.]

Traumatized consciousness, traumatized history, and traumatized bodies are, however, not only repositories of new ideas: they are also a threat. Traumatic events return through symptoms, reappearing in dreams, gestures, and stigmas. The traumatic past lingers transgressively in the present; vengeful, it haunts, captures and dominates the present. It takes a special kind of effort—an intentional "revision" of memory—to break away from this traumatic past and liberate the present. A defining feature of trauma is that its symptoms do not merely return from the past but are carried over into the future, so that the future becomes an already *lived-through past*. There are various ways to revive the present. *Transit culture*, as I understand it, is one of them.

2013, 2024

---

2   Jacques Derrida, *The Ears of the Other: Otobiography, Transference, Translation*, ed. Christie McDonald, trans. Peggy Kamuf (Lincoln: University of Nebraska Press, 1988), 57.

CHAPTER 1

Postcolonial Transit

Maidan: Revolution and Performance

The 2013–2014 Euromaidan protests in Ukraine were both a political and a sociocultural phenomenon, as is typical of major socially significant events. At the same time, they became a space of sociocultural performance, where new national, social, political, and gender relations were formed. Approaching and analyzing Euromaidan through the prism of performance theory does not diminish the political and ideological significance of the Ukrainian revolution.

Performance theory in no way reduces Euromaidan to aestheticization and play.[1] But opponents usually try to interpret its performative aspect one-sidedly, downplaying the political aspects of this phenomenon of civil protest that unfolded in the center of Kyiv and emphasizing its purely theatrical nature. One Russian blogger, who hides behind the nickname AK-47, resorted to a pejorative manipulation of these concepts to claim during the revolution that Maidan was a performance because the "Maidaniots," or rather the people masterminding them, were very concerned with the way Maidan looked and how the protesters behaved, all to impress their European sponsors and liberal audience ["libtards" in the original Russian—T. H.]."[2] The blogger claimed that Maidan had all the essential elements of performance: an audience (actually their handlers—the "sponsors" and "libtards"), a stage ("the time, place, and aesthetics of these ugly tents, tires, garbage . . . all the features were there"), and actors (Ukrainian politicians behaving "like People's Artists of Ukraine: dancers, musicians playing the bandura, spoken word artists . . . all in one package").[3]

Yes, there were many performances, art installations, and video projects during the Euromaidan protests, but their function was primarily sociocultural and political. For example, there was a performance on December 6, 2013 called

---

1   For the interdisciplinary reading of performance theory, see: Henry Bial and Sara Brady, eds., *The Performance Studies Reader*, 3rd ed. (London: Routledge, 2016); Caoimhe McAvinchey, ed., *Performance and Community: Commentary and Case Studies* (London: Bloomsbury Methuen Drama, 2014); Richard Schechner, *Performance Theory*, rev. and exp. ed. (New York: Routledge, 2003); Andrew Parker and Eve Kosofsky Sedgwick, eds., *Performativity and Performance* (New York: Routledge, 1995); Antonin Artaud, *Selected Writings*, ed. Susan Sontag (Berkeley: University of California Press, 1988); Victor W. Turner, *The Anthropology of Performance* (New York: PAJ Publications, 1986).
2   Ak47_416, "Maidan eto samyi bol'shoi performans za vsiu istoriiu ili byli bol'she?" [Is Maidan the largest performance in history or have there been bigger ones?], *Otvet.mail.ru*, 2014, https://otvet.mail.ru/question/165153241.
3   Ak47_416, "Maidan eto samyi bol'shoi performans."

"Bye-bye, Yanukovych," which its organizers defined as "an artistic manifesto of free Ukrainians." On January 19, 2014, there was another art protest, "Ukrainian Women Against a Vassal Future," in which women bombarded the Berkut riot police with children's toys. Theatrical performances accompanied the reimagining of classics that unfolded at the Maidan Square: the image of Taras Shevchenko, whose bicentennial was celebrated during those days, became especially popular during the revolution. The poet was "taken down from his pedestal," so to speak, and people talked to him, sang with him, hugged him, and took pictures with him. A new Ukrainian project, #Babylon'13, was born as a form of performative cinema during the revolutionary events: "D-moll (D minor) at Kyiv City Hall," "Shame," and "We Are Here." The project participants played the piano at Kyiv City Hall, sang for the soldiers manning the area, read poems by writers from the Executed Renaissance generation, and so on. An outdoor performance by an "extremist pianist" named Bohdan, who played the piano in the icy cold of January, also became famous.[4]

Euromaidan proved to be a fertile breeding ground not only for new political practices, but also new forms and genres of creativity. It was imbued with collective and individual theatricality and performativity. Since the late twentieth century, spectacularity has become an integral part of life, and particularly politics, culture, and sports. Theatricality and performance became a common thread running through the entire Maidan and tying it together, and from this perspective, this place and the sociocultural space it created were a product of the postmodern era and of the new mass practices aimed at the political, social, and cultural transformation of the world.

Maidan as an Intellectual Challenge

The Ukrainian revolution of 2013–2014 has many names. When the protest broke out in December 2013, Anton Shekhovtsov called it Euromaidan.[5] In 2014, Volodymyr Viatrovych described Euromaidan as an "anti-Soviet uprising,"[6]

---

4   M. Arker, "Ekstremist z Yevromaidanu dorvavsia do pianino" [Euromaidan extremist gets hold of piano], YouTube, January 26, 2014, https://www.youtube.com/watch?v=1JBjOe7B27k.
5   Anton Shekhovtsov, "Ukrainska revoliutsiia ye yevropeiskoiu i natsionalnoiu" [Ukrainian revolution is European and national], *Radio Svoboda*, accessed September 26, 2025, http://www.radiosvoboda.org/a/25203341.html.
6   Yaroslava Muzychenko, "Volodymyr Viatrovych: maidan stav antyradianskym povstanniam" [Volodymyr Viatrovych: Maidan became an anti-Soviet uprising], *Ukraina moloda*, April 2014, http://www.umoloda.kiev.ua/number/2445/222/86888/.

while Yaroslav Hrytsak considered it to be a "Revolution of Values."[7] Others said the Ukrainian uprising of 2013–2014 had given rise to a "Maidan of intellectual romantics"[8] and preferred the name "The Revolution of Dignity," which they believed most accurately defines the spirit of the events that unfolded at Kyiv's Maidan. This proliferation of names is an interesting phenomenon in itself which proves that Maidan became not only a major socio-political event, but also a synergistic phenomenon that prompted a powerful intellectual challenge and exposed the need for new sociocultural and geopolitical concepts and ideas.

Ideologically and symbolically, Maidan encapsulated democratic ideas and a true European spirit commensurate with the spirit of civil society. This was amplified by the post-Soviet and postcolonial contexts of the Ukrainian revolution and the somewhat revived and romanticized idea of national revolution. At the same time, Maidan gave rise to new geopolitical and cultural associations, while also spurring new syncretic forms of thinking. For Yuri Andrukhovych, for example, the real people on the Maidan resembled characters from classical literature, and because of these associations, Maidan turned into a Don Quixote-like masquerade in which hundreds of Ukrainians donned "colanders and pots" instead of helmets to express "their mocking and contemptuous disobedience" in such an "unwavering and indomitable manner."[9] It was a rebellious attempt to demonstrate dissatisfaction and contempt for any manifestations of totalitarianism.

What was even more interesting is that Maidan put forward new models of social practices. In retrospect, Maidan validated actionism and lent it a mass appeal. Ultimately, as Natalia Khoma has noted, over the past few decades, "political actionism has become firmly established as a form of social protest in Ukraine."[10] At the height of the human tragedy and mass killings on the Maidan, one philosopher argued that "Maidan offered the world its own innovations,"

---

7   Yaroslav Hrytsak, "Revoliutsiia tsinnostei" [Revolution of values], *Ukrainska pravda*, last modified November 7, 2014, http://life.pravda.com.ua/society/2014/11/7/183467/.
8   Svitlana Volnova, "Maidan sobral intelligentnykh romantikov" [Euromaidan gathered intelligent romantics], *Viva!*, last modified December 20, 2013, http://viva.ua/lifestar/news/24730-svetlana-voljnova-maydan-sobral-intelligentnih-romantikov.html.
9   Yurii Andrukhovych, "1984. 2014?" in *Yevromaidan. Khronika vidchuttiv* [Euromaidan. Chronicle of feelings] (Brusturiv: Dyskursus, 2014), 71.
10 Natalia Khoma, "Sotsializuiuchyi vplyv aktsionizmu: mystetsko-politychnyi syntez v proektsii modeliuvannia politychnoi povedinky" [Socializing influence of actionism: artistic-political synthesis in the projection of modeling political behavior], *Aktualni problemy polityky* [Current problems of politics], no. 53 (2014): 366–73. For a discussion of the actionism that unfolded in the 1960s and 1970s, see, for example: Peter Weibel, ed., *The Vienna Group: A Moment of Modernity 1954–1960: The Visual Works and Actions* (New York: Springer, 1997); Philip Auslander, "The Performativity of Performance Documentation," *PAJ: A Journal of*

which can be defined as "web confidentiality" (or trust) and "economic aspects of donation" (giving). He suggested that "the Maidan became a social network that unfolded in the topological space of confidential and trusting relationships, where geography played a minor role."[11]

Maidan became a harbinger of a *new social net-reality*, that is, a phenomenon of network reality created by a community resisting hierarchical corporate power. In other words, it is commensurate with network (nomadic) structures capable of fighting political regimes beyond geographical boundaries. Thus, Maidans as network communities can spring up anywhere. Their segments may be regional and professional communities, associations based on interest, or quasi-political structures akin to Narnia or the Vikings, their main hallmark being their opposition to hierarchical totalitarian power and ability to "stand up to the criminal-corporate system."

If we accept the thesis of a new society of network structures, Maidan did transform the social and geocultural ideas that existed at the time. Ukraine and Kyiv were no longer perceived as marginal backwaters on the edge of Europe—instead, they became outposts in the fight for European values. The philosopher and blogger Volodymyr Yermolenko defined the global framework of the performance taking place on the Maidan as follows: "Today, we need to think in terms of world history. Our stage today is not a minor European province. Our stage is an entire continent, the whole world."[12]

Sociocultural Codes of the Maidan

There is no doubt that politically, socially, and culturally, Euromaidan is associated with the most dramatic social changes of the early twenty-first century. In a sense, Maidan became an "institution" and a "form" of new consciousness. Exploring the Maidan culture, which had its own semiotic nature, necessitates dwelling on at least four codes of this event: Cossack, apocalyptic, carnival, and performative. These codes refer to the sociocultural signifiers that place

---

Performance and Art 28, no. 3 (2006): 1–10; Peter Weibel, ed., *The Vienna Group: A Moment of Modernity 1954–1960: The Visual Works and Actions* (New York: Springer, 1997).

11   Serhii Datsiuk, "Chto takoe Maidan?" [What is Maidan?], *Ukrainska pravda*, last modified February 20, 2014, http://blogs.pravda.com.ua/authors/datsuk/5305cb8896062.

12   Volodymyr Yermolenko, "Pro te, shcho nasha stsena—tsilyi svit" [About the fact that our stage is the whole world], *Krytyka*, last modified November 2013, http://krytyka.com/ua/community/blogs/pro-te-shcho-nasha-stsena-tsilyy-svit.

Maidan in historical and cultural contexts and enable us to perceive it as a meaningful text.

The Cossack code was one of the most powerful influences on Maidan. Appeals to the free spirit of the Cossacks and the revival of the Zaporizhzhia Republic became extremely popular in Maidan discourse. The presence of the Cossack myth as a nation-building force was explicitly declared in practice through building makeshift barricades, organizing battalions [*sotni*], and popularizing men's hairstyles featuring the characteristic Cossack *oseledets*, a long lock of hair on an otherwise closely shaven head. All these things revitalized Cossack imagery on the Maidan. The Cossack idea could be discerned on the Maidan not only at the level of external symbolic representation, but also at the level of receptive practices, particularly empathy. For instance, in the case of the "Cossack" Mykhailo Havryliuk, empathy and solidarity significantly reinforced the emotional associations generated by visual bodily strategies of representing Cossacks, such as in Ilya Repin's painting "Reply of the Zaporozhian Cossacks to Sultan Mehmed IV of the Ottoman Empire." The naked male body was perceived as the embodiment of vital (ancestral) Cossack strength. So when special forces soldiers humiliated Havryliuk by stripping him naked in the freezing cold and filming him, the activist's naked torso became perhaps the most striking embodiment of Cossack masculine physicality on the Maidan. The philosopher Taras Lyuty has highlighted the vitality of the Cossack myth at Maidan, noting that "figuratively speaking, the Zaporizhzhian Sich is one of those prototypes that manifested itself during Maidan with certain mythological attributes."[13]

Maidan was associated not only with the collapse of Viktor Yanukovych's regime, but also with the struggle between Good and Evil, the sacred sacrifice of the Heavenly Hundred who were killed during the Revolution of Dignity, and the emergence of a new Ukraine. The trauma of national memory is also present in the reception of Maidan. As Yaroslav Potapenko has noted, in Ukrainian public discourse, "it is quite common to perceive Maidan as a realm of triumph over fear, a topos of liberation from the paralyzing power of fear of a post-genocidal nation—to be punished for no reason and tortured in the most horrifying way."[14]

---

13 Maryna Dorosh, "Taras Liutyi: Yakshcho my ne osmyslymo radiansku epokhu, istoriia dali ne rukhatymetsia" [Taras Liutyi: If we do not comprehend the Soviet epoch, history will not move forward], Detektor media, last modified November 18, 2014, http://osvita.mediasapiens.ua/trends/1411978127/taras_lyutiy_yakscho_mi_ne_osmislimo_radyansku_epokhu_istoriya_dali_ne_rukhatimetsya.

14 Ya. Potapenko, "Spryiniattia Yevromaidanu v suchasnomu ukrainskomu informatsiinomu prostori" [Perception of Euromaidan in contemporary Ukrainian information space], *Visnyk*

At the same time, the eschatological myth plays an important role in the semiotics of Maidan, which has been transformed from a historical event into a cosmogonic spectacle. Independence Square in Kyiv is traditionally perceived as a sacred place. The Independence Monument symbolically marks this sacred space, while its historical and geographical centrality is reinforced by the Lach Gate and Kilometer Zero—the globe that indicates the distance to the capitals of the world and cities of Ukraine. Just as Kilometer Zero topographically marks the central location of the capital of Ukraine, so Maidan served as a kind of center of centers. As such, it has been endowed with a special nation-building symbolic meaning, and it has effectively become a temple where the fate of Ukraine is determined and glorified.

The eschatological codification of Euromaidan combined anxiety about the present and hope for the future, while also materializing Maidan in the form of a sacred body (sacrifice). For writers, the tragic events of the days of revolution evoked associations with liturgy. "It's almost like a Sunday service," Taras Prokhasko wrote. He went on to say: "Something is brewing during our revolution, this revolution so similar to a church service. The circumstances surrounding the revolution, the aspiration for a better Ukraine, all of this serves to bring out the lightness in people." For this revolution is "a war between good and evil," "a Sunday, a rare moment that encourages people to be decent."[15]

Associations with cordocentrism reinforced the sacred significance of the Maidan. Cordocentrism, where the "heart" is perceived as the spiritual center of human existence, is a philosophy close to the Ukrainian mentality that has been followed by many Ukrainian thinkers from Hryhorii Skovoroda to Pamfil Iurkevych. The well-known Ukrainian philosopher Dmytro Chyzhevsky considered it a defining characteristic of Ukrainian consciousness. The poet Ivan Tsyperdiuk associated the symbolic meaning of Maidan with an "invisible church" and "the beating heart of Ukraine." Maidan "is not just the place where the heart of Ukraine is beating. It is also where our great invisible church is, a temple where people go to pray and take communion, a temple they strive to preserve with all their might," he explained.[16] Tsyperdiuk also found an

---

Pereiaslavshchyny [Herald of Pereiaslav region], November 2015, http://visnik-press.com.ua/?p=44064.

15 Taras Prokhasko, "Oznaky zrilosti" [Signs of maturity], in *Yevromaidan. Khronika vidchuttiv* [Euromaidan. Chronicle of feelings] (Brusturiv: Dyskursus, 2014), 21.

16 Ivan Tsyperdiuk, "Vira" [Faith], in *Yevromaidan. Khronika vidchuttiv* [Euromaidan. Chronicle of feelings], by Taras Prokhasko, Ivan Tsyperdiuk, Yurii Andrukhovych, Serhii Zhadan, and Yurii Vynnychuk (Brusturiv: Dyskursus, 2014), 40.

interpretation of the eschatological plot of the spectacle known as "Maidan" within the pages of Holy Scripture. For it contains all the essential components of a biblical text which has traversed space and time and materialized in the spectacle on the Euromaidan, namely: the introduction (the promise of European integration), the course of events (the beating of students, numerous gatherings of hundreds of thousands of protesters), the continuation (clashes with the Berkut police, the construction of barricades, the takeover of Ukrainian House) and the climax on February 19, 2014, when almost a hundred protesters were shot dead, almost exactly a month after Epiphany and the first killings of protesters on the Maidan.[17]

Apart from the Zaporizhzhian Sich and the Apocalypse, the most powerful cultural associations that Maidan evoked were those of a carnival. There were at least two reasons for this: first, in the post-Soviet Ukraine of the 1990s, Carnival had become one of the most appropriate forms of self-awareness and sociocultural criticism, allowing for the ironic overthrow of and distancing from totalitarian symbols and socialist ideologemes; second, Maidan demonstrated that the use of modern information technologies such as the Internet, Facebook, blogs, stringer journalism, and street art—media benefitting from actionism, virtuality, and performance—are extremely effective during mass protests.[18] Carnival and performance were often intertwined on the Maidan, but there was a fundamental difference between them: carnival was primarily an aesthetic form, while performance became a new sociocultural practice during the Ukrainian Revolution of 2013–2014.

Carnival and Revolution

Many observers pointed out the carnival-like nature of Maidan. Hryhorii Nikonov, for example, noted that "up until Epiphany [January 19, 2014], the dominant sociopsychological and aesthetic feature of the protest in the center of Kyiv was its carnival-like nature," and it was only later that the carnival turned

---

17 Ivan Tsyperdiuk, "Kulminatsiia" [Culmination], in Prokhasko, Tsyperdiuk, Andrukhovych, Zhadan, and Vynnychuk, *Yevromaidan. Khronika vidchuttiv* [Euromaidan. Chronicle of feelings], 51.
18 For more on this topic, see: Liliia Tulupenko, "Maidan yak kultura protest" [Maidan as a culture of protest], *24 Kanal*, last modified February 25, 2014, https://24tv.ua/maydan_yak_kultura_protestu_n413494.

into a "theater of war."[19] Theatricality, playfulness, and spectacle were important attributes of Maidan. In a December 28, 2013 interview for Radio Liberty, however, Yuri Andrukhovych warned against turning Maidan into a carnival. Andrukhovych, himself an active creator and participant in the post-Soviet Bu-Ba-Bu carnival of the 1990s, recognized the difference between aesthetic play and political protest. In his novels *Recreations*, *The Moscoviad*, and *Perversion*, he had already shown that carnival can take many forms: it can be a fake, an organized political campaign, a military coup, or a pastiche replica from the past. He hinted that although actors and musicians can be cultural heroes, it is unlikely that they can carry the revolution on their shoulders. "In this regard, perhaps we shouldn't put so much hope in actors or musicians to save the situation there. They are all needed there, and they are all making an important contribution, but perhaps this is not the most important thing," Andrukhovych concluded.[20] And yet a performative nature, carnivalization, and theatricality became part of Maidan, even though the genre increasingly resembled an ancient tragedy. In this sense, the carnival nature of the 2014 Euromaidan was to an extent a replica of the 2004 Maidan, but at the same time, it went beyond it and even denied it.

The carnival nature of the 2014 Euromaidan allows us to trace the original sociography and geography of the phenomenon of the Ukrainian revolution of the early twenty-first century. The Maidan, as a closed space located in the center of Kyiv, and as a triangle formed by Independence Square, Hrushevskyi Street, and Instytutska Street, determined the location of the spectacle. It sometimes spilled out into the side streets, as in Andrukhovych's *Recreations*, but was still limited to the territory of Maidan. In his landmark novel, Andrukhovych symbolically defined the space of the characters' transformations through carnival, at the same time showing that this spectacle could be an imitation or ambivalent towards the authorities. In this context, one cannot overlook Renaissance carnival and the mocking popular culture that played a subversive role against the official and serious culture of the Middle Ages and became the basis for understanding the sociocultural function of carnival in history. Carnival itself is utopian in nature and always takes place in a limited space and within a limited period of time. Yet carnival in the social and cultural sense is an oppositional and

---

19   Hryhorii Nikonov, "Teatr boiovykh dii" [Theater of military operations], *Komentari: Cholovichi ihry* [Comments: Men's games] 3, no. 387 (2014), 41.
20   Aleksandra Tytorova, "Aktory i muzykanty, zvychaino, potribni Maidanu, ale tse ne naiholovnishe, vpevnenyi Andrukhovych" [Actors and musicians are certainly needed by Maidan, but that's not the most important thing, Andrukhovych is convinced], *Dzerkalo tyzhnia*, last modified December 28, 2013, https://dt.ua/UKRAINE/andruhovich-zasterig-maydan-vid-peretvorennya-na-karnaval-134809_.html.

subversive form of consciousness. Mikhail Bakhtin argued: "In times of great upheaval, reevaluation, and change, all our life in a certain sense takes on a carnival nature, the boundaries of the official world grow narrow, and this world loses its rigidity and certainty, while the boundaries of the square expand and its atmosphere permeates everything."[21]

Carnivalization became a hallmark of post-Soviet resistance,[22] later manifesting itself in the 2004 Maidan protests. Euromaidan, in turn, captured how the space and content of the carnival expanded during major socio-political upheavals. While Maidan was permeated from the start by the carnivalization of time and space, by carnival-like modes of communication and physicality, theatricalization, and a playful interpretation of everyday life, clothing, and leisure, it was not limited to "low," popular, humorous forms: it had more profound goals and ideas. What transformed the carnival belonged to the realm of actionism, or sociocultural performance, which stimulated the birth of both a new community (*maidanivtsi*, or people of the Maidan) and new identities (Maidan participants, volunteers, and supporters).

Let's try to look at Maidan as a social performance, thus going beyond the traditional aestheticized perception of carnival. Maidan undermined the boundaries of political, social, ethnic, generational, and gender relations during a period of crisis, giving rise to new forms of identity, often hybrid ones, in each of these areas. Maidan also emerged as a cornucopia of possibilities for choosing potential and reimagined identities. This phenomenon became one of the most important and defining markers of the development of the Ukrainian revolution.

From the very first days of the protest, carnivalization was a means of emotional and cultural bonding and the creation of the "body" of Maidan. Art, and not only political slogans, was instrumental in achieving this. During the revolution, one of the protesters noted in a tweet that Maidan was turning into a mini society, "where ancient traditions are brought to life with ultra-modern means. Maidan has everything: a chapel for prayer, kitchens, tents, student and community sectors, Wi-Fi points." In addition, Maidan emerges as a thoroughly creative space: the barricades look like artworks, and the famous Maidan Christmas tree is viewed as street art, revealing "the transformation of its meaning from a New Year's decoration—through a means of and an excuse for committing

---

21   Mikhail Bakhtin, "Dopolneniia i izmeneniia k 'Rable'" [Additions and changes to 'Rabelais'], *Voprosy filosofii*, no. 1 (1992), 154.
22   See, for example: Tamara Hundorova, *Pisliachornobylska biblioteka: Ukrainskyi literaturnyi postmodernizm. Rozvidka z komentariamy iz "kintsia postmodernu"* [Post-Chernobyl library: Ukrainian literary postmodernism. An exploration with commentary from "the end of postmodernism"] (Kyiv: Krytyka, 2013).

violence—to a symbol of the unity of people, flags from all corners of Ukraine, humor, and dignity."[23]

Decorated helmets and tires and exotic hybrid costumes highlighted the masquerade-like nature of social performance. This place of theatricality and carnival was transformed into an island of the improbable, revealing the cyclical nature of history, and becoming a hole in reality which the virtual broke through, although in fact real history was being made there. On the Maidan, the modern world, represented by devices, Wi-Fi, and TV, was confronted by the ancient Slavic *veche*; modernity (and postmodernity) turned out to be permeated by the Middle Ages and its attributes: catapults, shields, improvised masks, and helmets resembling those of knights. Ultimately, a Cossack Sich emerged in the center of present-day Kyiv, not staged, but almost real.

All of these codes—Cossack, apocalyptic, and carnival—were largely based on performativity. Maidan took on the form of a cultural event with all the elements of a theatrical performance, including a fixed stage, participants, and an audience. The tent encampments and barricades engulfed in flames became not just a battlefield and defensive structures, but also a popular tourist attraction: people came here to see everything with their own eyes, even on the day of fierce clashes on Hrushevsky Street. The touristification and commercialization of Maidan during the period of unrest were indicative of its belonging to the modern society of the spectacle, in which the most important thing is the "continuity of the spectacle."[24] The feeling of danger while photographing explosions and burning tires amplified the aesthetic pleasure of the tourist-spectators and gave them a sense of belonging to the Maidan community. Color also played an important emotional and conceptual role: just like during the Orange Revolution, it had a strategic purpose, since, as Abel Polese and Donnacha Ó Beacháin have noted, "a color, in many cases, has been a way to express dissent without speaking, has had a substantial visual impact, and has been a symbol that united the protesters, emotionally and politically."[25]

---

23 marisa_t, "Maidan yak performans" [Maidan as performance], *LiveJournal*, last modified December 17, 2013, https://marisa-t.livejournal.com/480580.html.

24 Guy Debord, *The Society of the Spectacle*, trans. Donald Nicholson-Smith (New York: Zone Books, 1995).

25 Abel Polese and Donnacha Ó Beacháin, "The Color Revolution Virus and Authoritarian Antidotes: Political Protest and Regime Counterattacks in Post-Communist Spaces," *Demokratizatsiya*, no. 2 (2011), 112.

Performance as Socialization

In general, all the forms of performance that unfolded on the Maidan and related to everyday life, clothing, physicality, time, and space were not an end in themselves, but functioned in the context of significant political, national, social, and linguistic transformations. Performance is an important sociocultural form and, as Natalia Khoma has noted, "a complex communicative action, where the roles of actors and spectators are equally important."[26] Khoma is primarily concerned with political performance, which mainly involves demonstrating political ideas in order to capture an audience's attention. But performance also has considerable sociocultural potential. On the Maidan, it was primarily a means of creating a *Maidan community*—a microcosm of the new Ukrainian society. Bakhtin has argued that carnival erases professional, religious, class, and family differences and barriers, giving way to a special form of familiar, intimate contact between people. The carnival community is like a universal cosmic body that exists in an eternal cycle of birth and death. At the same time, individual consciousness and particularity disappear in a mutual exchange between the top and the bottom, the spiritual and the down-to-earth.

Late twentieth-century postmodernism promoted the idea of the multiplicity of the individual self and different communities. In line with postmodern philosophy, the idea of a *multiple* (post-carnival) body was born, which is quite unlike the *collective* body of the traditional carnival. A postmodern emphasis in the cultural anthropology of Maidan enables us to clarify the ideology of carnivalized performance. Maidan became a catalyst and a place of change; in addition to uniting people of different social classes, ethnicities, races, religions, generations, professions, and genders into a single Maidan "body" (community), in addition to mixing geography—Ukrainian and global—it also grew out of new types of collective solidarity and network communities. This place and this space was accepting of people of different origins and professions, rich and poor, people from working-class and academic backgrounds, young and old, and representatives of different ethnic groups, who had come to Kyiv from big cities, small towns, and villages in Ukraine and from abroad. For them, Maidan became a common communicative space, one where individual aspirations, practices, experiences, and agency were not erased but continued to evolve and

---

26 Natalia M. Khoma, "Sotsializuiuchyi vplyv aktsionizmu: mystetsko-politychnyi syntez v proektsii modeliuvannia politychnoi povedinky" [Socializing influence of actionism: artistic-political synthesis in the projection of modeling political behavior], *Aktualni problemy polityky* [Current problems of politics], no. 53 (2014), 41.

be enriched, forming a new multifaceted community: dynamic, diverse, rhizomatic. Each brought their own world and experience, habits and behaviors to Maidan, but they were all united by a shared sense of duty, and human and national pride. They learned new models of social behavior, felt supported by each other, developed new perspectives, and became more urbanized.

A growing awareness of the value of civil society and democracy was an important consequence of Maidan. United by their protest against Yanukovych's corrupt regime and their sense of belonging to European civilization, Maidan participants embraced equality and pluralism as the ideal form of a new democratic Ukraine. At the same time, social hierarchies were being dismantled, the center and the periphery were being made equal, historical times were merging, and many different Ukraines were coming together in one Square. This self-awareness, role variability, and sense of connection became channels of communication for the protesters' growing agency in social, ethnic, and gender aspects.

Taras Prokhasko captured and recorded the ability of the community created by Maidan to unite all of Ukraine and go beyond the boundaries of the Square itself. In an ironic paraphrase of Taras Shevchenko, he wrote: "Everyone has the right to exist. Those who peacefully stand on the Maidan. And those who non-peacefully storm the positions held by the security forces. And the security forces, who do not like this at all, also have the right to exist. Some throw stones, and others defend themselves from them. Some do stuff there, in Kyiv, and others stay at home for now. To each their own . . . That is precisely what we are fighting for. [. . .] Some are thinking, some are staying quiet, some are fighting, others are providing food, and others are destined to become heroes . . . To each their own. [. . .] That is how we gain experience that we have never had before. This is how a connection between times is formed."[27]

In his blog, Prokhasko paid special attention to the diversity of the faces who were intellectually and aesthetically the opposites of those in Yanukovych's circle. He identified Maidan as an antizone where people from all walks of life gathered together and where the code of honesty and dignity was paramount: "Among these full-fledged people there are losers, morons, nerds, homeless people, homosexuals, paraplegics, cops, and four-eyes who refuse to live in a country ruled by thugs."[28] Similarly, Oleksandr Irvanets argued that despite the diverse nature of the Maidan community, the unique qualities and faces of individuals

---

27 Taras Prokhasko, "Kozhnomu svoie" [To each his own], in Prokhasko, Tsyperdiuk, Andrukhovych, Zhadan, and Vynnychuk, *Yevromaidan. Khronika vidchuttiv* [Euromaidan. Chronicle of feelings], 20-21.
28 Prokhasko, "Oznaky zrilosti" [Signs of maturity], 14.

created a unique collective portrait of the carnival—the Ukrainian revolution, in which they are the main actors: "Today's revolution has many faces... These are our faces! We are the main characters in this play."[29]

The performative strategy of Maidan challenged the notion of the homogeneity of Ukrainian society and its official authorities and encouraged people to go beyond purely binary oppositions such as "center/periphery," "us/them," "young/old." Maidan fostered the emergence of various network communities in the form of *sotnias* or "hundreds": there were art hundreds, medical hundreds, volunteer hundreds, female hundreds. Ultimately, the *Heavenly Hundred* became the embodiment of Maidan's spirit of sacrifice. In a sense, we can say that there were *many Maidans on the Maidan*, in terms of ideology, ethnicity, gender, generations, and geography. They reflected the diversity and multiplicity of Ukrainian society. There were many Maidans also in terms of the stages and phases of Maidan's development, beginning from December 2013 and up until February 2014.

Maidan as a Cornucopia of Possibilities

Maidan became a social and political phenomenon, where performance was a form of socialization and political education for citizens. Performative practice enabled new communication and also consolidated the emergence of new institutional forms: Maidan functioned as a theater, school, university, library, museum, hospital, and military headquarters. The performative nature of Maidan changed the carnival formula of the protest and turned it into a *cornucopia and factory of possibilities*. It expanded opportunities and broadened prospects for each and every participant, encouraging everyone to be creative and politically and socially active.

The theatricalization of the protest was what ensured this diversity: the right to speak out, to show initiative, to release creative energy. Suffice it to say that even people who had never written poetry in their lives took up rhyming and composing poems. On the Maidan, everyone sang, even if they had no singing voice, and everyone fought, even if they had no military experience. Students became fighters and cooks, retirees became barricade builders, and professors became waiters. In other words, Maidan turned out to be not only a platform for

---

29 Cited by: Oksana Zahakailo, "Poeziia i proza Yevromaidanu [Poetry and prose of Euromaidan]," *Dzerkalo tyzhnia*, last modified December 6, 2013, https://zn.ua/ukr/ART/poeziya-i-proza-yevromaydanu-_.html.

realizing the potential of each participant, but also a means of self-transformation. Maidan participants took on new social and cultural roles that were different from those they played in peacetime.

Kyiv's Maidan is a phenomenon of urban culture, and for Ukraine, where the rural population with its patriarchal laws constitutes a significant section of the population, assimilation into this urban space was particularly significant. People from big cities, in turn, acquired collective survival skills in conditions devoid of the usual amenities and, figuratively speaking, returned to a more natural lifestyle. This exchange of sociocultural practices accelerated the formation of the modern Ukrainian nation as a community of people who belong to their territory and live with a "sense of common good," as Serhiy Zhadan has pointed out. "And what is the common good?" he asked, before answering: "It's what enables us to stay together, what keeps us in our cities, within our borders. It's what gives us a sense of belonging to this territory."[30]

The postmodern era dictated new rules of communication and shaped new types of personalities. Given the fluidity of identities and cultural roles, theatricality, performance, and representation play a crucial role in this process. In the early twenty-first century, sociologists began to draw on the concept of performance, considering it one of the most significant social practices and ultimately associating it with the theory of society itself. The American sociologist Jeffrey Alexander proposed that social events be studied as performance, focusing specifically on the theatrical concept of performance. "Cultural performance is the social process by which actors, individually or in concert, display for others the meaning of their social situation," he explained.[31]

However, the general trend in performance theory is to take this category beyond the realm of theatricality and highlight the sociocultural significance of performance. According to Peter Snow, social phenomena become performances only when they activate the creative imagination and generate the ability to "imagine new possibilities," that is, "to imagine and enact those possibilities: in other words, to create them."[32] Creativity, or in other words, the ability to generate new forms of

---

30 Serhii Zhadan, "Pro spilne mizh riznymy Zakhodom ta Skhodom" [About what is common between the different West and East], in Prokhasko, Tsyperdiuk, Andrukhovych, Zhadan, and Vynnychuk, *Yevromaidan. Khronika vidchuttiv* [Euromaidan. Chronicle of feelings], 102.
31 Jeffrey C. Alexander, "Cultural Pragmatics: Social Performance between Ritual and Strategy," in *Social Performance: Symbolic Action, Cultural Pragmatics and Ritual*, ed. J. Alexander, B. Giesen, and J. Mast (London: Cambridge University Press, 2006), 32.
32 Stephen Slemon, "Unsettling the Empire: Resistance Theory for the Second World," in *The Postcolonial Studies Reader*, ed. Bill Ashcroft, Gareth Griffiths, and Helen Tiffin (London: Routledge, 1995), 83.

existence and alternative possibilities of self-expression, is one of the most compelling reasons to consider social phenomena as performances. Alexander argued that social performances "select among, reorganize, and make present themes that are implicit in the immediate surround of social life—though these are absent in a literal sense. Reconfiguring the signifieds of background signifiers, performances evoke a new set of more action-specific signifiers in turn."[33]

With regard to Maidan, it was the emergence of alternative possibilities and a "new set of more action-specific signifiers" that prompted action, helped reorganize the carnival, and became the creative force behind the new social, political, and cultural identities that emerged during the revolution. This understanding of the nature of Maidan helps us to better understand the formation of a new civil society that took place there. In other words, Maidan created an opportunity for change and brought to life a vision of a different reality, one that its participants sought to be part of. This reality was to constitute a solid foundation for understanding what a democratic society in Ukraine might look like. The social and political shifts immediately following Maidan demonstrated that the new skills and new intellectual horizons it unlocked in people would be further applied in their post-revolutionary activity.

With the benefit of hindsight, it has become clear that Maidan was indeed a heroic era, but at the same time, it raised the painful question of whether the Maidans were becoming a temporary form of government reconfiguration. Yet the social and cultural performance on the Maidan did give rise to new public initiatives and new cultural and aesthetic forms, such as #Babylon'13, the Maidan Library, the Maidan Museum, and many others. Maidan became part of the literary landscape and lent extra intensity to the debate about literary representation. Svetlana Alexievich, when browsing through *Chronicle of Eyewitnesses: Nine Months of Ukrainian Resistance (2014)*, a collection of social media posts, online publications, and speeches, noted that even a novel would be incapable of conveying that raw, unspoiled feeling that "has not been altered by time or literature" but is captured in the Maidan testimonies.[34]

Maidan also inspired the search for new revolutionary art symbolized, in particular, by the exhibition "Creativity of Freedom: the (R)evolutionary Culture of Maidan," which, incidentally, was held at the Ivan Honchar Museum, the

---

33 Jeffrey C. Alexander, "From the Depths of Despair: Performance, Counterperformance, and 'September 11,'" in Alexander, Giesen, and Mast, *Social Performance: Symbolic Action, Cultural Pragmatics and Ritual*, 94.
34 Svitlana Aleksiievych, "Vy rozghornete tsiu knyzhku i ne zmozhete zakryty . . ." [You will open this book and will not be able to close it . . .], in *Litopys samovydtsiv. Deviat misiatsiv ukrainskoho sprotyvu* [Chronicle of eyewitnesses. Nine months of Ukrainian resistance] (Kyiv: Komora, 2014), 3.

National Center of Folk Culture. Utilizing this interactive space, the exhibition demonstrated the scale and creativity of Maidan culture, presenting the personal stories of Maidan participants and items used by the protesters: flags and posters which had adorned the famous "yolka" Christmas tree during the revolution, Molotov cocktails, decorated helmets, and more. The performative element elevated post-Maidan art to a new technological level: visitors to the exhibition were invited to join in the performance by taking part in a virtual tour called "Maidan 3D," sharing their memories of the events on the "Stage of Stories," or recording their feelings and thoughts on a special wall called "Visitors' Voices."[35]

Euromaidan became a defining political and revolutionary event that highlighted the fundamental link between cultural and political practices. And, most importantly, it demonstrated that in the post-postmodern era, performance not only remains a timeless artistic phenomenon, but is also becoming a form of sociocultural practice that carries powerful creative and transformative possibilities.

---

35 "Interaktyvnyi vystavkovyi proekt 'TVORCHIST SVOBODY: (r)evoliutsiina kultura Maidanu'" [Interactive exhibition project 'CREATIVITY OF FREEDOM: (r)evolutionary culture of Maidan'], *Muzei Ivana Honchara*, accessed September 29, 2025, https://old.honchar.org.ua/events/interaktyvnyj-vystavkovyj-proekt-tvorchist-svobody-revolyutsijna-kultura-majdanu/.

"Internal Colonization" and Re-colonization

The concept of internal colonization as interpreted by Alexander Etkind gained significant traction in the 2000s and became one of the key concepts in post-Soviet discussions. Although the theory of "internal colonization" draws on the ideas of Western postcolonial studies, particularly Edward Said's *Orientalism*, it continues to be dominated by the position of the colonizer—that is, the one who forms and appropriates the positions of the imperial center. It is also worth looking at this theory from the position of the subjugated and colonized *other*, which creates yet another perspective from which to evaluate the Russian imperial experience. And the most contentious question here concerns the vectors of colonization itself, both internal and external.

The formation of the Russian Empire was a long and complex process. Paul Bushkovitch argues that even during the Petrine period, a transition was already taking place from the dynastic principle of self-determination to a state-based principle, and it was then that the concepts of the All-Russian Empire and the Great Russian Empire began to appear in diplomatic documents.[36] The assertion of imperial consciousness is closely linked to Russia's campaigns against the Turks and its conquests in the Caucasus. In general, the external colonization of various peoples (Bashkirs, Kalmyks, Don Cossacks, Ukrainians, Finns, Crimean Tatars) is inseparable from the Russian imperial project. Some regions of the Russian Empire, however, such as Turkestan or Siberia, resembled colonies more than others, such as Finland and the Baltic provinces.

Reflecting on textbook themes of Russian literature in "the comparative context of 19th-century colonial policy," Alexander Etkind, in his article "Russian Literature, 19th Century: The Novel of Internal Colonization," draws on the experience of Russia's imperial history: "Second only to the British Empire, Russian possessions stretched from Finland and Poland to Alaska and Manchuria, spanning the later boundaries of the USSR. The wars waged by Russia from 1815 to 1917 were almost all colonial wars, conflicts over territories that lay outside the national borders of the warring countries."[37] However, Etkind notes that "the

---

36 Paul Bushkovitch, "What is Russia? Russian National Identity and the State, 1500–1917," in *Culture, Nation and Identity: The Ukrainian-Russian Encounter, 1600–1945*, ed. A. Kappeler, Z. Kohut, F. Sysyn, and M. von Hagen (Edmonton: CIUS, 2003), 149.
37 This argument is repeated almost verbatim in two publications by Alexander Etkind. See: Aleksandr Etkind, "Russkaia literatura, XIX vek: Roman vnutrennei kolonizatsii" [Russian literature, 19th century: A novel of internal colonization], *Zhurnal'nyi zal* [Journal hall], https://magazines.gorky.media/nlo/2003/1/russkaya-literatura-xix-vek-roman-vnutrennej-kolonizaczii.html and Aleksandr Etkind, "Fuko i tezis vnutrennei kolonizatsii:

main paths of Russian colonization were aimed not outside, but at the interior of the metropolis: not into Turkey, not into Poland, and not even into Siberia, but into the villages of Tula, Pomerania, and Orenburg. Here the state distributed landed estates and subdued uprisings. Here community was discovered and folklore was recorded. Here ancient customs and strange religions were studied. From here, the capital's collections acquired deformities and rarities."[38] Etkind's conclusion, which he formulates following Chaadaev, is that the taking of control over Russia's internal regions is analogous to the acquisition of overseas colonies; hence, it is possible to speak about a form of "internal colonization."[39]

Etkind complements his argument about "internal colonization," formulated on the basis of Michel Foucault's theory of power, with an argument about "internal Orientalism," referencing Edward Said and the idea of knowledge as power. "Knowledge directs colonial power and is in turn generated by it," he writes.[40] In Etkind's opinion, the key difference between Russian and Western Orientalism is that "Russia colonized itself, took control over its own people. That was an internal colonization, self-colonization, a secondary colonization of its own territory," which led to the orientalization of its own people as its *other*.[41] That's why Russian *Orientalism*, according to Etkind, is directed onto its own people and not onto overseas colonies. One has the impression that this "internal colonization" is fueled by the ideas of Narodism ("Going to the People")—an extremely influential intellectual and spiritual trend in Russian philosophical thought of the nineteenth and twentieth centuries which sacralized the Russian people.

One of the fundamental mechanisms of colonial politics, as Etkind argues in his article "Foucault and the Thesis of Internal Colonization: A Postcolonial View of the Soviet Past," is "working with the cultural distance between power and its

---

postkolonial'nyi vzgliad na sovetskoe proshloe" [Foucault and the thesis of internal colonization: a postcolonial view of the Soviet past], *Zhurnal'nyi zal* [Journal hall], accessed September 29, 2025, https://magazines.gorky.media/nlo/2001/3/fuko-i-tezis-vnutrennej-kolonizaczii.html.

38 Aleksandr Etkind, "Russkaia literatura, XIX vek: Roman vnutrennei kolonizatsii" [Russian literature, 19th century: A novel of internal colonization], *Zhurnal'nyi zal* [Journal hall], accessed September 20, 2025, https://magazines.gorky.media/nlo/2003/1/russkaya-literatura-xix-vek-roman-vnutrennej-kolonizaczii.html.

39 Andreas Kappeler argues that the concept of internal colonization was employed by Ukrainian economists of the 1920s (M. Volobuiev, M. Slabchenko, M. Yavorskyi) and was later adopted and developed by Michael Hechter in his *Internal Colonialism: The Celtic Fringe in British National Development, 1536-1966* (Berkeley: University of California Press, 1975). See: Kappeler A. "Mazepintsy, Malorossy, Khokhly: Ukrainians in the Ethnic Hierarchy of the Russian Empire" [205: 178-79].

40 Etkind, "Russkaia literatura, XIX vek [Russian literature, 19th century]."
41 Etkind, "Russkaia literatura, XIX vek [Russian literature, 19th century]."

subjects—its study, exaggeration, demonstration, minimization, negation."[42] At the same time, a distinctive feature of Russian modernization and the colonization associated with it is, he believes, "the cultural difference between the upper and lower classes inherited from the agrarian society," and this is what fundamentally distinguishes it from Western societies and empires. The upper classes, the mainstay of a centralized state, act on the basis of on a written culture, while the lower classes act on the basis of an oral one. According to Etkind, these two worlds "were separated by an abyss," and "communication between them, if it was ever possible, turned out to be distorted, risky, and limited"—evidenced by Russian literature from Pushkin's *The Captain's Daughter* to Gorky's *The Life of Klim Samgin*.[43]

Thus, Russian ethnography as an imperial study of *the other* differs from British ethnography in that it is aimed at investigating its own people as *the other*. Russian Narodism, which became the Russian intelligentsia's love affair with the people, was undeniably a mix of "social guilt, mystical hopes, and academic curiosity, all regarding one's own people."[44] The uncivilized, infantile nature of one's own people is ultimately portrayed as a guarantee of a different, non-European path of development. This is what Etkind calls *"Orientalization of one's own culture."*[45]

Etkind offers the following conclusion: (a) Russia was reluctant to engage in distant imperial conquests: "the dynasty is opposed to all attempts at overseas expansion, considering them too difficult, profitless, or immoral: a strange attitude in light of the multidirectional colonialism which was typical of all its allies and adversaries in those decades"; (b) "in cultural, social, and economic terms, the empire developed from the outside in"; (c) colonization in Russia is characterized by settlement rather than conquest, and therefore the word "colonization" "is used in two opposite ways when applied to Russia and Europe," and "the paths of Russian and European colonization were so different from each another that they cannot be easily reduced to a single concept"; and (d) revolution in America and in Russia coincides with decolonization-colonization, but in America *external decolonization* leads to "national maturation," while in Russia *internal colonization* leads to "cyclical processes of its re-creation in new forms."[46]

---

42 Aleksandr Etkind, "Fuko i tezis vnutrennei kolonizatsii: postkolonial'nyi vzgliad na sovetskoe proshloe" [Foucault and the thesis of internal colonization: a postcolonial view of the Soviet past].
43 Etkind, "Fuko i tezis vnutrennei kolonizatsii" [Foucault and the thesis of internal colonization].
44 Etkind, "Fuko i tezis vnutrennei kolonizatsii" [Foucault and the thesis of internal colonization].
45 Etkind, "Fuko i tezis vnutrennei kolonizatsii" [Foucault and the thesis of internal colonization].
46 Etkind, "Fuko i tezis vnutrennei kolonizatsii" [Foucault and the thesis of internal colonization].

Despite abundant argumentation, the thesis of "internal colonization," just like the thesis concerning Orientalism in relations with one's own *other*, that is, *one's-own-not-one's-own people*, raises more questions than answers. This was demonstrated by a conference entitled "Russia's Internal Colonization," held on March 23–25, 2010, in Passau, Germany. Most of the speakers pointed out that despite the obvious similarity between internal colonization and modernization, the relationship between external, internal, and self-colonization remains unclear. Dirk Uffelmann underlined that "external Orientalization can lead to self-orientalization just as it can lead to self-colonialization." Alexander Etkind attempted to introduce the concept of hybridization into the notion of internal colonization (following Homi Bhabha), while Stefan Rohdewald, critiquing the binary nature of the proposed opposition between the external and internal vectors of colonization, proposed some terminological modifications. In particular, regarding discursive strategies prior to 1860, he suggests speaking of "an imaginary external colonization of the internal," and in discourses after 1860, especially those "concerning the southern and western Russian lands," of "an imaginary internal colonization of the external."[47]

"Internal" and "External" Colonization

Indeed, it would be a huge simplification to ignore, for example, the difference in national consciousness in Ukraine in the early nineteenth century and in the second half of the nineteenth century and the anti-colonial movements associated with the processes of colonization. In the early nineteenth century, given the dual (imperial) identity of the Ukrainian elite, it is still possible to speak of a certain imaginary colonization of Ukraine/Little Russia as the "*internal*," but there is no doubt that at the end of the nineteenth century, we can speak only of an imaginary internal colonization of the "*external*."[48]

Andreas Kappeler has noted that from the late eighteenth century onwards, when the Cossack elite began to be co-opted into the imperial nobility, it can

---

47 For a review of the conference materials, see Heinrich Kirschbaum, "Konferentsiia 'Vnutrenniaia kolonizatsiia v Rossii'" [Conference 'Internal colonization in Russia'], *Zhurnalnyi zal*, accessed September 29, 2025, http://magazines.russ.ru/nlo/2010/105/ge46.html.

48 For more on the dual ("amphibian-like") identity of the Ukrainian elite in the late eighteenth century, see Tamara Hundorova, "'Kotliarevshchyna': kolonialnyi kitch" ['Kotliarevshchyna': colonial kitsch], in *Kitch i literatura. Travestii* [Kitsch and literature. Travesties] (Kyiv: Fakt, 2008), 92–22.

be said that *"the Little Russians* were no longer considered by the center as an independent ethnic group": "Since the 'Little Russian' nobility was equal in status to the Russian nobility and increasingly perceived as Russian, all Ukrainians of the former Hetmanate were regarded as a regional variant of the Russians and dropped out of the ethnic hierarchy entirely."[49] Moreover, ethnic Ukrainians were subjected to internal colonization: the majority of the Ukrainian people were identified with the peasantry, an uncivilized mass of people, the *khokhly*.[50]

However, the rise of nationalism and the formation of the modern Ukrainian nation in the late nineteenth century changed the vector of colonization from an internal to an external one. The Russian government also changed its tactic of cooperation with the non-Russian elite: after the Polish uprising, not only did the Ukrainian language fall under suspicion, so did the representatives of the Ukrainian political and cultural elite, which fostered an anti-imperial disposition, federalism, and nationalism even among Ukrainian intelligentsia of an all-Russian or pro-Russian inclination (such as Mykhailo Drahomanov and Mykhailo Hrushevskyi). Eventually the entire twentieth century was permeated with anticolonial movements: on one side, the liberation struggles of Ukrainians for independence, and on the other, the various strategies of external colonization to which the governments of first the Russian and then the Soviet empires resorted.

The marked binarism that Etkind employs, consistently contrasting the European and Russian imperial experiences, remains insufficiently understood. It is also unclear why he strives so persistently to dismiss the issue of external colonization. To achieve this, Etkind resorts to the rhetorical device of fashioning an *imaginary* distinction. And even so, he attempts to construct this distinction in the most unexpected and paradoxical form possible to obtain discursive power over the realia of historical, cultural, and social life, and in this manner—through power—he brings about a re-colonization of the object being described. At the same time, the imaginary difference or "cultural difference," which, as Etkind reiterates, is the mechanism of colonial politics, has a *dual meaning*: on one hand, it *absolutizes* the foreignness of the imperial European experience of external colonization, and on the other, it *minimizes* the role of Russian external colonization. It is no coincidence that Etkind argues that, unlike European empires, which mainly exploited their conquered territories,

---

49 Andreas Kappeler, "Mazepintsy, Malorossy, Khokhly: Ukrainians in the Ethnic Hierarchy of the Russian Empire," in *Culture, Nation and Identity: The Ukrainian-Russian Encounters, 1600–1945*, ed. A. Kappeler, Z. Kohut, F. Sysyn, and M. von Hagen (Edmonton: CIUS, 2003), 168.
50 Kappeler, "Mazepintsy, Malorossy, Khokhly," 168.

the Russian Empire "granted its colonies economic and political privileges, creating opportunities for self-rule and self-sufficiency."[51] Etkind emphasizes that "the campaigns to subjugate the Caucasus, which after the annexation of Georgia found itself within the imperial territory, were of a non-colonial or at least a not entirely colonial nature."[52] Obviously, the experience of colonizing Little Russia, which led to the abolition of the Hetmanate's autonomy, is also considered "not entirely colonial." Neither is anything said of the various strategies to transform external colonization into an internal one, for example, through conferring the rights of nobility on Little Russian Cossack officers, and so on.

Etkind makes sure to mention that the significance of imperial conquests lies precisely in creating "ever new differences among those subjugated," and that imperial power itself involves generating "various strategies for manipulating these differences." In fact, Etkind himself manipulates the facts to a certain extent. In posing the question "When did Russian colonization begin?" he proposes a dilemma to which an answer must be chosen: "Did it begin with the occupation of ethnically foreign Kazan, or of ethnically similar Novgorod?" Evidently, he is not interested in historical reality; rather, he is concerned with the discourse being offered to the reader. Etkind goes on to insist: "Where were the Russian colonies—in the Chud lands, in the Urals and Siberia, where the classical process of mixing migrant and native populations was taking place, or in Little Russia, where the opposite was true, and the population, though ethnically similar to the metropolis, formed cultural and political differences that would prove decisive?" Ultimately, he presents the colonization of Ukrainians as a model of non-classical colonization, in which an ethnically homogeneous population (presumably of its own free will) merges into the empire, forming cultural and political differences of the *other-but-still-one's-own*. Thus, by mentioning "cultural and political differences that would prove decisive," Etkind pays tribute to political correctness, but he does not answer the question of where in fact these Russian colonies were. Neither does he see any particular problem in the external colonization of Little Russia, since its population is, he says, "ethnically similar to the metropolis."

The rhetorical maneuvers Etkind employs to construct his "cultural distances" and devise differences, which in fact turn out to be rules of identity and (hidden) power, only grow more pronounced and frequent. Ethnic and racial differences in the Russian Empire were not significant, the argument goes, and therefore the geographical and economic continuity of the empire "outweighed

---

51 Etkind, "Fuko i tezis vnutrennei kolonizatsii" [Foucault and the thesis of internal colonization].
52 Etkind, "Fuko i tezis vnutrennei kolonizatsii" [Foucault and the thesis of internal colonization].

all other differences—ethnic, linguistic, religious—melting them in a shared imperial pot."[53] Needless to say, in this "imperial pot" there was absolutely no melting, or melting away, of either cultural and political resistance to Russian colonization or of the struggle for the right of Ukrainian-language literature, theater, and scholarship to exist—a struggle that continued throughout the entire nineteenth century and even into the twenty-first century.

"Internal Orientalism"

Having elegantly acknowledged Ukrainians as almost "one's own," Etkind turns to an analysis of a famous painting by Ilya Repin, "Reply of the Zaporozhian Cossacks to Sultan Mehmed IV of the Ottoman Empire." On the one hand, having embraced the logic of appropriating the distinction of Little Russians as "others-but-still-one's-own," Etkind contrasts them with some external "others," namely the Turks. Yet on the other hand, he emphasizes the Little Russians' "oriental character." Etkind notes that although the Cossacks are also Eastern, this East is one's own—since, he writes, "they are all . . . Russians (or Little Russians)." Thus, it turns out that the Russian elite, according to Etkind's reasoning, carries out internal Orientalization of *its own people*, its own *other*, namely the Ukrainians.

Within the framework of the "internal Orientalism" proposed by Etkind, one's own East is contrasted with a more remote and "more unfamiliar" East—the Turkish one. Moreover, according to Etkind, the position that shapes all imperial cultural distances and differences in the painting is entirely rational, that is, Western. The legitimate representatives of the people, the Cossacks, are "depicted as an Eastern element, as children of nature, unlettered creators of folk culture. Their abusive exertions are addressed to a subject even more oriental than they themselves: the Turkish sultan. He is absent from the picture, only his name is there, but his distant presence/absence motivates all the participants: a situation characteristic of 'Eastern despotism.' The scribe, who does not look like the Cossacks (but does resemble Gogol), is vainly attempting to convey the carnival of folk culture in proper clerical language. In the person of the scribe, between the East of the Cossacks and the East of the sultans, stands the West with its literacy and rationality. Everyone here is from Rus (or Little Russian), but the cultural distance between the Cossacks and the scribe is obviously no less than

---

53 Etkind, "Russkaia literatura, XIX vek" [Russian literature, 19th century].

the cultural distance to the sultan. The Cossack in the center of the painting is clearly pointing backwards: that is where the sultan is, the letter's addressee, and that is the geographical East. Accordingly, the West stands in front of the painting in the person of the painter, and also of the viewer. The painting edifies the latter, declaring the powerlessness of writing before the spoken word, of professional culture before folk culture, of the West before the East. But the East is divided into two, and this, for us, is what is most important in all of history: the East of the Cossacks, an object of popular fascination, is radically different from the East of the sultan, an object of traditional Orientalism. The subject is refined and ironic. It also contains a parable about the indispensability of the West and of writing: even the Cossacks (and the sultan) need the scribe, and all of them need the painter and the viewer. In other words, the subject is read both as an oriental utopia of a Eurasian type, and also as its mocking deconstruction. The Second World is addressing the Third World, but they cannot do it without the First World."[54]

This rather lengthy quote not only describes the object of study, namely the *other Orientalism* produced by Russian imperial discourse, but also demonstrates that Etkind clearly identifies with the First World (and with the West and its methods of deconstruction). And this identification with the West enables him to ignore the history of colonial relations and the perspective of the colonized *other*. First of all, Repin, who himself was a native of Ukraine, depicts in the painting not abstract Cossacks, but real people of that time.[55] The painting was the result of a historical and ethnographic trip taken by the artist through the territory of the former Zaporizhzhia, planned by Mykola Kostomarov, a historian and researcher of the Cossack era, with ethnographer Dmytro Yavornytskyi as a consultant. Repin found quite a few of his models in the Katerynoslav province, but some were drawn directly from the artist's circle in St. Petersburg. Among them were the artist Jan Ciągliński, a teacher at the Imperial Society for the Promotion of the Arts and nephew of the Russian composer Mikhail Glinka; the Russian artist Porfirii Martynovych, who studied at the St. Petersburg Academy of Arts; Professor Alexander Rubets of the St. Petersburg Conservatory; and Fyodor Stravinsky, a soloist at the Mariinsky Theatre (and father of the composer Igor Stravinsky). Also pictured in the

---

54   Etkind, "Russkaia literatura, XIX vek" [Russian literature, 19th century].
55   Yurii Pukivskyi, "Illia Riepin 'Zaporozhtsi pyshut lysta turetskomu sultanovi'" [Ilya Repin 'Cossacks writing a letter to the Turkish Sultan'], *Lokalna istoriia* [Local history], last modified April 13, 2021, https://localhistory.org.ua/rubrics/painting/illia-riepin-zaporozhtsi-pishut-lista-turetskomu-sultanovi/.

painting are Georgii Alekseyev, Marshal of the Nobility in Katerynoslav province and Grand Chamberlain at the Russian emperor's court; the Ukrainian landowner and philanthropist Vasyl Tarnovsky, proprietor of the Kachanivka estate, where both Gogol and Panteleimon Kulish were guests, and Tarnavsky's coachman, Mykyshka. The model for Hetman Ivan Sirko was the Kyiv general Mykhailo Drahomyrov (later the Governor-General of Kyiv).

Thus, it is not "*others*" and not "*the people*" that we see in Repin's painting, but portraits of representatives of the Russian imperial elite and the Little Russian elite integrated into imperial culture. And the scribe is not a reproduction of some Gogolian type, as Etkind claims, but a portrait of Dmytro Yavornytskyi, a renowned Ukrainian ethnographer, historian and writer who was a passionate scholar of Cossackdom and Repin's principal consultant. So it is naive to identify the scribe as Western, and equally naive to look for a scribe who "does not look like the Cossacks (but does resemble Gogol)" in the painting, since almost all the so-called Cossacks in the painting "do not look like Cossacks," because they all are stylized (their models being Ukrainians, Great Russians, and Tatars). Gogol could only have been present in it as an artifice, pointing to the style of the painting itself, namely the *colonial style*. After all, Gogol was the creator of a fundamentally new genre in imperial literature—the genre of colonial stylization of which *Evenings on a Farm Near Dykanka* has become a textbook example.

The Symbolic Place of the Author: Who Is Writing?

Another question arising in connection with Repin's painting concerns the perspective of the image itself. In the painting, the scribe (Yavornytskyi) is indeed facing the viewer and depicted as a literate person. Since he represents the colonial subject, this means that the colonial subject possesses authentic writing. Is he a stranger in this colonial masquerade? Yes and no. He is not a stranger among the other (internally colonized) Cossacks, because he shares with them the spirit of carnival laughter and enthusiasm for Cossack history. In his memoirs, Repin writes that he noticed and captured Yavornytskyi's smile as the latter was looking through some humorous illustrations in a magazine. But at the same time the scribe is a stranger among the "Cossacks": the others have dressed up for the masquerade and have taken on their roles, but he, almost like an author among his characters, remains both within the painting and also outside of it. His mission is not (as Etkind believes) to convey the Cossacks' curse-laden oral speech "in correct bureaucratic language." Rather, the scribe himself is thinking up the next phrase while they are laughing at the preceding one.

An important role is played here by the muscle impulse associated with laughing. As the famous theoretician of decoloniality Frantz Fanon once noted, a colonized native encountering the colonial order finds himself in a state of constant tension and feels trapped: "The native's muscles are always tensed. You can't say that he is terrorized, or even apprehensive. He is in fact ready at a moment's notice to exchange the role of the quarry for that of the hunter."[56] This manifests itself in a distinctive sustained muscular tension in the colonized, as if he is patiently waiting for the moment when the colonizer finds himself undefended so that he can attack him. This perpetual muscular tension is reinforced by the native's obsessive desire to take the place of the colonizer.

The colonizer, for his part, is an exhibitionist by nature. He is simply overly concerned with his own security, and therefore constantly demonstrates his power and reminds the subjugated of his authority at every moment. Such relations resemble a kind of symbiosis and demonstrate the mutual psycho-affective dependence of the subjugated and the subjugator. They are based on an extreme and irreconcilable opposition which manifests itself in both muscles and body and constantly feeds an aggressiveness that requires release.

The release of the tension built up in the native's muscles flares up as violent clashes of intertribal strife and interpersonal conflicts. But one of the forms of anti-colonial resistance, especially at the stage of its rise and separation from the mass of rebel leaders, is the laughter of the oppressed, for it releases their muscular tension and frees them, at least for a moment, from their dependence. Laughter is a privilege of the colonial elite; it allows desires to manifest themselves and reorganizes aggression, replacing it with a sense of community, particularly national community. If Repin's painting is perceived as a colonial masquerade, then what the scribe is conveying is this psycho-affective release from colonial tension, achieved through laughter.

The image of the scribe can be identified as the symbolic place of the author: this is how Repin records and attests to a certain past in which (within which) he would like to be. The Cossack past becomes a mirror, a dream, an illusion in which the author places himself. The painting depicts various representatives of the empire, but the scribe is modeled after Yavornytskyi—a Ukrainophile and Cossackophile. Thus, it is with Ukrainophilia and Cossackophilia that the representative of the imperial center identifies, thereby joining the colonial masquerade.

---

56 Frantz Fanon, *Hnani i holodni* [The wretched of the earth] (Kyiv: Vpered, 2016), 18.

So the otherness of the scribe is not limited to the fact that he is *Westernized* while the Cossacks in the painting are *Easternized*. It would be an exaggeration to look for an *almost one's own East* in Repin's painting, since the masquerade East of the Cossacks is a costumed staging and a *discourse about colonialism itself*. This masquerade does not so much depict the Eastern flavor of the newly discovered Little Russian people whom Catherine II wanted to learn about in Gogol's *The Night Before Christmas* as it points to the existence of a completely different identity, that of the colonial *Little Russian elite* which, masked and in secret, opposes the supposedly homogeneous imperial community. In other words, if this is the East for the imperial center, then it is an East that is "*completely not one's own.*"

The dialogism and carnivalization in Repin's painting have an anti-imperial meaning and speak to the falseness (untruthfulness) of the empire. The colonized Third World turns out to be closer to the First, Western World, because it is ironic, and because, despite its seemingly obvious carnival spontaneity, it is rational and masquerade-like. Meanwhile, the Second (imperial) World remains in the grip of its illusory grandeur and power, which need to be rationally unmasked. This is exactly what Repin, together with Yavornytskyi, does.

What is at the center of this discourse? The unity of the empire and the homogeneity of the people of Rus? The laughter-filled folk culture and the authenticity of the Little Russian people so beloved by romantic writers? The assimilated and subjugated nearer East (Cossackdom), or the victorious and dominant West as personified by the scribe and the letter, as well as by the Western identity of the deconstructor himself?

These questions can be answered by changing the perspective proposed by Etkind. He argues that the Cossack standing behind the scribe is pointing towards the location of the sultan to whom the letter is addressed; but why not consider that the Cossack is pointing not to the East, but to the North? Then Repin's painting takes on a new, anti-colonial meaning: far from the metropolis, the carnival-like Cossack state, which definitely has both an ataman and a scribe, reveals that Russian internal Orientalism is an illusion. The subjugated and "almost one's own" East is in fact neither innocent nor submissive. Furthermore, the letter to the Turkish sultan could also have been addressed to the Russian tsar. Postcolonial criticism emphasizes that the position taken by the author himself, who is rewriting the colonial situation, is especially important. From the perspective of "internal colonization" and "internal Orientalism," Etkind explicitly associates himself with the West and writing, repeatedly retelling the Russian utopia story about the intelligentsia's love affair with the people, and including relationships with external colonies in that love affair.

Thus, when one engages in the "deconstruction of deconstruction," one can see that the claim that the colonization of Little Russia is exclusively "internal" is at least incomplete. The discursive strategy which draws on cultural differences creates and obscures these differences as desired. "One's own" adapted and somewhat simplified Ukrainian Cossack East is seen as an uncontentious part of *one's own* Russian people, and it turns out that "internal colonization" works best of all with regard to this not quite Russian, already previously colonized people. That is why the Orientalization and "othering" of the Cossacks in Repin's painting look like an imaginary internal colonization of the externally colonized, or, more simply, a *re-colonization*. Thus, ignoring the perspective of the colonized *other* leads to a new colonialism, this time through writing, analysis, and intellectual authority.

How did the postcolonial experience affect the underlying structures of post-Soviet novels in Ukrainian literature? If the main tension of these novels is uncovered, it can be concluded that it was caused by the experience of postcolonial life. In Oksana Zabuzhko's works, this experience is manifested through colonial trauma, which not only determines the twists and turns of the characters' lives but also influences their psycho-emotional state, physicality, psychology, geography, poetry, love, and sex. Out of this trauma emerges the theme of love coupled with the Ukrainization of the Russian-speaking lovers, and most importantly, the myth of brotherly solidarity between the two painter-sorcerers, representatives of colonized literature, in Zabuzhko's well-known novel *Fieldwork in Ukrainian Sex*. These are complemented by the imagery of the weak father crushed by the totalitarian machine and the eternally hungry, frigid mother traumatized by the Holodomor. But most importantly, the colonial experience turns out to be the collective subconscious of an entire people which determines the content of characters and conflicts bound up mainly with familial, lineal, and national destiny. Ultimately, the main theme of *Fieldwork in Ukrainian Sex* is the survival of the (national) family.

In Yuri Andrukhovych's *Recreations*, on the other hand, the colonial and totalitarian experience is expressed through a bifurcation of each of the characters, who are turned toward the past and try to somehow replay that past, repeat it, and reincarnate themselves in it in order to restore the full and complete identity of their own "I," stolen by history. That long-gone history—the Austro-Hungarian melancholy of pre-war Lviv, the ancestral sonority of the pre-Soviet Galician village—is reflected in *Recreations* through the traumatic experience of Andrukhovych's wandering, adventurous characters. The "recreations" are the break and, at the same time, the renewal that the characters want but are unable to achieve, because not only are they trying to overcome the experience of colonization, they are themselves colonized by their own past. Their colonization by a stolen and divided past has trapped them in a circle of repetitions and simulations. Such is the fate of the postcolonial subject. In *The Moscoviad*, this subject no longer seeks to restore its own "I" so much as it seeks revenge on the empire, fragmenting it and inverting the "top" and the "bottom," the center and the periphery; as well as voluntaristically and aggressively renaming the metropolis's topoi—and thus assaulting its already powerless late-Soviet body at the very heart of the empire. Without a doubt, it is the postcolonial worldview that fuels these first post-Soviet Ukrainian novels, which appeared in the 1990s.

Overall, the process by which postcolonial consciousness was formed in the post-Soviet space seems especially intriguing. Ukrainian postcolonial consciousness of the late twentieth century, in particular, was marked by the overcoming of cultural provincialism and marginality, including the *ressentiment* generated by anticolonial protest. Ukrainian literature of the Independence period emerges as the terrain where many decolonial and postcolonial models of thinking are articulated and where various forms of cultural identification are tested. The post-Soviet Ukrainian literature of the 1990s is imbued with sociocultural reflection that seeks to understand the relationship between the metropolis and the colony, "one's own" and "other," the dominant and the subjugated, the intimate and the social, the masculine and the feminine, the mono- and polycultural, the authentic and the stylized. As a whole, it signals Ukraine's entry into the zone of transitional postcolonial culture.

CHAPTER 2

Postcolonial *Ressentiment*

Ressentiment: Resentment and Colonial Resistance

The concept of *ressentiment* (resentment) entered modern Western cultural consciousness with Friedrich Nietzsche's *Genealogy of Morals*, written over twenty days between July 10 and July 30, 1887. The original source of this concept is Hegel's philosophy, which defines it as a consequence of self-assertion involving a clash (interaction) between two potential subjects, one of which ultimately asserts himself and becomes the master, while the other is transformed into the *other*, into an *object*, and becomes a slave. "This leaves the slave with a chronic awareness of his own otherness, creating fertile ground for *ressentiment*," which causes him to reevaluate the master from good to bad and himself from bad to good.[1]

Nietzsche defines this state as a "negative" perspective which becomes the starting point for self-identification for the weak and oppressed. Characteristically, Nietzsche notes that *ressentiment* in the modern era becomes a creative action and is an emotion that gives birth to values. *Ressentiment* in general, he believes, is a characteristic of those who, "deprived as they are of the proper outlet of action, are forced to obtain their satisfaction in imaginary acts of vengeance."[2] Nietzsche contrasts the self-esteem of aristocratic individuals (strong and wholesome personalities), whose *ressentiment* exhausts itself in an immediate reaction, with resentful individuals who are devoid of naivety, sincerity, and honesty and immersed in self-abasement and self-destruction, whose minds love to hide, preferring various nooks and crannies, hiding places and back doors, knowing the taste of silence and of waiting.

It therefore becomes essential to create an image of the enemy, with the elements of creation, creativity, and imagination playing a key role. The resentful person invents an "evil enemy" that he can use as an image from which to proceed. "While all aristocratic morality springs from a triumphant affirmation of its own demands, the slave morality says 'no' *ab initio* to what is 'outside itself', 'different from itself' and 'not itself'; and this 'no' is its creative act."[3]

Ressentiment becomes the concept to which Nietzsche assigns the function of an "instrument of culture" that influences change in cultural eras, social movements, the degradation of the human race, and the decadence of European civilization. It is thanks to Nietzsche that *ressentiment* is identified with a change in value-oriented *worldview*. Thus, the usual *affirmative* form of self-identification

---

1 William Strauss and Neil Howe, *The Fourth Turning: An American Prophecy* (New York: Crown, 1997).
2 Friedrich Nietzsche, *On the Genealogy of Morals*, ed. Robert C. Holub, trans., Michael A. Scarpiti (London: Penguin, 2013), 205.
3 Nietzsche, *Genealogy of Morals*, 205.

is transformed: it becomes *negative*, where the condition for self-affirmation is the denial of the other. Over time, *ressentiment* acquires a broad cultural meaning as a kind of "imaginary revenge" that drives the development of "counter-existence": being not *thanks to* something or someone, but *in spite of* them.

The concept of *ressentiment* was to become an important existential component in modern phenomenology, particularly in the work of Max Scheler. For Scheler, *ressentiment* means the intense experience and subsequent reproduction of a certain emotion, with the emotion itself becoming central to the self-awareness of identity. There is a constant return of the feeling, which triggers an "after-experiencing" or "re-experiencing" of the emotion. Notably, such emotion is negative and carries within it a certain shade of hostility.[4]

Scheler noted several fundamental characteristics of the emotional state of *ressentiment*, which he calls affect. Namely:

- *ressentiment* arises when envy is coupled with weakness, and this envy is directed outward, beyond the limits of one's own being;
- *ressentiment* directs feelings toward the valuables and possessions of others and is often an existential envy for the being of another; this is so-called existential envy, which is directed at the individual existence of another person. From the outset, such envy seems to deprive the other person of their right to exist, which is perceived as a "burden," a "challenge," and extreme self-belittlement;
- the elimination of *ressentiment* involves "expanding" the object, displacing or replacing it. When there is a delay in this expansion, the affect is directed at the subject himself, infecting him with self-criticism and causing incredible pain;
- the value illusion of *ressentiment* lies in elevating one's own sense of self-worth as a result of: a) humiliating the other or denying their worth; b) falsifying the value itself;
- *ressentiment* is a *physical* phenomenon: it generates a painful "body sensation" and disgust for one's own body, a distanced and objectified attitude toward one's own body as something foreign and separate, and also a desire to take revenge on oneself, to destroy oneself. The extreme tension between the impulse of envy on the one hand and powerlessness on the other is the critical point where affects take the form of *ressentiment*. The release of affect either becomes pathological or is transformed into a complex but productive cultural therapy.

---

4   Max Scheler, *Resentiment v strukture moralei* [Ressentiment in the structure of morals] (St. Petersburg: Universitetskaia kniga, 1999), 118.

Scheler's theory seems particularly productive for analyzing marginal and colonial consciousness affected by hostility toward the oppressor. Scheler's *ressentiment*, like Nietzsche's "will to power," is an important semantic category for describing the tense relationship between the "I" and the *other*, between the dominant and the colonized consciousnesses. Although the context of *ressentiment* has changed throughout the twentieth century, the aspect of opposition between the *strong* and the *weak* remains fundamental to its understanding. "Through its very origin, ressentiment is therefore chiefly confined to those who *serve* and *are dominated* at the moment," Scheler asserts.[5] The state of liberation from the gaze and power of the other can be considered a constitutive principle of *ressentiment*, since the latter is always present in the relationship between the subaltern and the dominant, the weaker and the stronger. *Ressentiment* stems primarily from emotional tension, rebellion, and resentment.

It is quite telling that *ressentiment* is associated not only with resentment, but also with phantasms. According to Scheler, *ressentiment* is the retention and after-experiencing of a certain emotion that is negative in nature. For Scheler, *ressentiment* is a self-poisoning of the soul which grows out of the repression of the experience of resentment and powerlessness, and is directed outward, beyond individual existence, fixating on existential envy toward the existence of the *other*. This appears similar to the *"illumination"* of true, genuine values with illusory ones. Therefore, *ressentiment* plunges one into a kind of *imaginary, unreal, fictional world* from which it is impossible to escape and see *what is really there*. This world of fantasies, myths, and magic is a special privilege of the colonized subject.

Existential philosophy, and particularly the existential philosopher Albert Camus, offers new insights into the understanding of *ressentiment*. Camus focuses on the positive aspect of value which is manifested by the person who rebels, as opposed to the "negative concept of bitterness" emphasized by Scheler. With his theory of the "rebellious man," Camus argues that the dominant feeling of *ressentiment* is not resentment, but passionate self-affirmation and self-creation. Rebellion is what brings out a person's dignity. "Contrary to Scheler, it would therefore be impossible to overemphasize the passionate affirmation that underlies the act of rebellion and distinguishes it from resentment. Rebellion, though apparently negative, since it creates nothing, is profoundly positive," Camus maintains, "in that it reveals the part of man which must always be defended."[6]

---

5   Scheler, *Resentiment v strukture moralei* [Ressentiment in the structure of morals], 127.
6   Albert Camus, "Buntivna liudyna [The rebel]," in *Alber Kamiu. Vybrani tvory: u 3 t.* [Albert Camus. Selected works: in 3 vols.] (Kharkiv: Folio, 1997), 194.

But while the rebel seeks only to reclaim his own existence, he is subject to the laws of spiritual enslavement and is not averse to gaining power over the world.

Camus's argument that rebellion "only makes sense within the framework of Western thought" because it is linked to the development of individualism is important here. It gives grounds for considering *ressentiment*, as interpreted by Nietzsche, Scheler, and Camus, as one of the forms in which modern Western consciousness unfolded. According to Camus, *ressentiment* as an existential rebellion is a component of Western society with its established theories of political freedom on the one hand and dissatisfaction with the actual level of individual freedom on the other.

In the late twentieth century, Jean Baudrillard reoriented *ressentiment* from the psycho-emotional to the aesthetic category and called it one of the signs of postmodern consciousness, in which nihilism is transformed into melancholy. The excessive referencing, simulation, and reappropriation characteristic of contemporary art, which "claims to be ironic," are in fact forms of threadbare irony, or "grave irony," as Baudrillard puts it. Thus, contemporary culture is both a parody and a palinody of art history, as it is a parody of culture by culture itself. It is therefore a form of revenge, a sign of radical disillusionment with culture. That is why *ressentiment*, according to Baudrillard, is characteristic of contemporary art, and it constitutes the last phase in art history, just as it constituted the last stage in the genealogy of morality (according to Nietzsche). "It is no longer the spleen or the vague yearnings of the fin-de-siècle soul. It is no longer nihilism either, which in some sense aims at normalizing everything through destruction, the passion of resentment (*ressentiment*). No, melancholia is the fundamental tonality of functional systems, of current systems of simulation, of programming and information. Melancholia is the inherent quality of the mode of the disappearance of meaning, of the mode of the volatilization of meaning in operational systems."[7]

Thus, the concept of *ressentiment* in the history of the twentieth century explains a wide variety of processes—from slave-master relations to religious and moral wars, intergenerational conflicts, the place of women and mothers in the family, theories of rebellion, and the subversion of canons. Given the powerful creative significance of *ressentiment*, which serves as a form of affirmation of the "weak" in relations with the "strong," it is reasonable to apply it to the analysis of colonial consciousness, particularly in terms of the self-affirmation of

---

7 Dragoslav Mykhailovych, *Koly tsvily harbuzy* [When watermelons bloomed] (Kyiv: Fakt, 2008), 228.

the colonized subaltern subject, who metaphorically intercepts and returns the colonizer's gaze.

The French psychiatrist and philosopher Frantz Fanon applied the concept of *ressentiment* to analyze colonial consciousness and, more specifically, the psychopathology of colonialism. Fanon, who argued that the colonial world is ordered according to Manichean principle and is strictly divided into colonized and colonizers, concluded that the weapon of the colonial world is violence, and that "the violence of the colonial regime and the counter-violence of the colonized balance each other and respond to each other in an extraordinary reciprocal homogeneity."[8] Not only do the colonizers subjugate the natives through violence, but the colonial subjects also gain their freedom in violence and through violence. The ethnic community is united by the psycho-emotional affect of violence, and for the individual, violence becomes a means of spiritual purification from their feelings of inferiority. Such use of force becomes the basis of the existential, physical self-affirmation of the colonized and gives meaning to their existence.

In his analysis of the tense relationship between colonizer and colonized, Fanon pays particular attention to the role of the body, muscle tension, and the unbearable sense of resentment that constitutes the very existence of the subjugated, but also leads to his suicidal self-eradication. More specifically, Fanon singles out two figures: the Mother, who identifies herself with the human race and believes in brotherhood, and the Rebel, who identifies himself with "resentment." The Rebel says of himself: "My family name: offended; my given name: humiliated; my profession: rebel; my age: the stone age." This colonial rebel may even direct his violence against his own son to prevent him from becoming an obedient slave. The colonial mother, on the other hand, prays for life and love for her son, protecting him from possible death at the hands of both the colonizers and the colonized. "The colonial mother protects her child from itself, from its ego, and from its physiology, its biology and its own unhappiness which is its very essence."[9]

Fanon also highlights the heightened emotional sensitivity in the colonial world: this sensitivity of the colonized extends to *the surface of their skin* and resembles *an open wound*. Being constantly under the power of the colonizer and feeling locked in a cage, the colonial subject experiences constant muscle tension and only relaxes during clan wars, fights between relatives, and magical rituals and dances. Since the entire existence of the local population in the colonial world is directed toward psychological and emotional survival, there are various

---

8   Fanon, *Hnani i holodni*, 45.
9   Frantz Fanon, "On National Culture," in *Literature in the Modern World: Critical Essays and Documents*, ed. Dennis Walden (Oxford: Oxford University Press, 1990), 226.

means of suppressing aggression: myths, fantasies, occult practices. Even collective suicide can be one of the ways in which the native strives to break free from the constant muscle tension.

This alternative is particularly evident against the backdrop of the mechanism of *ressentiment*, which consists of the painful emotional state caused by tension—envy, resentment toward the outside world, and the urge to appropriate others' existence—coupled with a feeling of powerlessness. Such powerlessness usually passes, but it can also linger and poison the consciousness of a marginalized individual. He succumbs to the destructive effects of self-deprecation and self-criticism, experiences moments of self-alienation and the moral and physical torment of self-flagellation, strives for the symbolic murder of his father, and feels hostility towards his mother. According to Scheler, a way out of *ressentiment* opens up when the object of envy expands, changes, or moves. Albert Camus offered a different interpretation of *ressentiment*, namely, not through the transformation or replacement of the object of envy, but on the part of the subject: the crushing resentment is overcome by an existential rebellion dominated by a sense of self-worth and a yearning for self-realization. Contemporary feminist theorists exploring postcolonial issues see an alternative to violent and masculine aggressive protest, which is based on *ressentiment*, in touching *another body*, which reveals the vulnerability of every human body—that is, through contact with *the other*.

Anticolonial resentment and postcolonial rebellion determine the range of the emotional manifestations of *ressentiment*. Whether social, ethnic, religious, gender-based, or racial, *ressentiment* often serves as the basis for contemporary terrorism, emerging as it does out of the protest of the "weak" against the "strong" and out of the long-repressed resentment of the subordinate toward the oppressor.

It is noteworthy that *ressentiment* has become part of postcolonial discourse, which from the outset has been aimed at anticolonial resistance in and through writing itself, and at deconstructing the traces of power embedded in this writing. When we speak of postcolonial criticism, we usually mean the rewriting of binary oppositions: Europe and *others*, colonizer and colonized, the West and the rest of the world. But the development of postcolonial studies reveals a rather complex system of relations between the colonizer and the colonized—what Stephen Slemon has called the "radical ambivalence of colonialism's middle ground."[10] This refers not only to the ambivalence of the relationship between the "I" and *the other*, but also to the appropriation of the "I"/*other*

---

10   Stephen Slemon, "Unsettling the Empire: Resistance Theory for the Second World," in Ashcroft, Griffiths, and Tiffin, *The Postcolonial Studies Reader*, 107.

binary inherent in colonial relations. The concept of resistance becomes particularly important here, with figures of anticolonial resistance inevitably permeating the consciousness and fate of the individual subject, because they are directed toward national liberation. Literary resistance manifests itself in places of ambivalence—between two systems, between two discursive worlds. It is hidden, but at the same time involved in both worlds.

Slemon even suggests talking about literary resistance, which he considers both narratively—as strategies for undermining the power embedded in the narrative, and receptively—through the techniques of reading a text and mediating structures common to the communicative community—such structures would deprive the texts of credibility. But how can this resistance be incorporated into writing itself? Slemon sees three problems here: first, the rewriting of the center/periphery as a figure of resistance can serve as an institutional form of preserving the dominant narrative; second, it can be assumed that literary resistance simply exists *there* in the text as a structure of intentionality and a social form of communication, but it is difficult to distinguish because it is a multifaceted and contradictory structure of subject-formations; thirdly, if we apply Michel Foucault's theory, power itself inscribes and contains resistance.

As Jenny Sharpe demonstrates in *Figures of Colonial Resistance*, the sites of anticolonial resistance are not easy to locate in the text, since resistance itself is an effect of the contradictory representation of colonial authority, and never a "reversal" of power.[11] Moreover, resistance itself is never purely resistance, never simply there in the text or in the interpretive community, but is always complicit in the apparatus it seeks to transgress.[12] Overall, anti-colonial resistance cannot be reduced to critical arguments or ideological slogans, as is usually thought, because it is *thematized* in the text itself.

Ressentiment embedded in a textual structure allows us to talk about anti-colonialism and postcolonialism and enables us to trace, both theoretically and practically, how anti-colonial and postcolonial critique of the imperial center differ. As already noted, the concept of *ressentiment* offered by Nietzsche, Scheler, and Camus was formed during the modernist era. Notably, it is modernist writers, such as Joseph Conrad, who are often identified with colonial discourse. Fredric Jameson even equates the emergence of the modernist style itself with the representation of a new world imperial system.[13] Generally, it cannot be ignored that the nature of

---

11 Jenny Sharpe, "Figures of Colonial Resistance," in Ashcroft, Griffiths, and Tiffin, *The Postcolonial Studies Reader*, 101.
12 Slemon, "Unsettling the Empire," 108.
13 Fredric Jameson, "Modernism and Imperialism," in *Nationalism, Colonialism, and Literature*, ed. Terry Eagleton, Fredric Jameson, and Edward Said (Minneapolis: University of Minnesota Press, 1990), 59.

modernist writing to some extent reflects a transnational view of the world; moreover, it is linked to disillusionment with colonialism and the culture it creates, with its defining features—"progressive temporality, linear cartography, and a unified European subject."[14] This undermines the foundations of imperial inviolability and the stability of the entire Western world, and white people experience anxiety, fear, and madness as they plunge into the "heart of darkness" of the East.

Also of relevance in this context is the generation gap, which leads to the removal of the father figure in modernist literature or the demonization of the father, who traditionally (for example, in Victorian England) embodied the patriarchal values of the imperial world.[15] All this influences the nature of the narrative and undermines the dominant discourse of Orientalism, characteristic of Western culture since the Romantic era. The anti-colonial resistance that emerged alongside modernism manifested itself not only in the rewriting of traditional relations between the center and the periphery, but also in a focus on marginality—which included bohemians, beggars, women, rebels, and drug addicts—in modernist and avant-garde works. Moreover, there were many immigrants and former residents of colonial countries among the participants of the avant-garde movement.

It is worth noting that the era of European modernism was a time when the genres of adventure novels and stories about travel—to India, Africa, Iran—were being actively developed. Rudyard Kipling's *Kim*, Joseph Conrad's *Heart of Darkness*, E. M. Forster's *A Passage to India*, and André Gide's *The Counterfeiters* testify to the power of the genre tradition of the colonial novel, although Conrad did admit: "I have smoked a pipe of peace at midnight in the very heart of the African Continent, and felt very lonely there."[16]

The genre conventions of the colonial novel usually imply the existence of two chronotopes—the metropolis and the colony, which can be juxtaposed or intersecting, but the author's main intention is to affirm the stability of the reader's self-esteem as a representative of the metropolis, to highlight his knowledge and depict his immersion in a familiar world both before the journey to the colonized space and during the journey itself.[17] In colonial adventure novels such as those by Rider Haggard, the journey from civilization to savagery is characterized

---

14 Simon Gikandi, *Maps of Englishness: Writing Identity in the Culture of Colonialism* (New York: Columbia University Press, 1996), 161.
15 Peter Childs, *Modernism and Post-Colonial Literature and Empire, 1885–1930* (London: Continuum, 2007), 19.
16 Joseph Conrad, "Geografiia i nekotorye issledovateli" [Geography and some explorers], in *Izbrannoe: v 2 t* [Selected works: in 2 vols.] (Moscow: GIKHL, 1959), 667.
17 For more on this, see: Childs, *Modernism and Post-Colonial Literature and Empire, 1885–1930*, 114.

by a monologic writing style that eschews multicultural and multilingual heteroglossia. In contrast, modernist texts frequently reverse this narrative and introduce twists and turns that disorient the reader and force together different linguistic, temporal, and spatial dispositions that destroy the stable picture of the world. A hallmark of modernist writing is that the colonial region, for example, the East, no longer signifies mere exoticism, but also remoteness from the West; and the return home, as can be seen in the works of Virginia Woolf, Graham Greene, Arthur Conan Doyle, and others, becomes a turning point for self-reflection (moral, psychological, and even civilizational).

In postcolonial texts, the mechanisms of writing are deliberately aimed at resisting and unmasking power and—through deconstruction and playful reversal of the center/periphery—at reappropriating values and restoring lost identity. How does *ressentiment* manifest itself in this context? I would suggest that *ressentiment* is an important component of postmodern consciousness, and that anti-colonial and postcolonial consciousness are not mutually exclusive, but are integrated practices in postmodernist texts.

Eastern European *(Res)sentiment*: Biography and Geography

The ideas of Europeanization and modernization have been intertwined in Ukrainian self-awareness since the late nineteenth century. "Psychological Europe" is an ideal professed by all supporters of modernization, from Mykola Khvylovy to Mykola Riabchuk. The latter even suggests "admitting the obvious fact that Ukraine is part of Europe and, more broadly, the modern world, and that it is impossible to return from this world to some 'golden age' of pre-modernity."[18] And it was not until in the late twentieth century that the ideal of Europe changed when several *Europes* were born. One of them is the *Europe* of Andrukhovych.

It is far from unique. Slavenka Drakulić, for example, talks about the Europe invented by Bosnians. In fact, just as in the case of Andrukhovych, it is a *ghost*. "It was us, the Eastern Europeans, who invented 'Europe', constructed it, dreamed about it, called upon it," Drakulić wrote. "This Europe is a myth created by us, not only Bosnians, but other Eastern Europeans, too—unfortunate outsiders, poor relatives, the infantile nations of our continent. Europe was built by those of us living

---

18   Mykola Riabchuk, "Za ogorozheiu Metternikhovoho sadu" [Behind the fence of Metternich's garden], in *Sad Metternikkha* [Metternich's garden] (Lviv: VNTL-Klasyka, 2008), 23.

on the edges, because it is only from there that you would have the need to imagine something like 'Europe' to save you from your complexes, insecurities and fears."[19]

And so a new construction of "Europe" begins, no longer from the perspective of the center, but from the former periphery of the "Europe" that the Romantics had envisioned. "'Europe' is an empty sound," Oswald Spengler claimed, and noted self-critically: "The ground of West Europe is treated as a steady pole, [. . .] for no better reason, it seems, than because we live on it."[20] It is precisely by feeling "at home" in the region and identifying themselves with the pole of "Europe" that the Romantics create the concept of Europe, employing mechanisms of rejecting and civilizing *the other* in doing so. As Larry Wolff notes, "It was also the Enlightenment, with its intellectual centers in Western Europe, that cultivated and appropriated to itself the new notion of 'civilization,' an eighteenth-century neologism, and civilization discovered its complement, within the same continent, in shadowed lands of backwardness, even barbarism. Such was the invention of Eastern Europe."[21]

Now, in the post-socialist world, the reformatting of "Europe" from the position of a marginalized *other* is marked by a sense of *ressentiment*. Slavenka Drakulić highlights this situation of post-Soviet *ressentiment* in her writing. A defining feature of what we might call post-Soviet writing is its polemical nature and opposition to the totalitarian past. Drakulić acknowledges that what unites post-Soviet authors is not just their shared communist past, but also the way in which writers seek to escape from that past and the direction in which they want to go. Very often, this feeling of *ressentiment* originates from a feeling of being perceived as "not quite Europe."

The Ideal Geography

And yet, even in this space of "not quite Europe," a different kind of "ideal geography" comes into play. In the idea of "small homeland" offered by the Polish writer Andrzej Stasiuk, feelings of resentment and *ressentiment* towards *the other* Europe have been surmounted, since Stasiuk has developed resistance to global virtuality and post-socialist homogenization and realized the value of his own

---

19 Slavenka Drakulic, "Bosnia, or What Europe Means to Us," In *Café Europa: Life After Communism* (New York: Penguin Books, 1996), 212.
20 Oswald Spengler, *Zakat Evropy. Ocherki morfologii mirovoi istorii: v 2 t.* [The decline of the West. Essays on the morphology of world history: in 2 vols.], vol. 1, *Geshtal't i deistvitel'nost'* [Form and actuality] (Moscow: Mysl', 1993), 145.
21 Larry Wolff, *Inventing Eastern Europe: The Map of Civilization on the Mind of the Enlightenment* (Redwood City, CA: Stanford University Press, 1994), 35.

time and space. That's why when he leaves Berlin, Stasiuk's narrator knows that "my soul has suffered no loss, gained nothing and wasted nothing, because it is resistant to the virtual, to states and cities that appear and disappear according to the rhythms of their inhabitants."[22]

For Stasiuk, "my Europe" is more of an odyssey, a voyage on a ship. It is not a virtual extension of his own reality, nor is it a linear narrative *ab ovo*. Neither "postmodern [. . .] freedom of choice" nor a "modernist striving for boundaries" can cover it.[23] Migration, journeying, "is always an escape," the Polish writer claims, so for him, moving from Warsaw to either the East or the West is undesirable. "In the first case, we were defeated by space, and in the second, it was time that got the better of us," Stasiuk asserts.[24]

He therefore draws on his own space—"circling" around his hometown, thus locking in the boundaries of desirable travels and transgressions. His "small homeland," described by "circling," is also an "ideal state" that rejects the very need for transcendence, that is, longing for another, better, and more desired world. "You must keep your feet firmly on the ground" is the requirement of this European time and space. "Ideal geography" is an expression of self-sufficiency achieved in a postcolonial situation, in which resentment towards the other is overcome, landscape and map merge, and reality and idea, eternity and the moment, are equated. Ultimately, one's own Europe is a circle of returns, and it exists only because it repeats itself, since Stasiuk is attracted by his own immobility, or more precisely, by the "continuity of reality."[25]

Thus, a pair of compasses traces a circle; the needle point pierces the spot where the narrator is and where he will remain; while the compass leg is placed where the writer "was born and spent most of [his] life."[26] A large 300-km (200-mile) circle around Wołowiec, the village he made home, marks the borders of "his own Central Europe."[27] Stasiuk describes his actual location as "the middle." However, in his Central European journey in a 200-mile circle on the map, he also acknowledges his "nostalgia for utopia" (Joseph Conrad). But this nostalgia has nothing to do with memory or history; rather, it is connected with a view: "This kind of nostalgia gravitates toward the ever-receding horizon, while utopia craves the view that can encompass the whole."[28]

---

22 Andrzej Stasiuk, "Korabelnyi shchodennyk [Ship's diary]," in *Moia Yevropa. Dva esei pro naidyvnishu chastynu svitu* [My Europe. Two essays about the most wondrous part of the world], by Andrzej Stasiuk and Yurii Andrukhovych (Lviv: Klasyka, 2001), 45.
23 Stasiuk, "Korabelnyi shchodennyk" [Ship's diary], 46.
24 Stasiuk, "Korabelnyi shchodennyk" [Ship's diary], 15.
25 Stasiuk, "Korabelnyi shchodennyk" [Ship's diary], 49.
26 Stasiuk, "Korabelnyi shchodennyk" [Ship's diary], 7.
27 Stasiuk, "Korabelnyi shchodennyk" [Ship's diary], 7.
28 Stasiuk, "Korabelnyi shchodennyk" [Ship's diary], 22.

And yet Stasiuk is also swept up in the great migration of peoples. He acknowledges that "we used to set out on a journey to make our lives more valuable, fuller, and simply better, broader, and more human. Now, living, we want to abandon our lives at any cost, we want to escape them and rush to become someone else."[29] In the West, this looks "more like a game than a drama." Further to the east, however, "the game imperceptibly turns into a drama."[30]

Europe as the "East-Central Part of the Body"

By contrast, the vision of "my Europe" and "ideal geography" in the East, as seen by the Ukrainian writer Yuri Andrukhovych, does turn into a "drama." It leads not to self-sufficiency and resistance to the virtual and homogeneous West, as in Stasiuk's case, but instead becomes the basis for a drama called *European revision*. In addition, the East-Central European revision takes on a distinctly autobiographical and historical quality. Andrukhovych writes about his belonging to East-Central Europe and associates himself with those whose "human 'I' lies in the east-central part of the body."[31] Memory, territory, and language come to the fore in private stories and autobiography: family myths about a German great-grandfather who gets off at Stanislau station in a "dirty provincial town" to start a new life, and his travels through the patchwork territory of "the most grotesque of empires"—"from patch to patch, from language to language, from landscape to landscape."[32]

In his East-Central European revision, Andrukhovych uses one of several possible paths to the "Europe" he is constructing—the mythological one. As Edward Said notes, "because of the presence of the colonizing outsider, the land is recoverable at first only through the imagination."[33] Of course, the myth of the good emperor and the happy Austro-Hungarian Empire has little to do with historical reality, but it carries with it a lightness of imperial existence that was aesthetically and mythologically created. In this way, Andrukhovych, along with other representatives of the Stanislav Phenomenon, turns to this aestheticized nostalgic myth, first, to affirm the European character of his native Galicia as a territory that was once part of the Austro-Hungarian Empire and to connect

---

29 Andrzej Stasiuk, "Pered zapravkoiu" [Before refueling], in *Fado* (Kyiv: Hrani-T, 2009), 83.
30 Stasiuk, "Korabelnyi shchodennyk" [Ship's diary], 84.
31 Yurii Andrukhovych and Andrzej Stasiuk, "Tsentralno-skhidna reviziia" [Central-eastern revision], in *Moia Yevropa. Dva esei pro naidyvnishu chastynu svitu* [My Europe. Two essays about the most wondrous part of the world] (Lviv: Klasyka, 2001), 125.
32 Andrukhovych, 83.
33 Edward Said, *Kultura y imperializm* [Culture and imperialism] (Kyiv: Krytyka, 2007), 225.

himself autobiographically with it, and, secondly, to reject another vision of Galicia that portrayed the region as part of the *brutal, unaesthetic* Soviet empire and the "Soviet people."

For Andrukhovych, opposition ultimately becomes the dominant revision strategy. Stasiuk finds his identity without seeking to reverse offend either his own or the other. Nor does he seek to take revenge on anyone else or to reclaim territories in the east, west, south, or north of the Central European circle he has outlined. In contrast, Andrukhovych's narrator is determined to mentally relocate himself, his place, and his time elsewhere, beyond the borders of Soviet Union.

In his imaginary travels, Andrukhovych's narrator finds it easier to recognize the imperial *other* as *his own*, while in *his own*, he recognizes the features of the *foreign*. It's displeased to him that his native Stanislaviv (now Ivano-Frankivsk) could even be conceived of as part of the same state as "foreign" cities such as Tambov or Tashkent, whereas "his own" Venice or Vienna are not.[34] The narrator identifies as a European, setting himself apart from his post-Soviet fellows who are "*confused, angry, and tired.*" These are the "millions of people with a stolen paradise" who make up the category of "former" residents of the socialist "paradise." To emphasize this dissimilarity, the protagonist imagines "two Ukraines": on the one hand, there is his grandfather, who fought for the *liberation of the region* and was traveling on a train carrying evacuated Ukrainians, determined to "fight back against the Soviets"; on the other hand, there is "a lieutenant named, let's say, Ivanenko, a native of Poltava, Sumy, or Kherson, the only one of his family to survive the great famine, a Komsomol member and a potential flying ace," who fires on the evacuation train.[35]

As Nietzsche showed, the impetus for the construction of counter-narratives and counter-histories is resentment, which sets a different perspective. The latter restores the *completeness of the world*, at least in the form of some ideal vision in which one's wishes could be fulfilled. This vision may be directed both to the past (a paradise lost) and to the future (a promised land), but most importantly, it offers an impression of the *completeness* of history. Andrukhovych, too, is oriented toward a happy vision of history, although his lyrical character admits with a touch of self-irony to an *obsession with the past*—said to be characteristic of all Ukrainians. That's why encounters between Ukrainian and Western intellectuals, he somewhat ironically notes, are marked by a lack of understanding between the "*representatives of happy communities*," who have no need of history,

---

34 Yurii Andrukhovych, "Erts-herts-perts," in *DezOriientatsiia na mistsevosti* [Disorientation on the ground] (Ivano-Frankivsk: Lileia-NV, 1999), 8.
35 Andrukhovych, "Tsentralno-skhidna reviziia" [Central-eastern revision], 95.

and the "representatives *of unhappy communities*," who are engrossed in contemplating their own history.

Galicia: A Collection of "Alternative History"

It is clear that the author of "East-Central Revision" does not want to lose history; moreover, he presents it as a *desirable future*, which in fact is synonymous with a *desirable past*. Within the Habsburg myth to which Andrukhovych refers, the utopian, happy "Galicia" becomes an ideal country. But this ideal country exists only in traces of the past. The author is aware that he is constructing it from *traces*—impressions of ruins and castles, of mostly hunched old men and women who "still knew Latin phrases from high school by heart and, in the days of Khrushchev and the Beatles, dressed as if they had come out to welcome Archduke Franz Ferdinand."[36]

Interestingly, old things are collected and become souvenirs—carriers of melancholic memory. "I find these fragments of the old way of life—artificial flowers, flowerpots, Christmas angels with baby lambs, tarnished coins, any kind of decadent jewelry, faded garters, music boxes, birds' nests—far more meaningful than any moral maxims," our I-narrator admits. "I am fascinated by old aquariums, fossilized fish, sooty bathtubs and sinks, whistles, squeakers, porcelain deer."[37] The narrator goes on to describe collections of old bottles, old maps, old train timetables.

It is noteworthy that these fetish objects of an old, fleeting era are items in a collection, freed from their authenticity. For, as Walter Benjamin maintained, the authenticity of a thing is "the essence of all that is transmissible from its beginning, ranging from its substantive duration to its testimony to the history which it has experienced."[38] The memories from which the narrator reconstructs his lost European "*Galicia*" are transformed into objects, and Andrukhovych's "*Europe*" itself is a highly distinctive object of desire for the postcolonial Ukrainian individual—a ghost, an aestheticized hiding place where one can hide from reality. Memory reveals desired feelings; ultimately, it is a home for nostalgia, and so the Habsburg myth is a nostalgic refuge from the *incompleteness* of colonial history for the colonized Ukrainian subject.

---

36   Andrukhovych, "Tsentralno-skhidna reviziia" [Central-eastern revision], 72.
37   Andrukhovych, "Tsentralno-skhidna reviziia" [Central-eastern revision], 77.
38   Walter Benjamin, "Mystetskyi tvir u dobu svoiei tekhnichnoi vidtvoriuvanosti" [The work of art in the age of mechanical reproducibility], in *Valter Beniamin. Vybrane* [Walter Benjamin. Selected works] (Lviv: Litopys, 2002), 58.

The affirmation of European identity through the Habsburg myth is a very specific form of decolonization. Built on a postmodern vision, Andrukhovych's anti-colonial myth is averse to the violence that Frantz Fanon considered a sign of decolonial resistance. But Andrukhovych's myth does make full use of another sign of anti-colonial resistance: the creation of a single national community. If there are elements of decolonization in the Habsburg myth, they are related to the creation of an imaginary community of those who do not want to be colonized. That's why resentment toward the history that *could have been different* is compensated by *a vision of true history* which the author can construct virtually and thus identify like-minded people. So while Stasiuk admits his distaste for virtual cities such as the reconstructed Berlin or Warsaw, which appear in place of the destroyed old cities, Andrukhovych, in contrast, turns his imagination toward virtuality. His vision of Galicia as the locus of *my Europe* is, above all, a virtual picture.

Several factors contribute to this. First, Andrukhovych, unlike his Polish fellow writer, resorts to an "ideal autobiography" rather than an "ideal geography." Second, the resentment that fueled the creation of the virtual *my Europe* in Andrukhovych's text is marked by a suspension in the abyss between the colonial past and the non-colonial future. The narrator nevertheless acknowledges the *inevitability of existence in the present* and declares the present as the true site of being. Significantly, the text includes a memory of the narrator's father's death—in saying goodbye to his father, the narrator is also bidding farewell to the colonial past. Thirdly, Andrukhovych completes his construction of a virtual Europe with the help of fetishistic souvenirs from the old way of life and myths about his great-grandfather, grandfather, and father, which, for him, serve as a replacement for actual history. Fourthly, the search for Europe manifests the predominant mood that permeates Andrukhovych's essay—nostalgia for one's home.

Ultimately, in "East-Central Revision," virtuality is neither complete nor absolute. The text clearly identifies the rifts between the real and the virtual, the historical and the textual, the narrator and the author. Right at the start, the narrator mentions a hiding place to which he can escape. This possibility is textual euthanasia: interrupted writing and the death of the author. "Even now, I want to stay there," Andrukhovych's narrator admits, "to get stuck on this fourth page, within the second excerpt, and not go anywhere, not write anything more, stop the river. I can still stay there, I yearn to linger in the old embrasure under the swallows and the rainbow. (Someone once told all of us about the 'death of the author,' and here is a variation on that: textual euthanasia)."[39] Ultimately, the word "death" did appear in "East-Central Revision," and it is not just virtual, but it is not the narrator who dies, but his father.

---

39 Andrukhovych, "Tsentralno-skhidna reviziia" [Central-eastern revision], 47.

The Ideal Autobiography

In his nostalgic "revision" (which is a different genre from Stasiuk's "ship's log," his arbitrary voyage across a map of the real Europe), Andrukhovych's narrator revisits (revises) his own history. He reconstructs it primarily with his imagination and presents it as a family myth. Using real facts, he creates an East-European, desirable autobiography. Andrukhovych invents the figure of his great-grandfather, a Sudeten German named Karl, and tells the story of another great-grandfather who travels to America to earn money. He reconstructs the image of his father, recounts his death and funeral, and finally experiences a moment of epiphany: "As I look down from the hill at the forest, I forget everything, stand still, and fall silent. And then suddenly: is it not *him* looking at the forest, is it not *his* gaze?"[40]

The ruins of the past, fragments of everyday life, fetish objects, eyewitness accounts, myths, and memories fill the void, because "we thought it was ruins and castles that preserved the 'distant past,' the message of completeness," the I-narrator admits.[41] This constructed "completeness" of existence is what forms the new existential body of the Central European-minded Ukrainian subject. Visions and fetishes compensate for his envy of the completed history of *other* Europeans. But if the story were only about the past, resentment would exhaust the colonial subject, pushing him out of the present. Here Andrukhovych makes a leap—he tells his father's story, recalls his death, his funeral, his difficult relationship with him; in short, he talks about his break with the past and in doing so returns to the present.

The idealization of the old Central European myth compensates for dissatisfaction with history so far and serves as a therapeutic means of overcoming the envy produced by the long years of the colonial past. Colonial trauma has a significant impact on the worldview of Andrukhovych's lyrical hero and his postcolonial reconstruction of Europe. Geographically and historically, he does not construct boundaries for his transgression the way Stasiuk does. Nor does he overcome his painful envy of the *other*, continuing to live in the romantic and infantile world of an open future. Ruins and decay are "the transformation of the past into the future," he says. "The future is basically another continent, a kind of America, a New World, a clean slate," his ego-narrator admits.[42] He doesn't like textual euthanasia either, because it cuts off the path to future books, poems, and actions.

---

40 Andrukhovych, "Tsentralno-skhidna reviziia" [Central-eastern revision], 124.
41 Andrukhovych, "Tsentralno-skhidna reviziia" [Central-eastern revision], 73.
42 Andrukhovych, "Tsentralno-skhidna reviziia" [Central-eastern revision], 79.

The romantic vision of self-realization in the "New World" and the image of the happy West for a colonial subject traumatized by an unfulfilled history remain "perfect possibilities" that persist for a long time. In Andrukhovych's writing, the archetypal image of this absolute longing for the West is that of a little boy, his great-grandfather. "I keep coming back to the image that still haunts me," the narrator admits, merging with the imaginary boy-great-grandfather. "A little boy is contemplating the river. Beyond the river lies the New World. Beyond the Danube lies America, that is, the future; beyond the Danube lies everything that will (and will not) come to pass."[43] The image of the Danube as a river beyond which lies another world—the world to which the protagonist travels in search of a happy homeland—has served since the Romantic era as a metaphor for the colonial aspirations that impel the protagonist to commit the act of heroism and take him to a foreign land.

Despite the twists and turns of individual fates, despite narrative pauses and breaks, Andrukhovych's narrative flows like a family chronicle. There are fateful turns of the river along the way, but the future itself is inevitably somewhere out there, in the future, beyond the river. This teleologism, this focus on the future, serves as a guarantee that somewhere out there, there is a personal *"Europe"* for every resident of Galicia. The family story of the great-grandfather who once traveled across the patchwork part of the world that would later be called East-Central Europe becomes one of the roads to Andrukhovych's ideal *my Europe*. This tale is a manifestation of just one of the possible stories that the author collects in his memory as he amasses his fetishized traces of the complete world.

For Stasiuk, the prototype of a European journey consists of sailing on an imaginary ship across a map—in essence, going round in circles—while for Andrukhovych, his European journey is a linear story. But even as he feels torn between the past and future—those two monsters that rob him of his vitality and prevent an Eastern European from finding his place—he is aware of the closed nature of his journey back and forth. "Yes, escape—but also return. Yes, the future—but also the past."[44]

Stasiuk, who has no need to restore his European identity because he is already part of it, admits that he does not like linear narratives. He does not resort to personalizing his history either. By contrast, the postcolonial Ukrainian subject with whom Andrukhovych's narrator identifies must construct his own individual and ancestral lineage—his personal history—in order to incorporate it into the already formed (long ago and without his involvement) European narrative. And yet it is simply impossible to construct this personal history in a

---

43 Andrukhovych, "Tsentralno-skhidna reviziia" [Central-eastern revision], 84.
44 Andrukhovych, "Tsentralno-skhidna reviziia" [Central-eastern revision], 84.

conventional way—starting from the moment of birth and proceeding through the usual succession of events—because whole sections of this history have been ripped out: events, people, facts, testimonies. The canon of European Ukrainian history has yet to be created. Admittedly, it is possible to borrow other people's European histories, and Andrukhovych does so, borrowing motifs, excerpts, and myths from the works of Bruno Schulz, Andrzej Stasiuk, Reine Maria Rilke, Robert Musil, Danilo Kiš, and others—hence the fragmentary nature of Andrukhovych's imaginary Europe.

Escaping into an aesthetically idealized virtual Central European vision, Andrukhovych the postmodernist knows that resentment toward an unfulfilled past is an abyss, that the past "prevents the future from becoming possible," that it "holds time in its grip." The Eastern European obsession with the past—incomprehensible, when all is said and done, to normal Europeans—has, as Jean Baudrillard noted, fatal consequences for Europeans themselves. According to Baudrillard, the unfulfilled past that post-Soviet people carry with them drags Europeans, too, into the void of someone else's past, prevents them from enjoying the present, and shatters the grand narrative of European history. This view of the East from the perspective of the *other*, namely the West and Europe, is also of interest in a discussion of Eastern European revision.

Baudrillard argues that the West's discovery of the Eastern Bloc countries is similar to the discovery of concentration camp survivors. "The danger is to feed them too quickly, since this kills them," he continues, extending the analogy with concentration camp victims. Baudrillard believes that these people live in a different world, they have been destroyed by a catastrophe, and they will never enter our (meaning the Western) world. The past could, of course, be erased from their memory, the philosopher goes on to claim, but it would be futile because it is they who are dragging us Europeans into their empty space in much the same way that the concentration camp dead and survivors are destroying our last hope for culture, the rule of law, and morality. The lure of emptiness is irresistible, and as a result, the West is being destroyed by the emptiness of communism, the emptiness of history.[45]

In Andrukhovych's case, however, it seems that the West has nothing to fear from the emptiness of the East. Stasiuk defines the limits of his desires himself and has no qualms about his empty past. Andrukhovych's protagonist, although fatally dependent on colonial history and the resulting schism between the past and the future, ultimately fills the void virtually. This enables Andrukhovych to break out of the vicious cycle of escapes-and-returns so that he can live "inside" the present. This "being 'inside' is always superior, more gratifying, and more

---

45 Jean Baudrillard, *The Illusion of the End* (Stanford, CA: Stanford University Press, 1994), 49.

noble," he argues, "because it signifies your inclusion, involvement, presence—as opposed to a separated, excluded, rejected existence 'in between.'"[46] This kind of being in the present can be correlated with the state of postcolonialism.

Looking from the Center and the Periphery

Stasiuk's and Andrukhovych's visions of "my Europe" are radically different, and not only because Stasiuk's *ressentiment* is compensated by his own "ideal geography," while Andrukhovych's is compensated by his "ideal autobiography," which is reinforced by the traumatic experience of colonial history, leading to juxtapositions of "us and them," "now and then," "completeness and emptiness." Andrukhovych's self-declared lingering in the existential present, or "inside," attests to a postcolonial state that is characterized by rather ambivalent feelings, in which the following coexist:

- coming to terms with one's colonial history;
- cutting oneself off from the "Western world";
- being frozen in the so-called mirror stage of self-identification, which leads to narcissism;
- accepting absurd rebellion (suicide) as a possible path leading to the release of *ressentiment*;
- acknowledging the end of the "parental era" and staying in the maternal cultural field—"inside," in the continuum of "presence."

It is this lingering "inside" that brings the postcolonial subject back to an appreciation of the maternal zone of marginality, which takes on a polymorphic form and draws the narrator's attention to ruins and traces, to fetishes and endless transformations of corporeality. Andrukhovych creates his postmodern Galicia as a polymorphous maternal marginalized country. In his collection of essays, "DisOrientation in Locality," Andrukhovych ambitiously claims that Central Europe is a provincial place "where everyone knows that they are actually at the very center, because the center is nowhere and everywhere at the same time."[47]

But in fact he is more concerned with marginality than with provincialism. Andrukhovych proves to be a faithful disciple of the hybrids and phantasms

---

46 Andrukhovych, "Tsentralno-skhidna reviziia" [Central-eastern revision], 98.
47 Yurii Andrukhovych, "Chas i mistse, abo Moia ostannia terytoriia" [Time and place, or My last territory], in *DezOriientatsiia na mistsevosti* [Disorientation on the ground] (Ivano-Frankivsk: Lileia-NV, 1999), 121.

created by Bruno Schulz, the incomparable master and king of maternal marginalia—side rooms that "follow their own time, measured by the ticking of clocks, monologues of silence" and the sleep of "wet nurses, broad and swollen with milk."[48] In Schulz's *Cinnamon Shops*, the expulsion of the father from the room, the image of the father's brother transformed into a "bundle of rubber tubing," and other things reveal the destruction of the center and the flow of action to the maternal space—forgotten rooms, backyards, alleys, and the edges of the town, overgrown with "precocious blossoming," "luxuriation and wilting."

The maternal archetype in Andrukhovych's fantasy worlds deserves special mention. We have already mentioned that the death of the father is a key theme in "East-Central Revision." Applying Jean Lacan's psychoanalytic concepts, we can say that the narrator is suspended in a world without the symbolic name of the Father, which centers the identity of the colonial subject. That is why the narrator turns to fictional revisions, to a mirrored self-identification with his grandfather, who is perceived as an ancestor who ties the protagonist to the West. Andrukhovych's autobiographical hero cannot break through to reality, and images of *the other* (the old way of life, other people's myths) serve as mirrors in which he sees his own complete history. The postcolonial Ukrainian subject feels lost, confused, unhappy that European culture as a whole is something separate from him, that it is not his mother, does not belong only to him, and does not satisfy only his needs. In order to fulfill his "I," the postcolonial individual fantastically and virtually appropriates this other culture, resorting to fetish objects and fetish narratives.

Immersed in a state of "presence" severed from the past, Andrukhovych acknowledges the end of the paternal era. As a writer, he creates a multifaceted, polymorphous, and many-named hero, and this polymorphism signals the absence of a defined, stable identity whose historical and sociological character would correlate with the Father's name. Habsburg or Soviet history could have been sanctified with this name, but both are now in the past.

The masquerade of roles and identities signals that there is no strong and powerful center that governs, supervises and cares—in other words, "the Father is dead." All in all, the past associated with the power of the father is receding—and that is why it is deliberately rejected by Andrukhovych's self-referential hero.[49]

---

48 Bruno Schulz, "Tsynamonovi kramnyti [Cinnamon shops]," in *Tsynamonovi kramnyti. Sanatorii Pid Klepsydroiu* [The cinnamon shops. Sanatorium under the sign of the hourglass] (Lviv: Forum vydavtsiv, 2004), 268.
49 It is noteworthy that Yuri Andrukhovych's essay "East-Central Revision" is deeply imbued with memories of his father, who died shortly before the essay was written.

CHAPTER 3

Post-Memory and Transgenerational Trauma

The Return of History

Marianna Hirsch has argued that post-memory is "a structure of inter- and transgenerational return of traumatic knowledge and embodied experience."[1] The handing down of transgenerational trauma has been a subject of research since the 1960s and has informed studies of the Holocaust, which affects the physical, mental, and social lives of the descendants of traumatized victims in the second and third generations. The inclusion of the transgenerational aspect in postcolonial discourse implies an expansion of psychological, social, and biological factors in contemporary postcolonial criticism.

As Karl Mannheim has noted, in order for a person to be identified as belonging to a particular generation, they need to have experienced and participated in the events that are decisive for their generation "with a common location in the historical dimension of the social process."[2] And yet in the late twentieth century, it became more common not to talk about what unites and brings generations together, but to focus on what divides them. The popular sociological theory devised by William Strauss and Neil Howe about the cyclical nature of generations in American history is entirely based on the generation gap.[3] The American sociologists' theory can be summarized as follows: they distinguish Generation X, Generation Y, and Generation Z. Generation X (also referred to as the Pepsi Generation or the Thirteenth Generation) is the demographic cohort born between 1961 and 1981. It is nomadic in nature and characterized by the awakening of revolutionary consciousness. The next generation, Generation Y (also referred to as the Net Generation, the Fourteenth Generation, and Millennials), consists of people born between 1982 and 2000. It's a generation of heroes, since it has had to take part in the culture wars. The next generation—Generation Z—includes those born after 2001. This generation is inherently artistic and highly adaptable to new circumstances, but lives in a world of crises and is being drawn into the war on terrorism.

As Strauss and Howe point out, it isn't just that history creates generations; generations also create history. Evidence that generations influence and

---

1   Hirsch, *The Generation of Postmemory: Writing and Visual Culture After the Holocaust*, 6.
2   Karl Mannheim, "The Problem of Generations," in *Essays on the Sociology of Knowledge*, ed. Paul Kecskemeti (London: Routledge, 1952), 290.
3   See William Strauss and Neil Howe, *Generations: The History of America's Future, 1584 to 2069* (New York: William Morrow, 1991); Strauss and Howe, *13th Gen: Abort, Retry, Ignore, Fail?* (New York: Vintage Books, 1993); Strauss and Howe, *The Fourth Turning: An American Prophecy* (New York: Broadway Books, 1997); Strauss and Howe, *Millennials Rising: The Next Great Generation* (New York: Vintage Books, 2000).

reinterpret history and shape contemporary history can be seen in the increasing relevance of the theme of generations in Ukrainian culture of the early twenty-first century. We can see this, for example, in the recent emergence of literary works where the theme of parents and children takes center stage. I'll name just a few of them. Yevheniya Kononeko's detective story *Nostalgia* (2002) is centered on the unraveling of the story of two parents, which leads to their suicide and binds their children with the mystery of the past. In her novel *Sweet Darusia* (2004), Maria Matios recreates a family history drawn to the past and specifically to the *sins* of parents. Sashko Ushkalov describes the lives of teenagers in a world "without parents" in his novel *Life Safety* (2007). Oksana Zabuzhko's novel, or, as the writer herself describes it, family saga, *The Museum of Abandoned Secrets* (2009) centers around the history of three generations and the theme of lineage. Lina Kostenko, in her *Diary of a Ukrainian Madman* (2010), also explores generational ties and family history against the backdrop of Ukrainian history at the beginning of the new millennium. Great historical narratives—true epics—appeared a little later: Vasyl Makhno's *Eternal Calendar* (2019), Maria Matios's *Beech Land* (2019), and Sofia Andrukhovych's *Amadoca* (2020). Chronologically these works span several centuries, they map local and geocultural communities, and recreate the multiethnic history of the peoples who have inhabited Ukraine, but generational history takes center stage in all of them.

Numerous anthologies that have appeared in Ukrainian literature since the 1990s reveal attempts at self-determination within the boundaries of generational identity. Special generational canons that have no overlap between themselves were formed: *The 1980s Generation: An Anthology of New Ukrainian Poetry* (1990); *Noun: An Anthology of the 1990s* (1997); *The 1990s Generation* (1998); *Beyond Decades* (1999) and *Beyond Decades-2* (2000), *Two Tonnes: An Anthology of Poetry of the 2000s* (2007). Ultimately, all the generations would come together on the Maidan to witness the formation of a new national community.

In Ukraine, the theme of generations in literature traditionally unfolds in two dimensions—through the narrative of generational conflict and through the revival of great family histories. These seemingly opposite narrative strategies are in fact connected. Perhaps their most general origins can be described through the concept of big and small stories. Drawing on the experience of postcolonial literature, we can recall that in these literary works, the two types of narratives particularly collide in some liminal zone—a borderline situation between different cultures, ethnic groups, religions, languages, and civilizations. In Arundhati Roy's novel *The God of Small Things* (1996), the twins Estha and

Rahel find themselves in such a liminal zone. They happened to be born and live in a border zone, in a town in southern India divided by different linguistic, religious, and social laws. It is they who have to pay for their mother's sin—her unlawful love for a carpenter, a man of a lower caste, or, as the novel puts it, for violating the Laws of Love, "the laws that lay down who should be loved and how. And how much."[4]

In Roy's writing, the big stories that deal with the existential matters of a nation are always connected with the concept of home and family history. As Slavoj Žižek has noted, the perception of a traumatic historical Real in the terms of a family narrative is becoming a fundamental ideological operation.[5] In today's globalized world, such family histories are transformed into ideological or national myths, but they also become commodities, prepackaged for convenient consumption. Such family histories and chronicles become collectibles; they are offered for sale like the jars of preserved exotic fruits in Salman Rushdie's novel *Midnight's Children*. Spiced with multiethnic flavors, often from a colonial past, they emerge as a *"local specialty."*

Yet there is an alternative that exists in opposition to this archiving of ancestral memory: a narrative that unfolds as an installation or collection of private details of life. These small stories are woven from the ordinary "small things" of everyday life. In Roy's novel, Ammu and Velutta, in love but forced apart by insurmountable caste prejudices, and with no future, entrust themselves to the God of Small Things in order to break out of the vicious cycle of their family history. "The Big Things ever lurked inside. They knew that there was nowhere for them to go. They had nothing. No future. So they stuck to the small things. They laughed at ant-bites on each other's bottoms. At clumsy caterpillars sliding on the ends of leaves, at overturned beetles that couldn't right themselves." In this way, they free themselves from the burden of history.[6]

Thus, small things (small stories) become the embodiment of life, *without* and *beyond* history. In Toni Morrison's novel *Beloved* (1987), the big story of slavery and the horrors it inflicted upon black people is ultimately transformed into a story about life in the terrifying house at 124 Bluestone Road, inhabited by real and imaginary people, and feared by neighbors. A dead daughter returns to the house to be with the mother who had killed her when she was a little girl to save her from a life of slavery that traumatizes both body and soul. The lives of

---

4   Arundhati Roy, *Boh dribnyts* [The God of Small Things], trans. Andrii Masliukh (Lviv: Vydavnytstvo Staroho Leva, 2018), 39–40.
5   Slavoj Žižek, *In Defense of Lost Causes* (London: Verso, 2008), 52.
6   Roy, *Boh dribnyts*, 339.

Baby Suggs, Sethe, Paul D, Sixo, Denver, and others are intertwined in this small story about a haunted house and correlate with *another* story—the real, terrifying story of the lives of black slaves at Sweet Home. In J.M. Coetzee's novel *Waiting for the Barbarians* (1980), a small story turns into the tale of a magistrate who wants to change the big story and takes on the guilt of the empire toward the barbarians, which results in his physical inability to love a barbarian woman, from whom he is physically separated by the impenetrable wall of the historical guilt of the colonizers toward the colonized.

The epic ancestral memory seemingly does not lend itself to the grand narrative description and disintegrates into a series of local memories, forming a dialogically complex and multifaceted picture of parallel, reverse, and alternative histories. This leads to the emergence of a method of memory archiving which Marianna Hirsch describes as album-like: a collection and assemblage of images and objects from the past based on old photographs, stories, and objects. Thus a destroyed world is reconstructed. And yet in postcolonial works, the big story exists as an ideal that challenges the Western farewell to *grand narratives, grand heroes, and grand journeys*—a phenomenon that Jean-François Lyotard claimed was axiomatic for the postmodern situation in the West in 1979.

The change in modality of the postcolonial novel is most clearly revealed by Salman Rushdie, who structures his novels according to the principle of breaking down, linking, and preserving fragments of history. We are dealing with the disintegration of the body, the fragmentation of consciousness, the permeation of people through history, and the bundling of smells and foreign words. In Rushdie's novel *Midnight's Children* (1981), this narrative comes in waves, sometimes reversing itself and removing similarities with fragments of fairy tales and myths, sometimes expanding and drawing in new names and new people. In Roy's novel *The God of Small Things*, the postcolonial narrative is similarly devoid of linearity and takes on a cyclical quality.

The generational gap in post-Soviet Ukrainian literature manifests itself either as the tragic echo of past parental sins or as the resentful ironic mask of the protagonist himself. In general, small stories coexist in Ukrainian literature with the unfolding of a grand family narrative, not out of a weariness with history, as is characteristic of the West, but out of a desire to rewrite history. The construction of family history takes on an uncanny and mythologized tone in Ukrainian literature, as demonstrated by Oksana Zabuzhko's *The Museum of Abandoned Secrets*, Taras Prokhasko's *The UnSimple* (2002), and Anton Sanchenko's *Wedding with Europe* (2008). The mythologization of *great* national history unfolds in the context of a reassessment of the values of the recent Soviet past, in particular the experience of parents and grandparents, and also on the basis of new alternative histories such as the history of the UPA, the history of the Holodomor, and post-Maidan history.

Any representation (presentation) of history, family narratives included, involves an imaginary repetition of what has been experienced. Paul Ricœur distinguishes between two forms of disposition, or two intentionalities, in relation to the past: *imagination*, directed toward the fantastic, the fictional, the unreal, the possible, the utopian; and *memory*, directed toward that which precedes, since precedence is the main feature of the thing being remembered. Imagination and memory can be in opposition to each other, but they can also confront, intersect, and interconnect. There is also the question of how to reconcile imagination and memory, recollection, and presentation. Ricœur emphasizes that recollection is a process that must involve the subject. It is a transition from "what?", i.e., the discovery of the cognitive resources of memory, to "who?", i.e., the focus on the appropriation of memory by a subject capable of recollection.[7]

Historical narrative speaks of history only when it cannot express everything, and this undisclosed core of the story, which cannot be expressed, is, according to Franklin Ankersmit, traumatic. This undisclosed core is what compels us to "tell" the story. Usually, these are traumatic events that need to be told but at the same time resist disclosure, emerging as something indescribable and unthinkable. The past is painful, if not traumatic, in its very essence, Ankersmit claims. What constitutes the core of historical experience comes from a special "combination of pain and pleasure in how we relate to the past."[8] Postcolonial rewriting of history naturally gravitates toward such a traumatic core, and it also makes generations the main agents of such traumatic experience. The narrative of postcolonial history, tailored to the post-memory of generations, becomes an exercise in "imagining."

Using Oksana Zabuzhko's novel *The Museum of Abandoned Secrets* as an example, we will set out to determine how traumatic experience, manifested through a generation gap, represents, or rather constructs, history in contemporary Ukrainian literature, and what narrative strategies are employed in it. Given the author's intention, the novel deals primarily with ancestral national history, and this history resembles a search for some kind of central, pivotal time. Typically for postcolonial novels, the work offers not a linear, rational view of family history, but a cyclical one, a return in the form of various biographical stories. The

---

7   Paul Ricœur, *Memory, History, Forgetting*, trans. Kathleen Blamey and David Pellauer (Chicago: University of Chicago Press, 2004), 4.
8   F. R. Ankersmit, *Sublime Historical Experience* (Stanford: Stanford University Press, 2005), 9.

latter erases the conflict between generations broken by the totalitarian machine that destroyed and devoured entire generations.

Archive, Museum, and the Female Body: Metaphors of Memory

Oksana Zabuzhko's novel is one of the most representative postcolonial novels in Ukrainian literature. Like other postcolonial writers, Zabuzhko must resolve the issue of the change in focus of the narrative and find a new internal structure for the story. Zabuzhko offers this structure in the first part of the novel: this must be a story where time is seen as a labyrinth; it draws closer, then hides from its contemporaries, but most importantly, it conceals mysteries and secrets that must be uncovered to restore the memory of the family and the memory of generations. This perception of time is reflected in the magical realism of the Latin American novel, and Zabuzhko makes full use of this temporal magic. She writes in the novel that in this shared time, "we all rub together unknowingly—the living, the dead, and the not yet born."[9]

The writer sees her role as articulating the traumas in twentieth-century Ukrainian history that have been deliberately hushed up—from the Holodomor to the underground movement of the OUN-UPA and dissidents of the 1980s—through the voices of the second and third generations. According to Yuliya Kazanova, this seems to be an attempt at overcoming historical amnesia and creating a national historical narrative.[10] Daryna, the protagonist and the author's alter ego, strives to overcome "this ineradicable attitude of superiority toward the past."[11] Zabuzhko reduces the concept of history to a Ferris wheel from the top of which, for a brief moment, one can see "a mere flash of a vista"—a narrative tapestry that leads us to believe that "EVERYTHING around" is woven together by threads of connections and memory: "A hundred, a thousand of them run invisibly through [Daryna] and into other people's lives, but to discern and comprehend the pattern they draw ... is impossible."[12] In this way, history—

---

9   Oksana S. Zabuzhko, *The Museum of Abandoned Secrets*, trans. Nina Shevchuk-Murray (Seattle: Amazon Crossing, 2012), chap. 2, Kindle edition.
10 Yuliya Kazanova, "'The Instinct of Resistance to Evil': Postmemory and the Ukrainian National Imaginary in Oksana Zabuzhko's Novel *The Museum of Abandoned Secrets*," *Memory Studies* 15, no. 2 (2021), https://journals.sagepub.com/doi/full/10.1177/17506980211044710.
11 Zabuzhko, *The Museum of Abandoned Secrets*, chap. 1.
12 Zabuzhko, *The Museum of Abandoned Secrets*, chap. 2.

like a great axial time, like a returning wheel, like an organism—is "threading together people from different centuries—let alone generations."[13]

Thus, Zabuzhko's novel appeals to the image of a "vista," or panoramic vision, and to the three allegories of postcolonial historical narrative: *the museum, the archive, and the secret*. The *museum* implies the demonstration or display of the stories themselves. The *archive* refers to the documents that record real and falsified biographies. *Secrets* allude to the silenced and hidden pages of history. All these stories revolve around Daryna, a journalist who works for a TV station and hosts a program about the hidden secrets of silenced history. When Daryna finds a photograph of UPA fighters among the archival materials, the image of the only woman in the picture catches her attention and sets off a chain of events. She also finds a random note written by her father in the margins of a book from her library, and this note helps her to understand her father's dissident history.

Paintings by Vlada, who dies tragically in a car accident, also become part of the archive and acquire magical significance. And the story of the adopted son of an old KGB agent, who is actually the child of a former OUN member, proves to be entirely archival. This is the triple framework of the historical narrative of this postcolonial novel, described by the Ukrainian dissident Leonid Plyushch in the blurb as a literary work about "three generations, three completely different eras, with completely different conditions." The author herself has maintained in numerous interviews that the title of the novel refers to the *hidden treasures* of national (ancestral) memory.

With its focus on postcolonial narrative, the novel is distinctly polemical in its opposition to the consumerist interpretation of national history. The novel's protagonist, journalist Daryna Hoshchynska, refuses to accept the perception of the past through a heroic-romantic "dramatically arched story with a handful of characters (parents, children, lovers, friends, and colleagues—anyone else?)."[14] Instead, in her almost cinematic vision, history becomes a virtual reality, programmed by the museum of *hidden secrets*, and is likened to a humongous, immeasurable "archive of things once witnessed, of footage that wants to be watched."[15] The footage can be reviewed at random, not chronologically, going back and forth, jumping here and there. This virtual model is based on the principle of reciprocal time mirrors: the 1940s look into the 2000s, while the latter, as if in a mirror, are projected onto the 1940s, and all three generations

---

13 Zabuzhko, *The Museum of Abandoned Secrets*, chap. 2.
14 Zabuzhko, *The Museum of Abandoned Secrets*, chap. 1.
15 Zabuzhko, *The Museum of Abandoned Secrets*, chap. 3.

are intertwined with chains of mystical associations and connections—with Adrian's dreams or Daryna's hallucinations.

It is worth noting that when describing magical time, the author borrows tried-and-tested techniques from the global postcolonial novel. Zabuzhko's novel is akin to Rushdie's *Midnight's Children* in its mystical knowledge that transcends time and space: this knowledge is carried by Saleem, the novel's protagonist, who tells the story of a thousand children born on August 15, 1947, at the stroke of midnight, the moment India declared its independence. In its focus on small objects, *The Museum of Abandoned Secrets* also resembles Roy's *The God of Small Things*. Capturing the "traces" of the past is possible through collecting "indeterminate bits and pieces" in the book of life. For life, as Zabuzhko writes in her novel, is "an enormous, bottomless suitcase, stuffed with precisely such indeterminate bits and pieces, utterly useless for anyone other than its owner,"[16] who takes it with them when they die. And yet it is from these scattered traces, hidden secrets, and "indeterminate bits and pieces" that the "lost secret code to the deep, subterranean core of the other person's life" is retrieved.[17] In Zabuzhko's novel, Roy's god of spontaneous small things is transformed into a collector of useless but existentially significant objects. It's also reminiscent of Dubravka Ugrešić's novel *The Museum of Unconditional Surrender* (1996), in which the metaphor of the museum is used to represent nostalgic mnemonic memory, rooted not so much in people and events as in objects and things that characterize the era.

These aspects of the postcolonial structure of Zabuzhko's novel form a metathematic narrative framework—the novel's form is explicitly stated and discussed by the protagonist, who represents the author herself. The narrative structure breaks down into a series of parallel novels that could stand alone. The novel also features various styles ranging from a romance to a mystical thriller and political commentary. The monologism of Zabuzhko's novel has been extensively discussed by literary scholars. Critics even argue: "It only makes sense to talk about polyphony in the context of characters as passive carriers of a certain ideology of the author."[18]

But the problem is not the pervasive monologism of the novel's narrative structure. After all, the narrative in Rushdie's *Midnight's Children* is threaded through Saleem Sinai's monologue, which ties all the diverse and multi-temporal stories

---

16   Zabuzhko, *The Museum of Abandoned Secrets*, chap. 1
17   Zabuzhko, *The Museum of Abandoned Secrets*, chap. 1
18   Vasyl Kostiuk, "Dyskurs nenavysti v obolontsi pornohlamuru [Discourse of hatred in the shell of pornoglamour]," *Krytyka* 14, no. 9–10 (September 2010).

together. All the voices in the novel are expressed indirectly through Saleem. But Rushdie's monological narrative is filled with foreign voices, woven from myths and allusions, and Saleem's language becomes the body that unites an entire nation.

In Zabuzhko's novel, the monological narrative is not elevated to the mythological level and remains distinctly original and subjective. The rational structure of the novel unpacks it into separate ideas, voices, and stories. These are linked by the postcolonial concept of ancestral time, which is outlined in the opening chapters. First, it seeks to affirm the "completeness" of national history and its transformation from marginal and peripheral to central and pivotal. Second, like a labyrinth, *hidden history* is meant to reveal the real history that lies buried in totalitarian times and has been suppressed from official historiography. Third, ancestral time is likened to a museum—the gathering, collecting, and exhibiting of historical (or imagined historical, fictional) facts—and serves as a performative act for revealing and reformulating history itself.

Zabuzhko not only challenges her characters to engage in ideological, political, and business discussions; she also lays bare the techniques of her storytelling. For instance, she pays a lot of attention to the question of what national history is and how it can be recounted. Here, Zabuzhko attempts (at least theoretically) to challenge the heroic-like or imitative stories, where history becomes a media performance—a kind of "story" reproduced by the mass media. History as such becomes a simulation; it can be rewritten or even erased so that it can originate from nothing, for example, from someone else's biography, which the museum curator and KGB agent Bukhalov can substitute for real history and recount to his daughter.

The idea behind *The Museum of Abandoned Secrets* is a fairly ambitious one: Zabuzhko seeks to show that in postcolonial history, the real history is not a documented factual framework or a glamorous social media "story," but an innermost, almost mystical *knowledge* that signifies belonging to it. That is why the novel's protagonist irrationally *knows* the truth about the past from the very beginning and therefore claims: "the whole story as I know it—know it anyway, without the SBU archives, but by feel, through my own life; through Artem's basement and its rickety desk; through Aidy, Vlada, love, dreams; by the same blind and unerring method through which I know the truth about my father's death."[19]

Zabuzhko resorts to several strategies to reconcile this knowledge within the scope of the postcolonial novel with its particular chronotope of a "museum of

---

19 Zabuzhko, *The Museum of Abandoned Secrets*, chap. 8.

abandoned secrets." Her strategies include political essays, parallel histories, alternative counterhistory, mass media projects, and autobiography. But perhaps the most important strategy for constructing the postcolonial novel is mystical knowledge: Gela, who died in 1947, allegedly "summons" Daryna to tell her about her death—"she tossed it to me from her photograph, like ball lightning."[20]

Such knowledge is eroticized, coming "in the instant of an accidental orgasm in an uncomfortable position, on a rickety desk, in a basement of a certain academic institute."[21] Ultimately, if we draw on Ankersmit's assertion that historical experience is elevated through its aestheticization, then in Zabuzhko's novel, we have an example of erotically sublimated historiography—a romance. This *erotic historiography* is defined, on the one hand, by a rupture between the past and the present, and on the other hand, by their merging. This merging of different historical events is manifested in parallel erotic scenes: in far-off 1947 in an insurgent hideout, and in 1997 in the basement of some institute. As a result, we have almost twins (the Adrian lovers) and three pregnant women (Olena Dovhan, "Rahel," and Daryna Hoshchynska).

Such mystical revelations take on special meaning in the novel under the influence of Gnostic philosophy, which is meant to affirm the protagonist's spiritual aristocracy and openness to mystical knowledge, in the Holy Grail, which the main character in Zabuzhko's novella "The Tale of the Guelder Rose Flute" sees in her *womb*. In *The Museum of Abandoned Secrets*, history is often associated with the female body, and the "abandoned secrets" hidden in the womb of bodily memory are erotic and mystical in nature. This heretical knowledge, which places the female body at the center of everything sacred, first appears in Zabuzhko's "Tale of the Guelder Rose Flute": Hanna, who has been gifted with an unusual sense of the otherworldly, knows that her belly is "like the church chalice bearing the blessed sacraments; when she first made this discovery, she recoiled in fear from such a blasphemous thought, but then each time she lowered her eyes, she found the same sight—a shallow chalice that glowed with a gentle pearly luster; it was here, inside her, it *was* her."[22] The Gnostic "truth," hidden in female physicality, in this hiding place of holy gifts and secrets, is postmemory. Postmemory repairs the generational gap and is revealed not rationally, but bodily, and to grandchildren, not children, because we need to take

---

20 Zabuzhko, *The Museum of Abandoned Secrets*, chap. 8.
21 Zabuzhko, *The Museum of Abandoned Secrets*, chap. 8.
22 Oksana Zabuzhko, *Your Ad Could Go Here: Stories,* trans. Halyna Hryn, Askold Melnyczuk, Nina Murray, Marco Carynnyk, and Marta Horban, ed. Nina Murray (Seattle: Amazon Crossing, 2020)., 40.

"a one-generation-long detour. Children aren't much use for this, but grandkids are perfect: Two generations is exactly the right distance, a systole-diastole, a rhythmic breathing, the pulse of progress."[23]

In Zabuzhko's saga, the world becomes an intricate web of symbolic analogies, dreams, events, destinies. Symbolic correspondences multiply and become blind signs—these are no longer magical connections, but analogies: Daryna becomes the reincarnation of Olena Dovhan, a Ukrainian Insurgent Army messenger who died in 1947, while Adrian becomes a guide to ancient family history, identical to another Adrian who died in 1947 in a UPA bunker.

The analogies and doubles multiply: Daryna's father is juxtaposed to Bukhalov's father, while Bukhalov's daughter, Veronika, is almost a sister to Daryna herself. Symbolic situations are also duplicated: Vladka's death is mystically linked to revenge, as she dies in a place where there was once a cemetery for those who died of starvation, and (as it turns out) Vladka's grandparents were among those who perpetrated the dispossession . . . Another character mentioned is Aunt Lyusya, who once brought a sack of flour from Western Ukraine, which was evidently given to her by Olena Dovhan, thanks to which Daryna's mother survived the post-war famine. In this way, Olena Dovhan programmed Daryna's future destiny. "Gela did not choose me—Gela simply followed her flour to find me. She followed the tracks of the life she once saved—in exchange for the one that had been cut short inside her," Daryna says.[24] The name of the man in the old photograph is also revealed intuitively: "and someone beside me (a woman's voice) prompts with the name Mykhailo! and in this single glimpse [. . .] I *recognize* him."[25] The union of Adrian and Daria also has a mystical background: "Those who died that night in the bunker, married us. They *knew*."[26] And most importantly, Daryna's unborn child turns out to be almost a reincarnation of Olena Dovhan's unborn child. The life analogies of the postcolonial novel testify to the magical harmony between the generations of grandparents, parents, and children.

Oksana Zabuzhko seeks not only to restore ancestral memory but also to incorporate the traumatic experience of generations into a new national consciousness. One of the strategies of such historiography is to rehabilitate the role of the symbolic Father, who centers and shapes national and cultural consciousness. The author's interest in the rehabilitation of the Father's name is demonstrated by the significant semantic load assigned to this theme in the novel.

---

23 Zabuzhko, *The Museum of Abandoned Secrets*, chap. 8.
24 Zabuzhko, *The Museum of Abandoned Secrets*, chap. 8.
25 Zabuzhko, *The Museum of Abandoned Secrets*, chap. 7.
26 Zabuzhko, *The Museum of Abandoned Secrets*, chap. 8.

A special, existential-magical presence is supposed to become a bridge between generations. This presence is formed through epiphanies in which past history magically comes to life on film, becoming part of the present life of Zabuzhko's characters. One such moment of epiphany occurs when the father is almost magically transformed from a failure into a dissident, and his daughter begins to admire him for his Sisyphean desire to fight despite fear. This effectively bridges the generation gap which was the opening scene of the piece, and the weak father of the Sixtiers generation who caused nothing but embarrassment during his lifetime becomes after his death, through the "traces" of his presence (such as the exclamation "this!!!" which he scribbled in the margins of a book while anxiously awaiting his arrest in the 1960s) *a person whom Daryna could admire.* "Not as my father—he had been gone too long for that—but as a person I could admire had I met him now."[27]

Daryna Hoshchynska is not the only character who turns to the figure of her father and ultimately finds a replacement for the "weak father" in the idealized image of a "father to be proud of." The family history of Pavlo Bukhalov and his daughter Veronika becomes a kind of mirror image of Daryna's relationship with her father. Daryna feels an intimate, almost mystical connection with this family. After all, when you consider the original idea of a postcolonial novel based on the principle of the wheel of history, which cyclically combines and mystically connects different times and different people, such intimacy no longer seems strange.

The family histories of the Hoshchynskis and the Bukhalovs turn out to be very closely intertwined: in 1947, Bukhalov the grandfather destroys the underground hideout while the pregnant Olena Dovhan, with whom Daryna identifies, is in it; in the 1960s, Bukhalov the son, taking pity on Daryna's mother when her husband is arrested, effectively saves her from imprisonment. But the very idea that the families could be friends infuriates Daryna: "And here was Pavlo Ivanovych seemingly stacking our parents' fates in the same file, seemingly saying we should be friends: the two invalid-father orphans, hello, Mowgli, we be of one blood, ye and I . . ."[28]

History separates these families with impenetrable ideological walls. Daryna comments that even the roles of the parents are different. Her father defended his truth, while Bukhalov Jr. deliberately distorted the truth, erasing entire lives from it. Bukhalov, who has access to the KGB archives, destroys materials related to the history of his own mother—a Jewish woman who carried messages for

---

27 Zabuzhko, *The Museum of Abandoned Secrets*, chap. 1.
28 Zabuzhko, *The Museum of Abandoned Secrets*, chap. 8.

the Ukrainian Insurgent Army (UPA) and hanged herself in her cell after being repeatedly interrogated and raped. To erase the traces of his mother, Bukhalov replaces her story with that of Leah Goldman, who died in the Przemyśl ghetto.

Zabuzhko lays bare the singular cynicism of the system which turned the son of a Jewish UPA member and her brother-in-arms into a loyal servant of the party. The child, born in a prison cell, is adopted by the NKVD officer who exterminated his family, and Bukhalov Jr. grows up to become a KGB officer. And yet Zabuzhko gives Bukhalov's son a chance—as a "little" person, he too has the right to his own life, he is not guilty of the crimes of his father and the system as a whole, and he is willing to sacrifice everything, even to rewrite his own history, for the sake of his daughter, who he wants to have everything he himself didn't have, including mastery of one's own fate. The whole story about Bukhalov and the strength/weakness of fatherhood becomes one of the counterpoints to the big "axial" story in which different, even conflicting fates and generations are intertwined.

Family rifts and generational conflict are one of the central predispositions to the conflict that unfolds in Zabuzhko's novel. The author further develops the criticism of parents, and of the 1960s generation in particular, that she introduced in her landmark 1996 novel *Fieldwork in Ukrainian Sex*. The author's criticism targets both the *frigid* mother whose routine was disrupted by the hungry 1930s, and the *weak* father infected with fear of arrest. He has no power over anyone or anything but his daughter, whom he can control both mentally and physically.

In *The Museum of Abandoned Secrets*, the protagonist's father in fact represents the entire generation to which he belongs—the dissidents of the Sixtiers generation. The novel is fiercely critical of the artificial *glorification* of the Sixtiers generation caused by the rewriting of history, where it is easy to join the ranks of heroes who fought against the totalitarian system by fashioning "a glamorous, [. . .] almost-dissident biography."[29] A Sixtiers legend—a "well-known poet" with "a vague victim-of-the-regime claim"—comes in for particularly harsh criticism in the novel.[30] Zabuzhko reduces her to a "hefty, lumbering old woman with a bad bite," whose grievance about the past stems from the fact that on her fiftieth birthday (celebrated the same year that "Stus was sentenced to a second term") the Writers' Union failed to send her a birthday telegram.

But dividing the Sixtiers generation into "real" and "fake" is not the author's main goal. Zabuzko's generational utopia, in which the very form of the

---

29 Zabuzhko, *The Museum of Abandoned Secrets*, chap. 1.
30 Zabuzhko, *The Museum of Abandoned Secrets*, chap. 1.

postcolonial novel seeks to remove and eliminate generational conflict, is a symptomatic phenomenon. The writer Ihor Bondar-Tereshchenko places the new generational consciousness of the nineties generation in the category of "hobnobbing" and "postmodern self-indulgence." Characterizing the confrontation between the Sixties and the nineties generations, he says in his extravagant way, not without cynicism: "On one side of the 'revolutionary granite' live anxious countrymen with suicidal tendencies, who strive to look nationally conscious until their last breath, reluctant to work as security guards or watchmen for commercial firms. On the other side are infantile young people in velvet 'rebel' gloves, the darlings of patrons and Mossad agents, practicing visionaries and functionaries, the golden children of postmodern self-indulgence."[31]

A member of the last Soviet generation, who were born in the early 1960s, Oksana Zabuzhko (born 1960) began her writing career in the 1980s, but became well-known in the 1990s. The 1980s generation is a fairly powerful literary phenomenon with talented representatives such as Yuri Andrukhovych, Oksana Zabuzhko, Vasyl Herasymyuk, and Ihor Rymaruk. This generation introduced a distinctly new, multi-format poetics to Ukrainian literature. Their strong national and ethical focus, which they shared with the Sixtiers, sets them apart from subsequent generations.

A secret is a mystery, but it's also something unrevealed, hidden in a traumatic past, which should (and must) be revealed in order to understand the present. Secrets also play an important role in interpersonal relationships and internal psychological processes. In particular, a secret becomes a mark of transgression (upsetting the equilibrium in relationships between people and between generations), a sign of the disintegration of language and time. At the same time, it signals the need to restore equilibrium, connect the community, and build a coherent and understandable message.

Anne McClintock defines the colonial journey as moving forward in *geographical* space, but backward in *racial* and *gender* time, "to a prehistoric zone of linguistic, racial and gender degeneration."[32] That is why women's issues in postcolonial novels are closely intertwined with aspects of linguistic, gender, and racial identity. Women become victims of class and caste conflicts in Arundhati Roy's *The God of Small Things*. The female face of colonial victimhood is

---

31   Ihor Bondar-Tereshchenko, "Oksamyt Ukrainy [Velvet of Ukraine]," *Yi*, no. 34 (2004), http://www.ji.lviv.ua/n34texts/ibt.htm.
32   Anne McClintock, *Imperial Leather: Race, Gender and Sexuality in the Colonial Contest* (New York: Routledge, 1995), 369.

embodied in Jean Rhys's novel *Wide Sargasso Sea* (1966). The fate of colonial India is associated with women in Amitav Ghosh's novel *Sea of Poppies* (2008).

Postcolonial criticism usually focuses on the analysis of male-female relationships, conflicts within the family rooted in alienation, and women's nostalgia for childhood as a place where the spontaneity of childhood (girlhood) was experienced physically and emotionally. Postcolonial writing frequently makes women not only victims but also tools of violence. Frantz Fanon, for example, raised the question of the role of revolutionary women in anticolonial protest. At the same time, he masculinized the protesting women and emphasized their erotic power. In Fanon's view, women are not independent actors; they embrace their revolutionary mission instinctively. They hide men's pistols, bombs, and rifles under their skirts, infiltrate foreign communities, and carry out subversive and terrorist acts. But even while protesting against the colonizers, the women remain mysterious and threatening to their male countrymen. Therefore, their role and place had to be clearly limited; even in a new, independent nation, women had to exist within the confines of a somewhat transformed but strong heterosexual family.

In many colonial cultures, the national narrative is usually organized around a father figure. When Oksana Zabuzhko moves in the direction of the past, she sends her heterogeneous agents—a woman and a man (Daryna and Adrian)—on ahead. The goal of the journey, however, is to rehabilitate the symbolic name of the Father, thereby emphasizing the need for the sociocultural normalization of contemporary Ukrainian society in terms of national memory.

The fact that the present is drawn into the past is particularly significant for the emerging postcolonial Ukrainian novel. In the postcolonial novel, as we know, fatherhood is not simply a matter of biology. Salmon Rushdie argues that when writing about fathers, the contemporary author of the postcolonial novel is in fact writing about himself and creating his own history, since it is very difficult to rewrite the history of fathers without saying anything about oneself. And yet "children make fictions of their fathers, re-inventing them according to their childish needs. The reality of a father is a weight few sons can bear," Rushdie warns.[33] In Oksana Zabuzhko's novel, it is Daryna, as the daughter of her father, who strives to bear this weight. Thus, the rehabilitation of the symbolic Father becomes one of the hallmarks of the Ukrainian postcolonial novel, which has a womanly face.

---

33 Salman Rushdie, *The Moor's Last Sigh* (New York: Vintage Books, 1997), 331.

CHAPTER 4

Post-Soviet Transit

Farewell to the USSR: Donbas Transit and the Last Soviet Generation

Voroshilovgrad Transit

The new migration of peoples, is the main theme of the Serhiy Zhadan—the leading figure of the 2000nd. Zhadan opens up a new theme in Ukrainian literature, through which the last Soviet generation identifies itself—the state of transit—thereby capturing the situation of global migration that defines early twenty-first-century existence. Zhadan links the theme of transit to an Eastern Ukrainian myth that is quite unlike the bohemian-nostalgic Habsburg myth celebrated by the writers of the Stanislaviv Phenomenon. The difference between Zhadan's artistic vision and that of Andrukhovych is quite telling. Andrukhovych's bohemian hero, the bearer of the Habsburg legacy, who wanders the highways and byways of Europe, has no sympathy with the new European immigrants who worship at the Brandenburg Gates. Rather, he travels through the centuries and across borders like an old gentleman of fortune, exercising his ancestral right to belong to Central Europe and carrying out an Eastern European revision. Like Orpheus, he seeks to bring his Eurydice—the good old days of Austrian Galicia—back from oblivion. Modern Ukraine and modern Europe are of little interest to him; he lives on dreams and illusions about the past. In this, he is the opposite of Zhadan's migrant hero, who does not cross European borders so freely, but identifies with the new arrivals who bring a new spirit to the West, often an Eastern one. In his acclaimed work *Death in Venice*, Thomas Mann embodied the drama of old Europe and its culture founded on the worship of ancient beauty. Even as it gazes into the mirror of beauty, old Europe is dying of a disease brought by the eastern winds and merchants from the East. Eastern winds are precisely what Zhadan is interested in.

Serhiy Zhadan's novel *Voroshilovgrad* (2010) is about eastern transit, particularly Ukrainian transit. It is a movement not only between the familiar and the foreign, but also between the similar and the different, the past and the present. Where is the place that the migrant occupies, and what remains of his past when he is on the road, and where are the doors of memory through which he can enter? Zhadan's essay "Immigrant Song," published after the release of *Voroshilovgrad*, holds the key to understanding the novel. It can be read as an author's commentary. The essay explores how Zhadan's personal biography intersects with the biography of Europe, and how migration is not simply forgetting and losing oneself, because migrants always retain something *of their own*, such as memories of their home, their landscape, and their childhood.

Zhadan essentially declares that the entire modern world is migrating. The widespread mass migration from Ukraine which began in earnest in the 1980s "seems never to have stopped," Zhadan writes in the essay. "Sometimes I think that everyone was always emigrating. Friends and classmates were emigrating. Communists and dissidents were emigrating. Teachers and unemployed people, men and women—everyone was emigrating [. . .].[1] But this applies not only to Ukraine. The whole world is moving, resettling, and migrating, even within the same country, and this is creating a new geography and giving rise to new literature. It is no secret that many of the new literary works that are generating widespread interest and receiving prestigious international awards are written by immigrants (V.S. Naipaul, Salman Rushdie, Arundhati Roy, Jhumpa Lahiri, etc.).

Zhadan's novel *Voroshilovgrad* tells the story of Ukraine in transit—a country moving from a Soviet past to a capitalist society, from mono-ethnic rootedness to transnational migration and multicultural communities. Ukraine is also becoming a country of migrations, a meeting place between West and East. Zhadan also unfolds his myth about Slobozhanshchyna, a historical region in northeastern Ukraine, and about memory and "one's place" in the post-Soviet transit world. Voroshilovgrad is not just a geographical location in the eastern Ukrainian borderland; it's also the chronotope of the state of transit in which people in the post-totalitarian era live. It should not be identified with a specific city; rather, it is a dark hole that sucks the past in like a vacuum cleaner and through which a new subjectivity is transformed as it moves into the future. It is also a topos of memory where time and space merge.

Zhadan attempts to give this "territory" a very specific social and local— Eastern Ukrainian (characteristic of Slobozhanshchyna)—flavor. He also draws fairly clear boundaries for this "territory," constantly playing with geography: north, south, the distant Carpathians, the nearby Donbas. Here, in this chronotope, childhood memories are erased, favorite belongings are lost, familiar landscapes are destroyed, and old friends are forgotten. But this is also where a new sense of self is born, one that feels a kinship with the people around, takes root in its territory, and is prepared to defend it.

German reviewers described the translation of *Voroshilovgrad* as a "virtuoso western," a "road movie," a "crime novel about raiding," and a "cinematic journey," irrespective of whether "its protagonist is traveling by bus or train, walking

---

1   Serhii Zhadan, "Immigrant Song," *Krytyka* 14, no. 9–10 (September 2010): 35–39, https://krytyka.com/ua/articles/immigrant-song.

across the steppe, or running with a ball across a soccer field."² In Ukrainian reviews, *Voroshilovgrad* is framed as the personal story of the thirty-three-year-old protagonist against the backdrop of the "lost generation" of the 1990s,³ and the novel is examined through the lens of "solidarity and shared responsibility"⁴ and the "pervasive motif of return."⁵ There are also reviews of the novel that call it an "apologia for Soviet nostalgia" and an "'anthem' of solidarity, mutual support, resistance, and leftist and (quasi) anarchist sentiments."⁶ American critics, on the other hand, point out that although *Voroshilovgrad* is set in 2009, it is "the novel of our present moment," almost "an intimate sojourn in a long-neglected Soviet borderland"⁷ where the Russo-Ukrainian war is now raging.

Voroshilovgrad is a palimpsest novel whose central theme is the post-Soviet transit experienced by an entire generation and manifested in the categories of social and individual memory, geocultural identity, and transnational migration. Donbas thus emerges as a borderland, a heterotopia where time stands still, life resembles a train station, and the territory is associated with "emptiness." The key concepts at work here are migration and displacement on the one hand, and the revision of memories of the totalitarian past on the other.

Although the theme of migration is not central to the Ukrainian reception of the novel, it is symbolically alluded to in the title of the German translation, *Die Erfindung des Jazz in Donbass* [The Invention of Jazz in Donbas] (Munich: Suhrkamp, 2013). This is a paraphrase of an inserted chapter in the novel titled "The History and Decline of Jazz in the Donetsk Region," and at first glance

---

2   Efim Shuman, "Nemetskie kritiki o vostochnoukrainskom vesterne Sergeia Zhadana [German critics about Sergei Zhadan's Eastern Ukrainian western]," *Deutsche Welle*, last modified February 14, 2013.

3   Alina Zemlianska and O. Strilets, "Trahichnyi obraz ukrainskoi molodi u romani S. Zhadana 'Voroshylovhrad' [The tragic image of Ukrainian youth in S. Zhadan's novel 'Voroshylovhrad']," *Naukovi zapysky Kharkivskoho natsionalnoho pedahohichnoho universytetu imeni H. S. Skovorody, Literaturoznavstvo* [Scientific notes of H. S. Skovoroda Kharkiv National Pedagogical University. Literary studies] 1, no. 95 (2020): 114–16.

4   Les Belei, "Khymernyi sotsrealizm Serhiia Zhadana [The whimsical socialist realism of Serhii Zhadan]," *Litaktsent*, October 29, 2010, http://litakcent.com/2010/09/27/dvi-recenziji-na-voroshylovhrad/.

5   Lina Kostenko, "Ukraina yak zhertva i chynnyk hlobalizatsii katastrof [Ukraine as victim and factor of globalization of catastrophes]," *Den*, no. 76 (April 2003), http://ukrlife.org/main/evshan/kostenko_l.htm.

6   Vasyl Kostiuk, "Dyskurs nenavysti v obolontsi pornohlamuru [Discourse of hatred in the shell of pornoglamour]," *Krytyka* 14, no. 9–10 (September 2010): 42–43, https://krytyka.com/ua/articles/dyskurs-nenavysty-v-obolontsi-pornoglamuru.

7   Marci Shore, "The Bard of Eastern Ukraine, Where Things Are Falling Apart," *New Yorker*, November 26, 2016, https://www.newyorker.com/books/page-turner/the-bard-of-eastern-ukraine-where-things-are-falling-apart.

seems to have little to do with the main narrative. It is an excerpt from a book read by the novel's protagonist, Herman. Herman returns to a kind of heterotopia—his hometown near Voroshilovgrad, where, by immersing himself in the past and developing a connection with his home turf, he undergoes an initiation and sets out on a journey to the future.

This inserted chapter acts like a mirror, bringing out and revealing the transcultural themes of the novel that permeate the symbolic fabric of the text. The book is given to Herman by Pasha, a former drug addict who is now the presbyter of a Baptist community, through Tamara, a woman of Roma origin. It tells the story of two Black women who came to Donbas from the United States as Baptist missionaries and popularized spirituals, a genre which grew out of the songs of former enslaved Black people brought to America. This transnational chapter, as a "text within a text," is the key to one of the main themes of the novel—global transit and large-scale migration, which stretches from East to West across Ukraine. Moreover, Donbas, which was historically and culturally perceived as "emptiness" and served as the frontier of the Eurasian Wild Steppe, is revived as a geocultural, spiritual, and mental matrix. The idea of transit is the main theme of the novel, which has its counterpoints, including male friendship, love, responsibility for "one's home turf," post-Soviet memory, and the motif of the coming of age of the last Soviet generation.

The main image of the novel—Voroshilovgrad itself—is a chronotope of initiation in which the post-totalitarian person lives, uprooted from their homeland and suspended in the air. It is difficult to call this place a specific city; it is rather a "territory"—a dark hole that sucks the past in like a vacuum cleaner and through which a new history is transformed as it moves into the future. Donbas could be compared to some kind of Castaneda-esque void, but Zhadan seeks to give this "territory" a very specific Donbas flavor, even though he calls it an "emptiness." Here, memory and history are lost, Donbas is associated with heterotopia, that is, "another place" where time turns back and space is absorbed by post-Soviet phantasms. Here, in this metaphysical chronotope, childhood memories are erased, favorite belongings are lost, familiar landscapes are destroyed, and old friends are forgotten. But in fact, this is a space of transition and initiation.

The new post-Soviet era in the novel is unequivocally associated with the resettlement of peoples, with a worldwide global migration—this is not just about individuals moving somewhere, but entire nations traveling across the globe. Thus, the novel unfolds against the backdrop of transit—the post-Soviet blurring of bordelines. Zhadan gives this theme an Asian twist, echoing Mykola Khvylovy's *Asian Renaissance*. Migration and transit in these eastern Ukrainian lands are linked to war and proximity to the border. One of the characters talks about the anxiety that the steppe must have caused German tank crews, who had ventured so far from their homes for the first time, to feel when they ended up in Ukraine's east during World War II. These borderlands are a shapeless space where you can lose yourself. "'And when you finally find yourself here,' Ernst said, his finger circling in the air, 'you get this eerie feeling, you realize how good you had it till then, because here [...] everything you thought you knew about war, about Europe, about landscapes, is nullified, because endless emptiness begins right on the other side of that fence, emptiness without content, form, or connotation. It's real, absolute emptiness, and there's nothing to hold on to.'"[8]

Donbas emptiness—be it metaphysical or physical—is what the novel sets out to analyze. It turns out that the local people's fault lies precisely in the fact that they cling too much "to this emptiness."[9] The territory becomes increasingly feminized and transforms into the body of the motherland: it absorbs water, light-filled grass, soil, lakes, skies, gas fields—everything standing out like gold veins on the Motherland's skin.[10] It grows out from damp ground in the sunny haze, "light and deep," and sprawls out to the east and south. Voroshilovgrad ceases to exist as an empty memory and becomes a symbolic place of remembrance. Ultimately, the author acknowledges this himself: "It is a kind of return to the past, a return to emptiness, falling into a time hole from which he [Herman—T.H.] will try to escape," Zhadan has commented. "This is a novel about memory, about the importance of memory, about the continuity of memory, about the need to remember everything that has happened to you, because this allows you to shape your future. It is a novel about the need to defend yourself, your loved ones, your principles, your territory, your past, and your future. It is a novel about resistance, a novel about confrontation, about defending your principles from external pressure."[11]

The main character in the novel is Herman Korolyov, a seemingly unremarkable young man with an equally unremarkable career: formerly a historian, he is now a self-described political expert. Zhadan presents him as a typical representative of his time—the transit period of the 1990s, when most young people, just like Herman, had no permanent home or steady income, and therefore they

---

8   Serhii Zhadan, *Voroshilovgrad*, trans. Reilly Costigan-Humes and Isaac Stackhouse Wheeler (Dallas: Deep Vellum Publishing, 2016), 145, ebook.
9   Zhadan, *Voroshilovgrad*, 303.
10 Zhadan, *Voroshilovgrad*, 189–190.
11 "Serhii Zhadan: 'Voroshylovhrad' ne prypade do dushi tym, khto upodobav 'Depesh Mod' [Serhii Zhadan: 'Voroshylovhrad' will not appeal to those who liked 'Depeche Mode']," *Hrechka*, September 23, 2010, https://gre4ka.info/kultura/111-68serhii-zhadan-voroshylovohrad-roman-pro-zakhyst-svoikh-pryntsypiv-vid-zovnishnoho-tysku/.

"edited speeches, held seminars for up-and-coming leaders and workshops for election observers, constructed political platforms for new parties, chopped wood at Bolik's father's country house, advocated for the democratic process as guests on TV talk shows, and laundered, laundered, laundered the dough being funneled through our accounts."[12]

This life in transit is like being at war, because just as they do in wartime, people in transit are in the process of changing their memories and identity. Wars are ever-present and ongoing in *Voroshilovgrad*: wars with gas workers, corn farmers, aviators, farmers, businessmen. For some reason military fatigues are the fashion here: a Bundeswehr jacket, an SS cap, tanker pants, a camouflage T-shirt, a British fireman's jacket, a German belt with the words "God is with us" on it, a German military jacket, a British military jacket, heavy soldier's boots. In short, just like war. The characters also resemble brothers in arms: Herman points out several times that "a solution would only be found when your brothers in arms were standing alongside you."[13]

At the same time, the idea of brotherhood is much broader and more diverse: the brothers (and sisters) in Zhadan's novel include not only the semi-criminal Kocha, but also friends from his youth, people he played soccer with in the 1990s, as well as Roma, Baptists led by a former drug addict turned preacher, a former historian called Ernst who now guards an abandoned airfield, and the unfamiliar and mysterious women with whom Herman makes love. All of them end up on one team, fighting on the same side of the front, because their moral code is to "stick together, keep outsiders out, and protect your land, women, and homes."[14] Shared responsibility and shared gratitude are what unites them all on the same side of the front, because, as the presbyter taught them, "I had them and they had me.[15]

Among the brothers is the "older brother," who never makes a personal appearance in the novel. Such "absences" are not unusual in Zhadan's work. In his 2004 novel *Depeche Mode*, the stepfather who kills himself is a semimythical figure; it is news of his death that the three friends are supposed to bring to the fourth one, his stepson. In *Voroshilovgrad*, the absent figure is the older brother. It is tempting to view these figures as post-totalitarian allegories, in which case the stepfather's death can be associated with the collapse of the Soviet Union and the older brother's leaving with the loss of the Russian "older brother." But

---

12   Zhadan, *Voroshilovgrad*, 12.
13   Zhadan, *Voroshilovgrad*, 109.
14   Zhadan, *Voroshilovgrad*, 411.
15   Zhadan, *Voroshilovgrad*, 421.

Herman's older brother has nothing in common with the Russian older brother, because he is someone who "dug himself into the ground and fired in all directions, unwilling to give up his territory." He is prepared to fight to the death "for this empty land," while the younger brother, Herman, has no trouble "letting go of emptiness, trying to rid [himself] of it."¹⁶ The older brother is, rather, the ideal Ukrainian *other*, personifying rootedness and belonging to this Donetsk land.

Herman had left his hometown, gone to university, and lived in a dormitory in Kharkiv, but now he lives in a rented apartment surrounded by other people's furniture. Early one morning, he receives a phone call that connects him to his past and his family (a call from an old friend, his brother's business partner). His brother ran a gas station in Herman's hometown, but now he has left (for either Berlin or Amsterdam), and in the meantime, the gas station has been taken over by racketeers. Herman is thirty-three, and he could have written in his resume: "I've been living on my own for a while, and quite happily, too. I rarely see my parents and have a good relationship with my brother. I've got a completely useless degree. I've got a dubious job. I've got enough money to support the lifestyle I'm used to. It's too late to get used to anything else. I'm more than happy with my lot. If something's not going to make me happy, I don't bother with it."¹⁷

Herman, like his friend who took the name of the German communist Ernst Thälmann, might have considered himself a *loser*. They both grew up in Soviet times and were inspired by aviators and cosmonauts. But their "tickets to heaven" turned out to be fake. "'When we were kids,' Ernst said, 'we all wanted to be aviators. We wanted to fly and touch the sky! [...] What happened to our dreams? Who took our tickets to heaven away from us? I ask you, why have we who love the sky been ostracized? Why have we been forced into seclusion?'"¹⁸ The former airfields are now planted with corn, and the hero of the new era is the "corn farmer"—a farmer who is willing to turn all the surrounding asphalt into corn fields.

Ernst and Herman rise up against the corn-growing businessmen, and so do the soccer players—a former soccer team that symbolizes a form of brotherhood—and the displaced Roma and Baptists. Zhadan remains faithful to his previously proclaimed poeticization of war and reconstruction. Militarism is a key theme in *Voroshilovgrad*. Militarism is validated not only by wars, but also by sports. Soccer is what unites the past and the present, and it is also a team sport, which is why Herman's hallucination, in which he and his former teammates

---

16 Zhadan, *Voroshilovgrad*, 90.
17 Zhadan, *Voroshilovgrad*, 14.
18 Zhadan, *Voroshilovgrad*, 142–143.

play a match against the gas workers and Herman ends up as the hero of the hour, is a prelude to the defense of the airfield.

The social environment of the 1990s is united by football, in which "racketeers and collaborators, soccer players and under-age hooligans from the new block" can come together and form a team. Soccer becomes a battleground for ideological conflicts and political slogans, but at the same time, it is a field of freedom, emotions, and desires. Zhadan's novel makes a connection between sport and life under a totalitarian regime, as sport becomes the channel through which personal freedom manifests itself. In this respect, it is reminiscent of Dragoslav Mihailović's gritty novel *When Pumpkins Blossomed*, in which boxing and hooliganism become substitutes for power and sex because boxing can make you fearless and teach you to "beat up a man like a sack."[19] Sport becomes a substitute for power, and camaraderie combined with violence serves as a prototype of brotherhood.

The Balkan complex, which blends violence, multi-ethnicity, loss of homeland, business, death, the Roma, sex, and emigration, is a distinct genre and has migrated (largely due to the influence of Emir Kusturica) into Ukrainian literature, including Zhadan's works. The theme of migration is also part of this complex. In Mihailović's novel, Ljuban, a former boxer, now an immigrant in Sweden, never stops dreaming about Yugoslavia, and even the petrol at the Austrian border, which he smears on his face, hands, and hair, smells like Yugoslavia to him. "And over time, the fact that you left will stop hurting you as much as it did," he admits, "but it will not stop weighing on you."[20] The only hope of return for Mihailović's Ljuban, the erstwhile "Champion," is the prospect of some "small-scale, reasonable war," "because if it came to that, then they would definitely call me" home. A small-scale war is also what called Herman home in Zhadan's *Voroshilovgrad*.

Memory as a Palimpsest

The blurb for the Ukrainian edition of *Voroshilovgrad* reads: "A harsh, melancholic, and realistic novel. As realistic as socialist realism can be."[21] The reference to socialist realism is no accident. In addition to the oxymoron of "realistic

---

19 Dragoslav Mykhailovych, *Koly tsvily harbuzy* [When pumpkins blossomed] (Kyiv: Fakt, 2008), 17.
20 Mykhailovych, *Koly tsvily harbuzy* [When pumpkins blossomed], 122.
21 Zhadan, *Voroshilovgrad*.

socialist realism," it suggests the ever-present shadow of the Soviet past in the novel. This idea is encapsulated in the title, *Voroshilovgrad*, which refers to past Soviet history while also pointing to its simulacral or phantom nature, since this city no longer exists, although its shadow has left a trace in many people's lives. This phantom memory is clearly shown in the protagonist's account of how when he was at school back in Soviet times, in their German class the children had to talk about the world around them using postcards "with views of the city of Voroshilovgrad," which mainly featured administrative buildings and monuments. "But what can you really say about something you've never *actually* seen?" Herman notes in the novel.[22] Stories like this are analogous to socialist realism: just as socialist realism reflected the "almost real" world around them, the children in the class talked about the "almost real" city of Voroshilovgrad which they had never seen. Herman summarizes this paradox in strikingly simple terms, referring to his own history: "I exist. But there's no Voroshilovgrad anymore."[23]

And yet individual memory is written like a palimpsest. Another character in Zhadan's novel, Olha, says the picture postcards "are my past. Something they took away from me and forced me to forget. But I haven't forgotten, because those really are a part of me."[24] The palimpsest function of the narrative in the novel is vividly illustrated in a scene in which Herman sees "the outline of Lenin's profile" inside a building in the border zone, a building that has been repurposed as a Shtundist church but looks as if it used to be a village house of culture. A profile portrait of Lenin once hung there and has left a mark on the faded fabric of the canvas that traces the outline of the Soviet leader. Now there's a crucifix hanging there instead, as if "somebody had crossed out the tenets of Marxism-Leninism once and for all," the narrator comments.[25] In effect, Zhadan is arguing that contemporary history is being written in the place of the past and in its traces, because the past cannot simply be crossed out or erased; it is already etched in people's life stories and memories.

The Lenin profile, like the phantom city of Voroshilovgrad, frozen in time and isolated in space, is not only a sign referring to socialist realism, but also a "trace"—a metaphor for the virtual memory of Soviet life. The palimpsest is written over such "traces" through the process of "erasure" and "writing" as exercises of "working through" memory. A palimpsest is a means of accumulating and

---

22 Zhadan, *Voroshilovgrad*, 182.
23 Zhadan, *Voroshilovgrad*, 183.
24 Zhadan, *Voroshilovgrad*, 437–38.
25 Zhadan, *Voroshilovgrad*, 245.

archiving social memory, and, as Aleida Assmann, one of the leading researchers of memory categories, has noted, it becomes "a bearer of different writings."[26] According to Assmann, social memory is inseparable from individual memory and is a shadow that "runs" alongside the present. Individual research on memory is not necessarily imbued with nostalgia and fueled by a desire to return to the past. But social memory is not only a museum, but also an archive. In *Voroshilovgrad*, memory is predominantly a form of writing, in which the quest to find one's place in contemporary history unfolds against the backdrop of the shadows, traces, and phantoms of socialist history.

The palimpsest in Zhadan's novel develops against the background of a particular individual memory, which the protagonist in Zhadan's memoir and travelogue *Anarchy in the UKR* (2005) refers to as "private socialist realism."[27] It is "primarily external, outdoor, graphic," devoid of ideological "clichés about social guarantees and the joy of communist labor," and it has become etched in memory like "the ABCs of my childhood."[28] *Anarchy in the UKR* can be considered a preface to *Voroshilovgrad*, an almost autobiographical narrative that reconstructs Zhadan's own memory of the 1980s and 1990s. At the forefront of *Anarchy in the UKR* is the story of the last Soviet generation, perceived through the unity of geography, biography, and corporeal memory. The narrator maintains that the "utilitarian aesthetics" of Soviet-era signs, slogans, and inscriptions are embedded into memory "like the red color of flags and workers' slogans is etched on my retinas, like iodine seeps into an open wound."[29] *Anarchy in the UKR* is also a memoir about an autobiographical hero, a representative of the last Soviet generation, whose coming-of-age coincided with a period of "strange and painful things happening all around us."[30] Arguably, the defining event of that time was the collapse of socialism and the Soviet Union, when "life was destroying our country," "breaking our parents," and "discarding all those who were superfluous and unnecessary."[31] But for the teenagers of the last Soviet generation, this story was not just part of official history, but also a scene from their personal life stories. Even if we set aside history, Zhadan's protagonist in *Anarchy in the UKR*

---

26   Aleida Assmann, *Cultural Memory and Western Civilization: Functions, Media, Archives* (Cambridge: Cambridge University Press, 2011), 142.
27   Serhii Zhadan, *Anarchy in the UKR* (Kharkiv: Folio, 2008), 72.
28   Zhadan, *Anarchy in the UKR*, 72.
29   Zhadan, *Anarchy in the UKR*, 71.
30   Zhadan, *Anarchy in the UKR*, 110–11.
31   Zhadan, *Anarchy in the UKR*, 111.

asks, "Who would dare to deprive all these people of their biographies? And what would be offered in return?"[32]

In his poetry and prose collections of the late 1990s and early 2000s (*Quotations*, *Big Mac*, and *Depeche Mode*), Zhadan captured the post-totalitarian ontological homelessness of the last Soviet generation, for whom time was associated with an endless train. In *Anarchy in the UKR*, he analyzes the coming of age of this generation, summoning the demons of childhood, mapping out the landscapes of remembering, and returning to "places of memory." Tatjana Hofmann calls this type of narrative "literary ethnography" and notes that Zhadan does not "museumify space as a historical and cultural landscape"; on the contrary, his sketches are protected from the exoticization and "museumification" of Eastern Europe "as a heterotopia in relation to the rest of Europe or a rejected province."[33] Zhadan constructs landscapes of memory against the backdrop of the image of Donbas, which is imagined as a stagnant and lost world, and Ukraine's eastern frontier zone, where active transit processes—social, migratory, and criminal—are taking place.

In *Anarchy in the UKR*, Zhadan is creating a new kind of *coming-of-age memoir* in which personal memories become a way of reanimating the *space of memory* inscribed, as in Andrukhovych's vision of "my Europe," in *geography and biography*. But Zhadan's perspective is different—it unfolds in the eastern Ukrainian borderlands and is devoid of Andrukhovych's nostalgic Habsburg escape. Geoculturally, it is a story of taking root in "one's own home turf," rather than a biography of existence in the zone of Eastern European transit, as in Andrukhovych's writing. Zhadan conjures up "ghosts from the past," unfolding the archive of his memory year after year—from "my eighties" to "the red nineties"—and captures iconic places of memory: the Park of Culture, hotels, train stations, dormitories, Kharkiv's main square, and the dilapidated Palace of Pioneers. In his memory, there are recollections of "my past, someone else's past, and our collective past," childhood and adult life, and each of the witnesses of the past has their own personal file in the archives. Zhadan equates the "inhabiting of space" with the "inhabiting of the memory which is connected to that space." In fact, Zhadan registers his frustration with the "mechanical build-up of space," as well as with the "endless unraveling of this memory."[34] Hence, the descriptions of houses, roads, and places have nothing to do with "geographical

---

32 Zhadan, *Anarchy in the UKR*, 152.
33 Tatjana Khofman, *Literaturnye etnografii Ukrainy: proza posle 1991 goda* [Literary ethnographies of Ukraine: prose after 1991] (St. Petersburg: Aleteiia, 2016), 201.
34 Zhadan, *Anarchy in the UKR*, 14.

or topological attachment," as the narrator claims. Rather, they primarily reflect "an attachment to myself, a dependence on myself, on my own experience, which does not let go for a moment, forcing me to return again and again to places where I felt unspeakably good or unspeakably bad."[35] The Soviet past described in *Anarchy in the UKR* was still warm and tangible, still within reach, like "one's well-worn hockey sticks stored in the upper cabinets and in the garage."

In *Voroshilovgrad*, Zhadan conveys through Herman the toned-down biography of a post-Soviet teenager who has grown up, no longer lives at train stations, and is no longer homeless, but is essentially a loser, unrooted in life. He runs away from any responsibility, leaves home, and feigns both friendship and work. His name, Herman Korolyov, is a symbolic Soviet name and refers to the Soviet dream of space (Herman Titov, Serhii Korolyov). "We all wanted to become pilots. The majority of us became losers," says his historian friend, who guards an abandoned airfield once used for agricultural aviation as the last remaining territory inherited from the Soviet era.[36]

In *Voroshilovgrad*, unlike *Anarchy in the UKR*, Zhadan employs museumification reminiscent of Dubravka Ugrešić's novel *The Museum of Unconditional Surrender* (1996). Ugrešić compiles entire lists of "traces" of things and objects from socialist everyday life that are connected to her individual life story and the social and cultural changes in her family: her parents' *first* bedroom, the *first* gas stove, the *first* Nikola Tesla radio, the *first* rubber doll, the *first* gramophone, the *first* washing machine, and so on. Zhadan also assembles entire collections—signs of the Soviet past and the hybrid transitional period—creating a kind of catalog of "everyday socialism."

He also collects topoi of socialist everyday life (a sanatorium, a pioneer camp, a house of culture, an apartment from 1991) and works with family albums, using the effect of *post-memory*. This way of "saying goodbye to yesterday" corresponds with both cultural and communicative memory as conceptualized by Jan Assmann.[37] On the one hand, the collected items are clearly symbolic cultural signs of a specific time, and they can be seen as museum collages on display. On the other, his memory is biographical and communicative—it encompasses memories of the recent past and transmits generational memory of the last years of Soviet rule and the transitional 1990s and does so by appealing to common

---

35 Zhadan, *Anarchy in the UKR*, 127.
36 Zhadan, *Voroshilovgrad*, 30.
37 Jan Assmann, *Kul'turnaia pamiat'. Pis'mo, pamiat' o proshlom i politicheskaia identichnost' v vysokikh kul'turakh drevnosti* [Cultural memory. Writing, memory of the past and political identity in the high cultures of antiquity], trans. Mariya Sokol'skaya (Moscow: IASK, 2004), 52–53.

codes according to which this history can still be read. In a sense, Zhadan's collage collections in *Voroshilovgrad* play the role of anthropological ethnography and resemble post-Soviet second-hand goods, echoing Svetlana Alexievich's book *Second-Hand Time: The Last of the Soviets* (2013).

The novel contains quite a few devices that preserve anthropological field materials and document collections. Hera, as Herman's friends call him, lives in Kharkiv in an apartment let by "an old, embittered retiree, a former cash collector named Fedor Mykhailovych," whom his friends called "Dostoyevsky." The apartment is a repository of old things, almost a Soviet-time museum where time has stood still, and all the rooms are stuffed with "1930s furniture, tattered books, and stacks of old *Ogonyok* magazines from the Soviet days,"[38] as well as piles of colorful clothing from the past and jars of honey, vinegar, and walnuts jumbled together with copper coins, beer bottle caps, and buttons from army overcoats. There were also "porcelain Lenin figurines, enormous fake silver forks," and scribblings on the walls—"some random telephone numbers, addresses, and bus routes," as well as "cutouts from calendars and photographs of unknown relatives."[39]

The passengers on the ghost bus—Donbas entrepreneurs from the 1990s—also turn into museum exhibits (wax figures): "women in bras and sweatpants with bright makeup and long fake nails, tattooed guys with wallets hanging from their wrists, also in sweatpants and Chinese-made sneakers, and kids in baseball caps and athletic uniforms holding bats and brass knuckles."[40] The driver's seat in the Ikarus bus is the epitome of post-Soviet transitional hybridity, with quasi-sacred objects collected and archived on the windshield as if on an iconostasis. Alongside Orthodox icons, there are "all sorts of sacred things," such as "teddy bears and clay skeletons with broken ribs, necklaces made out of rooster heads, and Manchester United pennants" as well as "pornographic pictures, portraits of Stalin, and Xeroxed images of Saint Francis."[41]

Carriers and drivers, buses and fixed-route minibuses become an embodiment of transit time, a visual representation of the processes of displacement experienced by a post-Soviet person. The old, dilapidated buses to which Zhadan ultimately leads his protagonist serve as a place of refuge, a kind of multinational transit zone where one can find safety from the dangerous and unfamiliar roads of the new life. They also resemble a church.

---

38 Zhadan, *Voroshilovgrad*, 7–8.
39 Zhadan, *Voroshilovgrad*, 8.
40 Zhadan, *Voroshilovgrad*, 23.
41 Zhadan, *Voroshilovgrad*, 23.

The photographs from the Soviet past collected in Tamara's family album acquire symbolic meaning, too. There, "grown men and women, children and old people, students, soldiers, blue-collar workers, high school seniors wearing white graduation aprons, [...] and infants with their favorite toys" seemed to be waiting "for someone to meet their eyes, some color, some black and white, to ascertain what it was that kept them together, what they were living for and why they'd passed on."[42] Old photographs primarily capture events that stand out against the backdrop of everyday life, showcasing status symbols for "glorifying and immortalizing important events in family life."[43] These photographs are of typical recreation spots and status symbols of Soviet life: seaside promenades with "men wearing old-fashioned swim trunks standing still on a seacoast, old Soviet cars, silly children's toys, factory entrances, university lecture halls, school hallways, and train compartments."[44] The photographs from the family album concretize and visualize the collective memory of the past and remind Herman of a kind of "extended family"—acquaintances, friends, classmates, neighbors, relatives—with whom he shared a common history. It was "an endless throng of faces, portrait and profile, shadows from the past, from every moment of my life, every moment of my memory," he realizes.[45]

Zhadan also takes his protagonist to special places where the presence of the past is mummified. These include a "time-worn sanatorium" for retirees and a former pioneer camp with a room dedicated to Lenin. The retirees are people from the past—petrified and grotesquely monstrous—including the former director of an oil depot with "Lenin's slyness in his eyes" who has been "working for the Party since '52." Overall, there are quite a few pensioners in the novel: "men on crutches gnashed their brittle yellow teeth, while the women, whose arms were almost all in casts, smiled effusively, their thick lipstick making them look like sadistic clowns."[46]

Each of these "rich descriptions" (Clifford Geertz) is recognizable, albeit somewhat erased as to their details and contexts, since they are all exhibits in the museum of post-Soviet transit on the site of the former USSR. This is symbolically demonstrated by the collage in the trailer where Herman's friend Kocha lives. The collage on the wall is composed of clippings from newspapers and magazines, fragments of faces, outlines of bodies, and shreds of crowds,

---

42 Zhadan, *Voroshilovgrad*, 334.
43 Pierre Bourdieu, *Photography: A Middle-Brow Art* (Stanford: Stanford University Press, 1990), 19
44 Zhadan, *Voroshilovgrad*, 335.
45 Zhadan, *Voroshilovgrad*, 338.
46 Zhadan, *Voroshilovgrad*, 173.

beer bottle labels, political pamphlets, photos from fashion magazines, and soccer team calendars. All of this is united by "some bizarre pattern": "a solid light-green, claylike background littered with letters and symbols, broken lines, and contrasting colors wrapped the whole construction together." It's a map, "probably a map of the USSR—the Carpathian Mountains, the Caucasus, and Mongolia were in sandy clay, the taiga and Caspian Lowland were in light green, and, apparently, the deserts were signified by a chalky dry area, where the sandy clay had hardened. The Pacific Ocean was dark, dark blue and the North Sea was light blue.[47] In this way, Zhadan outlines a global dimension for his phantom "Voroshilovgrad." Like the collage pasted onto the map of the former Soviet Union, the stories of the various characters that Zhadan narrates are also written on a mental map of the "fake" world that was the Soviet Union.

The essence of such a place-as-emptiness is Voroshilovgrad—the central toponym of the novel. Voroshilovgrad exists as a kind of simulacrum, because its name has no roots, it is random, easily appropriated and just as easily discarded. The city was renamed Voroshilovgrad twice (in 1935 and 1970) and twice stripped of this name (in 1958 and 1990). Back in November 1935, the name of the Soviet commander Kliment Voroshilov was attached to the great city of Luhansk, transforming this originally imperial city into a Soviet one. Indeed, Luhansk had been developed as an imperial city since its establishment. Officially founded on September 3, 1882 by order of the Russian emperor, the city was built on the territory of the Luhanske settlement (lands seized by the tsarist government from the Kalmius Palanka of the Zaporizhzhia Cossack Army), which stretched around an iron foundry established by order of Catherine II in 1795. Luhansk has been a city of migrants since its inception: craftsmen and workers were brought here from the Russian hinterlands, peasants were resettled here from the Yaroslavl province, and engineers traveled here from England. Thus, since the days of the Wild Field, this area has seen a constant migration of both peoples and toponyms.

Donbas and Global Migration

Another central theme in *Voroshilovgrad*, which characterizes post-Soviet transit and at the same time relates to the global situation of our time, is the "resettlement of peoples," or global migration. In the novel, Zhadan not only collects signs and traces of the Soviet past, but also introduces the reader to various

---

47   Zhadan, *Voroshilovgrad*, 44.

migrating social groups (communities)—gas workers, farmers, Shtundists, carriers, and displaced persons. None of these groups are rooted; they migrate across the Donbas Wild Field like nomads, feeling like aliens and living as if they were at a train station.

The transitional time of displacement and great movements has engulfed the modern world, but it is especially active in the borderlands. Zhadan's space is the eastern borderlands of Ukraine, traditionally known as the Wild Fields, and later as Donbas. The area is described as "featureless—no trees, no towns, no signs of life or death."[48] Bordered by the Donets River valley, it is associated in the novel with "emptiness." Looking from the West at this eastern borderland, it seems that here, any idea "about Europe, about landscapes, is nullified, because endless emptiness begins right on the other side of that fence, emptiness without content, form, or connotation. It's real, absolute emptiness, and there's nothing to hold on to."[49] East-West migration routes now run through it. Even for Hera, who grew up in the area, this territory has little significance. He is puzzled as to why his brother chose to stay here, "unwilling to give up his territory," while he and his father found it easy to leave it behind. Hera admits that his brother "would be capable of fighting to the death for this empty land," while he has "no trouble letting go of emptiness, trying to rid [himself] of it."[50]

Two stylistic streams—harsh prose where life is permeated with brutality, fear, and sex, and profound lyricism—converge in the architectonics of the novel. In contrast to the godforsaken, shapeless "emptiness," there are waves of poetry that Zhadan uses, like an aura, to encase this territory with its endless cornfields, hills, and valleys, borders, and random stations. The poetic component in *Voroshilovgrad* lays bare the author's deep attachment to his homeland. In his reveries, Herman feels the earth breathing, sprouting roots, and being filled with underground gas. The earth is a living thing, like an organism or body, lying under the flat skies, "like a herd left behind by its owners." But, the narrator says, "If you choose just the right spot, sometimes you can feel all these phenomena together—roots intertwining, rivers flowing, oceans filling up, planets soaring across the sky, and the living moving along the earth's surface like the dead move beneath it."[51] "A light and deep emptiness" unfolds to the east and south, but above it, somewhere in the south, "the gates of Voroshilovgrad sliced cleanly through the sky."[52]

---

48 Zhadan, *Voroshilovgrad*, 309.
49 Zhadan, *Voroshilovgrad*, 145.
50 Zhadan, *Voroshilovgrad*, 90.
51 Zhadan, *Voroshilovgrad*, 235.
52 Zhadan, *Voroshilovgrad*, 190.

Rising above and sinking into the ground, which consists of roots, stones, grass, a yellow layer of sand, and a white layer of clay, Herman finally comes to understand his connection to it. "The clay we'd exposed had a sweet and piquant smell. I had dug up something valuable, something I'd always suspected was there. I never would have imagined that it was right there under the surface this whole time," he feels as he roots himself in his "home turf" not only rationally, but also physically.[53] A local businessman and lawmaker, meanwhile, insists that Herman and all the "locals" need to stop "clinging to this emptiness" and leave and look for "a better place to live" instead.[54]

The borderlands are a space of mirages, smuggling, and crime, where smugglers have set up camp, transporting counterfeit electrical appliances, lawnmowers, refrigerators, microwaves, and chainsaws across the border to the imaginary East, to the North Caucasus, "somewhere in Ossetia or Ingushetia." From the east, from Russian territory, come fuel trucks that look "like elephants meandering out of some desert land with valuable and aromatic fuel supplies in their black wombs."[55]

On the geo-cultural map, the border is marked by a railway embankment and a railroad that stretches from nowhere and leads nowhere. But the border's "emptiness" actually turns out to be a body, a cosmogonic matrix. In a semi-delirious state, Hera imagines a universal movement that reigns over him, transcending borders and lying beneath them. Animals cross the border: snakes slither across it, red foxes run through it, crows fly over it. The crossing, the overcoming of borders, is a cosmic movement, for everything alive is in motion: roots persistently break through the soil and reach for water, silver veins of water bypass the bodies of the dead and move into obscurity. Deep within the earth beats the black heart of coal, while the fresh milk of natural gas curdles in subterranean deposits, giving the roots the strength to withstand the winds.

Movement also reigns on the land, where massive waves of migration flow from Eurasia to the West. On a map titled "Eurasia" in the refugee camp, "routes outlined with a red ballpoint pen stretched from the east, from Tibet and the regions bordering China, from the Great Wall and Mesopotamia, all the way to Rostov, in Russia, and continued on through our area."[56] In his nighttime reveries, Hera sees a great "migration of peoples." A massive stream of unknown people silently passes by him, heading towards the West. It is the Orient itself in

---

53 Zhadan, *Voroshilovgrad*, 227.
54 Zhadan, *Voroshilovgrad*, 303.
55 Zhadan, *Voroshilovgrad*, 261.
56 Zhadan, *Voroshilovgrad*, 314.

motion seen through the eyes of a Westerner: ethereal men of tall stature with long hair tied in ponytails or mohawks and tattooed faces; women with their hair in buns or dreadlocks, some with bald heads, their skulls painted red and blue.[57] They carry sleepy, hungry children on their backs, children with big empty eyes. Further ahead, herders drive the livestock and sweep away their tracks with harrows.

Herman encounters refugees (displaced persons, nomads) once again, this time in real life, when he accidentally stumbles upon some amid endless cornfields shrouded in fog. Among them, the dark-skinned Karolina explains, there are Mongols, Tibetans, and Africans, but all of them are fleeing "to the West." Hera's perception of the East is clearly orientalized, as is typical for a Soviet person, and shaped by stereotypes from Western culture. In Hera's mind, all migrants from the East are associated with "Mongols." For Karolina they are "Mongols" too: "They don't have any documents or normal names. Those Mongols really are strange, but they're kind."[58] The refugee camp resembles a train station where they speak "some Asian language, no doubt discussing the pressing Mongolian issues of the day."[59]

Ultimately, everything beyond the border is associated with the East, since for Soviet people, "everything south of Rostov is the Caucasus."[60] Orientalism is also marked by gender: in the novel, the two retired women who are stuck in the past, one of whom is wearing "a multicolored sundress dating back to the Soviet days, peppered with images of tropical flowers and herbs," are also referred to as Easterners (Spanish or Roma women).[61]

The world in transit is inherently hybrid and transnational. The Orient is embodied not only by refugees from Eurasia, but also by the Roma, who are sometimes called "Georgian gypsies" and other times associated with the Balkan community. They "looked more like Serbs than Georgians," Hera realizes.[62] Emir Kustirica's influence in the depiction of the Roma in *Voroshilovgrad* is evident, as are the Balkan contexts. Zhadan's novel is reminiscent of Dragoslav Mihailović's gritty novel *When Pumpkins Blossomed*, in which boxing and hooliganism become ambivalent substitutes for power and sex. Sport becomes a substitute for power, providing pleasure in self-realization, and camaraderie combined with violence serves as a prototype of brotherhood. In general, the

---

57 Zhadan, *Voroshilovgrad*, 59.
58 Zhadan, *Voroshilovgrad*, 334.
59 Zhadan, *Voroshilovgrad*, 311.
60 Zhadan, *Voroshilovgrad*, 201.
61 Zhadan, *Voroshilovgrad*, 158.
62 Zhadan, *Voroshilovgrad*, 201.

Balkan complex, which blends violence, multiethnicity, loss of homeland, business, death, the Roma, sex, and emigration, is a distinct genre in modern culture and has migrated (largely due to the influence of Emir Kusturica) into Ukrainian literature, including Zhadan's works.

The Roma belong to a community of Shtundists led by a presbyter. A wedding band plays at their funerals, "the trumpet player, drummer, and violinist picking up the tune," and they sing a special hybrid post-Soviet anthem in honor of Romanistan ("Live on, Romanistan, the magnificent and free land untainted by the pernicious influence of transnational corporations").[63] The anthem combines church hymns ("When the Lord takes you by the hand"), everyday life ("the weather and utilities causing constant vexation"), lyrics from the anthem of the Ukrainian SSR ("Sing to the Motherland, home of the free," "bulwark of peoples in brotherhood strong"), and quasi-Romani expressions ("Nalače maguša pchendle, z romujuvale; lače manuša pchendle z ame solovji"[64]).

The Roma call Herman "friend" and "gadjo," lend him money to repay his debts, and eventually offer to help him fight the corn raiders who want to turn all the land in the east into endless cornfields. All of them—as "worn yet durable" as their vehicles—show up for the meeting with the corn raiders to defend the now useless but iconic agricultural airfield. Ironically and not without affection, Hera refers to them as "a funeral procession" and compares them to "taxi drivers waiting for fares outside a train station."[65]

The idea that Zhadan entrusts the presbyter to convey to the people is that all who live in this territory, "baptized and unbaptized people, Shtundists and barefoot, semiliterate villagers," were born and raised on this land and there are no enemies among them. "As long as you're together as a team, you've got nothing to fear," the presbyter declares.[66] He gives Herman a book about the history of jazz in Donbas, passing it on to him through the dark-skinned Tamara. At first glance, this inserted story has nothing to do with the plot. But in fact it is connected to it, primarily through jazz and its transnationality. Indeed, jazz is present in the novel from the very beginning, when Herman leaves the city on his road trip and listens to CDs of the famous Black saxophonist Charlie Parker (1920–1955). "The music made the Volkswagen tremble, like a glass jar

---

63   Zhadan, *Voroshilovgrad*, 205, 207.
64   "Nalače maguša pchendle, z romujuvale; lače manuša pchendle z ame solovji" ("Bad people said that Gypsies were lice-ridden; good people said that we were nightingales"), "Kultura tsyhan [Roma culture]," 4ua, n.d., http://4ua.co.ua/moscow/yb3ad68a4d43b89521206c37_1.html.
65   Zhadan, *Voroshilovgrad*, 387.
66   Zhadan, *Voroshilovgrad*, 445.

someone was drumming on with a stick,"[67] and "Parker's alto ripped through the air, exploding like a chemical weapon wiping out an enemy camp. He was blowing out a golden flame of divine wrath. His black fingers buried themselves deep in the toxic wounds of the air, extracting copper coins and the dried fruits of his labor."[68] The music of the brilliant Black musician accompanies the characters everywhere in *Voroshilovgrad*.

As Zhadan argued in *Anarchy in the UKR*, music creates a community of like-minded individuals. Just as soccer created a community of friends and the presbyter gathered a community of Shtundists, so, too, the African-American Parker—whose music breathes a "golden flame of divine wrath"—creates a non-conformist community that Herman feels part of. In addition, jazz embodies the idea of global transcultural transience, which is illustrated by the inserted section "The History and Decline of Jazz in the Donetsk Region." For the melody of one of the spirituals written by Gloria Adams, who brought American jazz to Donbas and cultivated it there, would later be performed by "renowned jazz musicians such as Chet Baker or Charlie 'Bird' Parker."

Voroshilovgrad tells the story of *another* Ukraine—a country that is transitioning from a Soviet past to a capitalist society, from mono-ethnic rootedness to transnational migration and multicultural communities. Ukraine is also becoming a country of migrations, a meeting place between West and East, and a part of the processes of global migration. Zhadan also rewrites the individual and even the collective memory of the Soviet past, reclaiming the right to the biography of the last Soviet generation. In *Voroshilovgrad*, he debunks the myth of the eastern Ukrainian borderlands as an "emptiness." For the characters of his novel, this territory really does turn out to be their "home turf," land that they are willing to defend and protect as their "last territory." It can be argued that in a general sense, *Voroshilovgrad*, with its central narratives addressing the issues of identity in a situation of transit—location and dislocation, rootedness and uprooting—can be categorized as an example of postcolonial migrant literature, a rare genre in Ukrainian literature.

Six years after the publication of *Voroshilovgrad*, Zhadan wrote *The Orphanage*, a novel about the war in Donbas, in which he addresses the self-determination of the "last Soviet generation"—now on the front line which their "home turf" has become. After *Voroshilovgrad*, his characters know where their home is, and they know that "even this territory, it turns out, may be desirable [and] dear," that "you want to hold on to it for dear life," because here "you hear that motherland

---

67 Zhadan, *Voroshilovgrad*, 17.
68 Zhadan, *Voroshilovgrad*, 19.

forms in darkness, / like the spine of a teenager living in a boarding house"⁶⁹ ("She's fifteen, sells flowers at the train station," 2016). And yet war once again tests this "emptiness," and in *The Orphanage*, Zhadan further develops the theme of the transience of Donbas and "the rootlessness of life, feeling disconnected from one's homeland." Ultimately, both novels form a kind of Donbas diptych, united by a common theme—the birth on the eastern Ukrainian frontier of what Serhiy Zhadan calls a "sense of one's country, its distinctiveness, and one's belonging to it."⁷⁰ Twelve years before Russia's full-scale invasion of Ukraine, Zhadan speaks prophetically of Ukraine's center of gravity shifting to the East. It is on the eastern Ukrainian borderlands that a new Ukrainian identity has been fiercely fought for and forged since 2014.

---

69 Translated from the Ukrainian by John Hennessy and Ostap Kin.
70 Pavlo Stekh, "Skhid Serhiia Zhadana: pysmennyk rozmirkovuie pro dytynstvo v Starobilsku ta identychnist rehionu [Serhii Zhadan's East: the writer reflects on childhood in Starobilsk and regional identity]," *Svoi.City*, July 9, 2019, https://svoi.city/articles/36462/shid-sergiya-zhadana-pismennik-rozmirkovue-pro-ditinstvo-v-starobilsku-ta-identichnist-regionu.

CHAPTER 5

Biopolitics and The Post-Totalitarian Generation

The Phenomenon of the "Sick Body"

The role of generations in post-totalitarian society is quite significant. This is reflected in the phenomenon of post-memory in the generation of children of Holocaust survivors. German historian Jörn Rüsen has suggested that we look at the history of German Nazism and the assessment of the Holocaust through the prism of the perceptions of different generations, namely through their genealogical connection with the generations involved in the crimes. According to Rüsen, it is the third generation that restores the connection between generations, while simultaneously rejecting the "collective silence" and "moral distancing" of the first two generations. The third generation formulates a new attitude towards the past, which is not cut off, but linked to the present. Rüsen came to the conclusion that "the objective genealogical chain of generations has become a structural element of the historical perspective within which German identity is formed."[1]

Unlike the German experience of trauma caused by Nazism, in Ukraine, the process of coming to terms with the experience of totalitarianism was delayed (and only began after 2014). This is reflected in the symptoms of generational rifts at the beginning of the twenty-first century. As Hannah Arendt noted, the experience of totalitarianism becomes an even greater problem when totalitarianism itself disappears. Totalitarianism destroys the private world and eradicates the individual, condemning them to loneliness. However, Arendt says, "even the experience of the materially and sensually given world depends upon my being in contact with other men, upon our common sense which regulates and controls all other senses and without which each of us would be enclosed in his own particularity of sense data which in themselves are unreliable and treacherous."[2] The youngest generation is the successor to the privacy and rootedness destroyed by totalitarianism, and therefore trusts only the unreliable and deceptive organs of its own senses.

Virginia Woolf noted in 1930 that considering how common illness is, it is strange indeed that it has not taken its place with love, battle, and jealousy among the prime themes of literature.[3] It can be assumed that after surviving

---

1   Jörn Rüsen, *Novi shliakhy istorychnoho myslennia* [New paths of historical thinking], trans. Volodymyr Kamianets (Lviv: Litopys, 2010), 240.
2   Hannah Arendt, *The Origins of Totalitarianism* (San Diego: Harcourt Brace Jovanovich, 1973), 475–76.
3   See, for example, Tamara Hundorova, *Lesia Ukrainka. Knyhy Syvilly* [Lesia Ukrainka. Books of the Sibyl] (Kharkiv: Vivat, 2023). The book explores Lesia Ukrainka's work and illness from a cultural and anthropological perspective.

Covid-19, the world will place illness at the forefront of culture. Illness in the post-postmodern world is not only a threat to a person's spiritual, mental, and physical state—as a phenomenon of biopolitics, it raises questions about human nature itself and its limits. Until recently, the processes of modernization and cultural evolution were based on the idea that "human plasticity is practically infinite," which made it possible to socially construct human behavior and create social and cultural utopias to which human nature was expected to conform. In other words, the assumption that human nature is limitless and susceptible to endless transformations became one of the linchpins of the modern era. However, "although human behavior is plastic and changeable, these properties have certain limits: at some point, deeply rooted natural instincts and behavior patterns rise up and undermine the best plans of social engineering."[4]

One such stage is experienced in the post-totalitarian period, when human nature itself rebels against the radical social and technological experiments carried out on humans by the modernizing spirit of the age, embodied in socialist doctrine and expressed in forms of totalitarian control and violence over not only the spiritual but also the biological nature of humans. These biotechnological and social experiment can be characterized as traumatic, and the post-totalitarian state can be called post-traumatic, marked by a regression into infantilism and illness. It is this biopolitics that finds its characteristic reflection in post-Soviet literature of the early twenty-first century.

The post-totalitarian experience is deeply traumatic primarily because it significantly involves the experience of the older generation, which is forced to radically reevaluate its values. But post-totalitarian trauma also shapes society's unconscious and plunges the younger generation into a state of uncertainty, instability, and homelessness. By the end of the twentieth century, as the transition to a post-industrial information society was underway, the role of so-called youth subcultures had significantly increased. A distinctive feature of these subcultures is generational solidarity, which is reinforced by a series of signs, symbols, myths, and rituals that enable the maintenance and reproduction of a particular group identity. The special role of such generational identities and subcultures lies in the fact that they are selective in relation to the heritage of their "parents," and thus break down the distances established by tradition and society and help to change the paradigms of cultural movements, liberating biological instincts and adapting sociocultural practices to living conditions.

---

4   Francis Fukuyama, *Nashe postchelovecheskoe budushchee. Posledstviia biotekhnologicheskoi revoliutsii* [Our posthuman future. Consequences of the biotechnological revolution], trans. M. B. Levin. (Moscow: AST, LIUKS, 2004), http://alt-future.narod.ru/Future/Fnpb/fukunpb.htm.

As Karl Mannheim has argued, individuals born in the same social and cultural context are potentially a generation, but they become an actual generation when they are caught up in the whirlwind of social change and experience processes of dynamic societal destabilization, for example, during times of war. Mannheim claimed that "the quicker the tempo of social and cultural change is, then, the greater are the chances that particular generation location groups will react to changed situations by producing their own entelechy."⁵ Moreover, it is among representatives of generations that have experienced radical upheavals that skeptical and destructive thinking can be encountered.

Slavoj Žižek argues that "the symptom arises where the world failed, where the circuit of the symbolic communication was broken."⁶ In the early twenty-first century, such symptoms of *broken* symbolic communication are clearly emerging. Broken communication symbolizes existential loneliness, but it also reflects postcolonial and post-totalitarian confusion. From the perspective of biopolitics, this is manifested in the phenomenon of the *sick body*. The symptom of the *sick body* primarily points to the inseparable connection between social disorder and the somatic state of the individual, such as digestive problems, sexual disorders, difficulty breathing, and fear of death. This phenomenon signals a shift in post-postmodern consciousness from anthropocentrism to biological and zoological anthropology, which Rosi Braidotti considers a new political and affirmative figure for the contemporary post-human world.⁷ This state reflects the replacement of the didactic mode of socialization characteristic of Soviet subjectivity with performative and staged socialization.

It is worth mentioning the peculiar autistic spectrum of post-Maidan young people's fiction of the early twenty-first century. The typical motifs of the fiction of the 2000s generation mostly revolve around the generation gap, the loss of parents, life without a mother, homelessness, travel, depression, alcoholism, the rejection of social identifiers, and the deconstruction of social and cultural myths. The ideals, guidelines, and tastes of these writers are not rooted in the present: for them, time either hangs in limbo or shifts into a kind of frozen past. The past, however, is not historical: the era of history has come to an end. Rather, the past has been replaced by selective images of the past, with its problematic areas and places. Moving into the past is not painful because immunity

---

5   Karl Mannheim, "The Problem of Generations," in *Essays on the Sociology of Knowledge*, ed. Paul Kecskemeti (London: Routledge, 1952), 310.
6   Slavoj Žižek, *Vozvyshennyi ob''ekt ideologii* [The sublime object of ideology], trans. Vladyslav Sofronov (Moscow: Khudozhestvennyi zhurnal, 1999), 79.
7   Rosi Braidotti, *The Posthuman* (Cambridge: Polity Press, 2013), 104.

to historical traumas and troubles has already been developed. Moreover, there is no desire to be rooted—either in history or in the present.

The authors' self-identity is defined in a closed manner, namely, within the subculture of their generation, groups, publications, blogs. As Ihor Bondar-Tereshchenko noted at the time, "Today, an electronic online diary on the LiveJournal network is no longer considered bad taste and moral exhibitionism. There are fewer and fewer random visitors to your virtual corner, the circle of close friends is becoming even more marginalized, and the 'literary process' seems to be reappearing before our eyes. At least that's the impression you get, occasionally wondering where the former active authors of 'live' literary life in Ukraine have disappeared to. And they *are* disappearing, losing their meager social connections and remaining moral virtues in the cyberspace of LiveJournal."[8]

There is an overall shift of focus to "living contemporaries" and *topical* literature: the main thing is that it should interest *you* and *your* like-minded peers. Such sentiments are primarily expressed in the punk literature which emerged in Ukrainian literature and culture in the late twentieth century. It was primarily represented by the early works of Serhiy Zhadan, which were imbued with moods of protest, anarchism, and nonconformity, as well as the generational resentment characteristic of the "last Soviet generation," to which the writer belonged. Zhadan's poetry collection *Quotations* (1995) and his novel *Depeche Mode* (2004), landmarks of the punk subculture of the 1990s, found their continuation in the 2000s. Generally speaking, representatives of this generation are focused on escaping society and its laws. Their tastes and references, on the other hand, are directed and confined to those who are similar to them, and their ideals are essentially escapist in nature. Their characters are not rooted in the present—their ideal is transported somewhere to the 1960s, that is, to the period that sociologists usually allocate for the formation of a generation. In a sense, the generation of the 2000s seeks to live the life of the previous generation, symbolically erasing the experience of their parents. This gap arises from a distrust of the cultural practices of previous generations, especially those of the so-called adults, which have been distorted by the totalitarian system.

When you search for non-communicativeness or auto-communicativeness in youth punk culture, they are revealed by the symptom of the *sick body*, which turns out to be not a whole, self-identical biological object, but rather a *dissociated* and *performative* one. In modernist works, the body typically appears as

---

8   Ihor Bondar, "Zhyttia v ZhZh," *Chetver*, no. 28 (November 2007), http://chetver.com.ua/n28/01.html.

lustful flesh, a repository of self-consciousness and of various, frequently divergent desires, and as a text inscribed with diverse cultural signs and practices. The body as performance is a phenomenon of the postmodern era, with the falling away of the belief that divergent life currents disconnect the body and virtual corporeality crosses boundaries, or, as Valery Podoroga calls them, *thresholds of existential territories*. These existential territories are neurotically colored, as the body, broken, finds itself at the center of vitally necessary compromises between the unconscious and the conscious, as well as becoming a field of (non)encounter between the self and the *other*.

Thus, the postmodern concept of corporeality is that "individual life is not confined to the body-threshold, as in a dungeon, but is always a whirlwind, a whirlpool, a fall between depths and surfaces, a change of bodily states independent of stable, visible bodily forms."[9] This circulation of corporeality and its existential thresholds seems infinite. After all, since the mid-twentieth century, as Donna Haraway notes, all "biomedical discourses have been progressively organized around a very different set of technologies and practices, which have destabilized the symbolic privilege of the hierarchical, localized, organic body."[10]

In the paradigm of the organic body, illness is associated with the incorrect transmission of information, or "communications pathology," which manifests itself as a violation of the boundaries of the "strategic assemblage called self."[11] In the postmodern paradigm, where the body is fluid, changing, and evolving, illness, on the contrary, is associated with the continuity of repetitions, reincarnations, fragmentation, and recombination of this body. This ability to undergo various bodily transformations is possessed by Wozzeck, the mentally ill eponymous hero of Yuri Izdryk's novel, which has become a kind of hallmark of Ukrainian postmodernism. It is his illness that gives Wozzeck hallucinatory dreams, as well as the demiurgic power of bodily recombinations. He particularly appreciates the fact that "the people in your dreams were not bound to their physical shells, and you could mix and match—put several people in one body or divide one person into several different ones, shuffle them, swap them around, try different people in different people's bodies or even objects or things,

---

9   Halyna Pahutiak, *Zapysky Biloho Ptashka* [Notes of the White Bird] (Kyiv: Ukrainskyi pysmennyk, 1999), 20.
10 Donna Haraway, "The Biopolitics of Postmodern Bodies: Determinations of Self in Immune System Discourse," in *Feminist Theory and the Body: A Reader*, ed. Janet Price and Margrit Shildrick (New York: Routledge, 1999), 210.
11 Haraway, "The Biopolitics of Postmodern Bodies," 211.

because the essence of things was not fixed once and for all, but manifested itself in its original richness of all possible variations."[12]

The postmodern body is inorganic; it is both *the same* and not the same, or *different*. This is embodied, in particular, by monstrous corporeality, as a monster is neither entirely alien to the self nor entirely familiar to it. Monstrous corporeality in general has become an emblem of contemporary post-totalitarian society. Such monstrosity, which manifests itself in the appearance of various kinds of non-humans, hybrid shape-shifters, and fantastical creatures, is a consequence of unresolved traumatic memories of the Soviet past. Applying Sigmund Freud's ideas about the uncanny and melancholy as an insurmountable loss, scholars have explored the phenomenon of melancholy in the post-Soviet era, in which the oblivion and repression of memories of the totalitarian past return to literature in the form of phantasms.[13] However, it is also important to discuss the biopsychological symptoms of catastrophism, as the phantasms of the post-totalitarian era are largely based on biocultural violence against nature, particularly against the body—this violence served as the foundation for both modernization processes and socialist experiments.

The post-postmodern literature of the early twenty-first century, having survived a period of euphoria induced by postmodern ideas of the circulation of corporeality, is returning in various ways to the values of individual lived experience, autobiography, and traces of lived as opposed to textualized life. In Ukrainian literature, this is particularly evident in Taras Prokhasko's *One Could Make Several Stories Out of This* (2005) and Yuri Andrukhovych's *The Secret* (2007). Prokhasko claimed that his postmodernist work *The UnSimple* was more of a framework or outline for a novel (more precisely, a collection of narrative stories). However, his next novel (in one of his interviews, he referred to the book as a novel, which was eventually published as a collection of reminiscences, *One Could Make Several Stories Out of This*) is supposed to be a novel in its own right, with everything that was omitted in *The UnSimple*: conversations, thoughts, and experiences. Essentially, this shift from a collection of narratives about a story to the story itself signals the end of postmodernism.

A notable feature of Prokhasko's postmodernist writing has always been its philo-bio-textuality, where the textual recombinations produced by the

---

12   Izdryk, *Votstsek & votstsekurhiia* (Lviv: Kalvariia, 2002), 47.
13   For more on melancholy as a condition of cultural and gender identification resulting from an unresolved rupture with the maternal body, see: Hundorova, Tamara. *Femina melancholica. Stat i kultura v gendernii utopii Olhy Kobylianskoi* [Femina melancholica. Gender and culture in the gender utopia of Olha Kobylianska] (Kyiv: Krytyka, 2002).

imagination overlap with the biological fluidity and organic nature of life, while the viruses of textuality itself, multiplying the number of recombinations and variations, ultimately spread into extra-textual reality. This strategy is best illustrated by his short story "Necropolis": the very title of the story, which is about the writing of the novel *Necropolis*, represents the necrophilic idea of weaving textual recombination from dead, formalized chains of words. However, the main problem lies in how to incorporate all the diversity of living meanings of being into such a recombined verbal form, because even a simple register-description of the recombination scheme turns out to be limitless. Ultimately, as the narrator was aware, there are countless ways to write *Necropolis*—as a lyrical story, a script, a treatise, a list, and a map of existence.

Prokhasko's *One Could Make Several Stories Out of This*, on the other hand, embodies a different aesthetic paradigm: the core of the work is the spontaneity of life and the impressions it offers. The book is a flowing river of memories and stories, rich in details of Soviet life, recollections of Brezhnev and the Druzhba foreign literature shop , the army, his father, his brother Yurko, his uncle, his grandfather Mykhailo, and even the detached house that they began to build in 1937. This rehabilitation of the naturalness of the self, the body, and the details of everyday life shows that artistic narrative moves in parallel with the flow of life, rather than attempting to create life itself.

This experience of *rehabilitating reality* from the shackles of textuality, which is becoming a hallmark of post-postmodern culture, prompts us to wonder whether the transfiguration of corporeality also has its limits and whether what Arthur Kroker called "the flesh-eating 90s" are behind us.[14] Almost all the 1990s postmodernist novels of Yuri Andrukhovych, Oksana Zabuzhko, and Yuri Izdryk captured the destruction of the self and the differentiation of the individual, as well as the formation of parallel or contrasting virtual bodily identities. Such fragmentation can be considered a sign of a postcolonial situation, in which the central axis of the colonized subject's identity has been disrupted. Thus, despite the apparent integrity of the characters, in Andrukhovych's novels the virtual variations of a certain psychotype of the Ukrainian post-Soviet bohemian hero were Yurko Nemyrych, Hryts Shtundera, and Khomsky (*Recreations*); the Ukrainian poet Otto von F. was inseparable from his Soviet incarnation, the KGB agent "Sashka" (*The Moscoviad*), while Stakh Perfetsky (*Perversion*) disintegrated into "countless faces and countless names."

---

14   Arthur Kroker, *Hacking the Future: Stories for the Flesh-Eating 90s* (New York: St. Martin's Press, 1996).

In Oksana Zabuzhko's *Fieldwork in Ukrainian Sex*, the image of the protagonist is also split between virtual personas—thief, poet, little girl, lover, ghost. Perhaps the most differentiated in terms of various bodily-existential, spiritual, and virtual planes is Yuri Izdryk's Wozzeck—an archetypal character for the 1990s who breaks down into "a series of incomprehensibilities associated with the ambiguity of the relationship between the 'self,' 'you,' and 'he'. That is, between me, you, and him. That is, between Wozzeck and Wozzeck Incorporated."[15] The disintegration of the self is captured not only in grammatical forms, but also in the perception of oneself from the outside, from within the body, from the surface of the body, and from the perspective of another body.

The search for the self is directed inside the body—through optical magnification, as in an ultrasound examination, computer games, or animated cartoons—but it also moves deeper, "through the hydraulics of the heart and blood vessels, the twilight peristalsis of serpentine tubes, and the childlike liveliness of the thinnest epithelium."[16] Another way to search for the self is through the surface of one's own body.

And yet all these ways of articulating oneself through the concepts of "I," "you," and "he," combining them with the physical, biological shell, create only a series of combinations, since *the body as such does not exist*. That is why Wozzeck felt like a biorobot—"not a body, not his usual self, not a person, but a certain pulsating substance that could be inside you and behind you, take up the space of a poppy seed or grow to the size of a room."[17] As *a non-body*, Wozzeck can fit a metal bed, a white-painted stool, a light bulb, a window, a floor, a ceiling, walls, and a toilet, and ultimately "a good third of the globe" inside himself "without any discomfort." "All of it was you, and you were all of it," the narrator says in summary.[18] In general, Wozzeck interprets illness itself as the only thing that can make our existence meaningful. Illness helps you not only to be a body without organs, but also to construct a spontaneous and illogical, fragmentary text, free from the sequence of events. Illness also relieves the pain of pathological communication—*"not meeting people"* becomes a habit for Wozzeck.

The breaking down of closed organic physicality and the virtual "devouring" of flesh in each of these seminal works of the 1990s are symbolic of post-totalitarian consciousness. The profound changes marked by the break with the Soviet past, the freedom brought about by perestroika, and the reevaluation of all previous

---

15 Yuriy Izdryk, *Votstsek & votstsekurhiia* (Lviv: Kalvariia, 2002), 23.
16 Izdryk, *Votstsek & votstsekurhiia*, 34.
17 Izdryk, *Votstsek & votstsekurhiia*, 34.
18 Izdryk, *Votstsek & votstsekurhiia*, 36.

officially accepted values led to a different way of existing, particularly to the discovery of one's own bodily self. However, it turned out that the integrity of the bodily self had been largely maintained through totalitarian coercion and control, as all space between people was destroyed and they would press against each other, as in the overcrowded public transportation of Soviet times or the phenomenon of standing in line so characteristic of the Soviet era. When all other ties are weakened, it turns out that the past—the colonial, Soviet, totalitarian past—devours not only the present, but also the body.

In the 1990s, illness became a metaphor for post-totalitarian inorganic identity, causing painful transformations and fragmentation of personality, as well as searches for the lost "self," as seen in Izdryk's *Wozzeck*, and communication breakdowns, as in his *Double Leon* (2000). But illness also made Stakh Perfetsky's Orphic wanderings in time and space possible in Yuri Andrukhovych's *Perversion*. In the 2000s, illness became a metaphor for a new, consciously constructed identity that enabled you to go beyond reality into a virtual world. Illness becomes desirable, and literary characters enter into it as if it were their own existence. It was in the 2000s that people began to talk about how, as a result of the biotechnological revolution, "it will be possible to maintain normal bodily functions practically indefinitely," and the central issue of the so-called post-human existence of the world will be, on the one hand, the assimilation of post-human subjectivity to multiple levels of coding, and on the other hand, the identification of boundaries/limits, the definition of which changes the localization of the "I"/"self".[19]

The generation of the 2000s is witnessing and participating in the Anthropocene crisis, which was actively discussed at the end of the twentieth century. Against the backdrop of new technological breakthroughs, environmental crises, and post-catastrophic thinking, a new consciousness was born. It was all about the possibility of transcending the universal anthropocentric dimensions of culture, altering the biological concept of humanity in response to technological progress, the emergence of eco-critical consciousness, and phenomena such as cyberfeminism, transhumanism, and cyberpunk, among others. It was accompanied by a reevaluation of the concept of the biological body, a shift in the boundaries and surfaces of corporeality brought about by various technologies: piercing, bodybuilding, tattooing, cloning. All these biotechnologies promised a transformation of human nature itself, leading to the emergence

---

19 N. Katherine Hayles, *How We Became Posthuman: Virtual Bodies in Cybernetics, Literature, and Informatics* (Chicago: University of Chicago Press, 1999), 300. Hundorova cites the Ukrainian translation by E. Maricheva (Kyiv: Nika-Tsentr, 2002), 363.

of the cyborg body in culture. Such work with the body demonstrated how, in place of the Soviet vision of the future with its "iron communards," the phenomenon of hybrid posthumanity—machine and organism—emerged. As the founder of cyberfeminism Donna Haraway argued, "it seems to be that no matter how technologically advanced the society becomes, technology cannot replace the personal bonds that tie humans to humans, humans to animals, and humans to their own senses.[20]"

In Mykhailo Brynykh's *Electronic Plasticine*, the organic body, which is organized by the coincidence of consciousness and its material embodiment, as well as by the boundaries and limits of corporeality, is literally lost: as a result of coding and system failure, the characters presented here are constantly being recoded and renamed, and the body itself becomes interchangeable, ultimately a thing and a material. A certain "patron" buys the bodies of homeless people and "makes art out of them," so that the body is transformed into a decorative material. "The point is to present fragments of bodies as decorative material. Here they're just corpses, but after the right treatment, they become like plastic. You would never say these are real bodies," one of the characters explains.[21]

In the trashy literature favored by Brynykh, the body is denatured and becomes monstrous, like the ugly, overweight body of Ivan Hakkerel (*Electronic Plasticine*). Ultimately, in Brynykh's work, the fleshly body ironically and grotesquely disintegrates like a mechanical automaton and melts like plasticine: "First his eyes popped out: they bulged and swelled, the whites of his eyes cracked, and brown blood poured out of the cracks [...]; his body jerked like a passenger in an electric chair, and his heart rolled out of the gaping hole in his chest—it splattered on the floor, bounced, and rolled under the table; one after another, his ears fell off [...], then, almost all at the same time, Vova Karlovych's limbs came off [...], his spine melted like sugar in a teaspoon over a gas flame; a few minutes more, and Vova Karlovych's torso was completely liquid."[22]

Monstrosity is also inherent in the esoteric characters of Lyubko Deresh's *Cult*, where the summoning of the monster Yog-Sothoth, the Weaver of Shadows, and the Great Worm coincides with journeys into the subconscious, which are both threatening and desirable. The monstrous body—a symbiosis of organic matter and machinery—evokes a maddening fear: "The brain went mad with fear

---

20 Donna Haraway, "The Biopolitics of Postmodern Bodies: Determinations of Self in Immune System Discourse," in *Feminist Theory and the Body: A Reader*, ed. Janet Price and Margrit Shildrick (New York: Routledge, 1999), 276.
21 Mykhailo Brynykh, *Elektronnyi plastylin* (Kyiv: Fakt, 2007), 35.
22 Brynykh, *Elektronnyi plastylin*, 129-30.

because it saw a giant pale worm, infinite in time and space, a living, nightmarish eternity, pale and transparent, covered with scales, a monster-worm, a representative of a separate race and civilization, a race as alien to humans and to living beings as it is possible to be."²³

The transformation of non-humans (monsters, in other words) and evil forces into the main characters of novels and short stories means displacing humans outside the aesthetic system and undermining the traditions of European humanism of the Modern Age. However, this displacement of humans, which some scholars consider an attribute of the return of a Gothic, criminal-barbaric society, can also be viewed from another perspective, namely through the symptom of the "sick body," which signifies the situation of the rebirth of post-Soviet society. And then it is worth bearing in mind that "the large-scale violence experienced in the twentieth century became a normative emotional experience not only for eyewitnesses and participants in the events, but also for their descendants. Clearly, the consequences of the traumatic experience of continuous terror [...] have become woven into the fabric of the history of three generations of Soviet people. The psychological, moral, and social perversions caused by this experience have yet to be truly [...] assessed."²⁴

Since youth subcultures make active use of styles such as trash, camp, punk, etc., the body in these subcultures resembles a masquerade and performance at the same time. This body is extravagant. The prominent psychiatrist Ludwig Binswanger, a representative of the phenomenological approach in psychology, argued that extravagance is based on an extreme dependence on social rules, which can deprive patients of their "personal qualities and uniqueness" and leave them "a mere copy of some general way of life."²⁵ In other words, this state of inauthenticity can be viewed as "a profound loss of individuality, independence, and freedom that arises from excessive social pressure." Extravagance is a variant of transforming existential elation into a pretentious way of self-presentation, a certain kind of *role-playing behavior*. Binswanger explains: "For only where the *communio* of love and the *communicatio* of friendship is missing and where mere intercourse and traffic with 'others' and with one's self has taken over the exclusive direction of our existence, only there can height and depth, nearness and

---

23 Liubko Deresh, *Kult* (Lviv: Kalvariia, 2004), 242.
24 D. R. Khapaeva, "Tsena zabveniia: Rossiiskoe goticheskoe obshchestvo" [The price of oblivion: Russian gothic society], Fond imeni D. S. Likhacheva [D. S. Likhachev Foundation], http://lfond.spb.ru/programs/likhachev/100/stenogrammi/hapaeva.html.
25 Ludwig Binswanger, "Extravagance, Perverseness, Manneristic Behaviour and Schizophrenia," in *The Clinical Roots of the Schizophrenia Concept*, trans. J. Cutting, ed. J. Cutting and M. Shephard (Cambridge: Cambridge University Press, 1987), 86.

distance, present and future, have so much importance that human existence can go too far, can attain to *an end* and a *novo* from which there is neither retreat nor progress. In such a case, we speak of conversion into *Extravagance*."[26]

The illness we are talking about can be more accurately defined as extravagance, with an absence of *communio* (love) and *communicatio* (friendship) observed in relationships with others, while in the circle of those similar (identical) to oneself, *communion* and *communicatio* overlap. Effectively, it is something akin to narcissism—friendship and love for those who are similar to us. Existence in the constant present, or more precisely, in the timelessness of the present, and asociality allow one to avoid growing up, to fall into dreams and hallucinations, in other words, to get stuck in the present. Ultimately, extravagance, just like a body without organs and like monstrosity, becomes a discursive phenomenon. These form a special text of homology and totality, where there are no connections with the *other* world and *other* people, where the characters are homogeneous, and entire chunks of text can be lifted straight from LiveJournal.

The melancholic sublimation of the sick body involves supplementing it with an ideal, or canonical, body. Valery Podoroga argues that "the canonical body is objectified, it is an ideal norm, that is, a set of behavioral norms, following which we distinguish between the correct and incorrect use of the human body."[27] The space of contemporary culture, into which the canonical body is inscribed and from which it seeks to be extracted, is primarily represented by various images of physicality that are fetishized by popular culture, associated with beauty, reproduced, and packaged as a commodity. This is the fetishized body. In youth cultures, the fetishized body, presented in its kitsch form, plays a particularly significant role.

For many characters in young people's fiction, the canonical body exists as a replica of the bohemian world of the 1960s, a particularly appealing period for contemporary young people's fiction. As everyone knows, in the 1960s, hippies, the Beat Generation, pop culture, camp, and rock music exhibited the hallmarks of bohemian, anti-bourgeois culture. The main character of the Bu-Ba-Bu carnival of the 1990s, which originated with a literary performance group of the same name, was also a bohemian hero who escaped the uniformity, control, and violence of Soviet society, overturning and transforming its values. Serhiy Zhadan also frequently references the 1960s in his works, starting with the "corrupt

---

26 Binswanger, "Ekstravagantnost," 293–98.
27 Valerii Podoroga, *Fenomenologiia tela. Vvedenie v filosofskuiu antropologiiu: materialy lektsionnykh kursov 1992–1994 gg* [Phenomenology of the body. Introduction to philosophical anthropology: materials of lecture courses 1992–1994] (Moscow: Ad Marginem, 1995), 21.

poets of the 60s" and "quality music" from the 1960s and 1970s which could have served as the basis for his "perfect radio station" ("Live fast, die young"). Drawing on the Bu-Ba-Bu group and largely following in Zhadan's footsteps, young authors of the 2000s borrow many scenes, plots, and bohemian topoi from the works of Andrukhovych, Izdryk, and Zhadan.

The reluctance to grow up, infantilism well into old age, distrust of the maternal body of the motherland, and the paternalistic society—all these experiences were shared by the hippies and the beatnik generation, who created pop art, a popular culture based on pleasure and affirmation. But this era cannot be repeated, except perhaps through fetishes, masquerades, and irony. As we can see in Zhadan's short story "Ten Ways to Kill John Lennon," the encounter with the generation of Havel, John Lennon, and the hippies is not quite idyllic: "Imagine the late Lennon at eight o'clock in the evening when he'd started drinking at eight in the morning, his glasses all fogged up from the alcohol fumes, with those round lenses, you know, proper John Lennon glasses."[28]

The attitude of the 2000s generation towards the rock stars of the 1960s is not at all nostalgic, but rather melancholic—like a loss that can never be compensated for. They therefore seek to fill that loss by turning to fetishized images onto which the memory of their idols is transferred. Nostalgia is a recollection that gradually overcomes the feeling of loss by selecting and reassembling acceptable fragments of past events, thereby inserting them into memory and forgetting the source of the loss. Melancholy, on the other hand, keeps the feeling of existential loss alive through memories (and souvenirs).

In the 2000s, the former rock idols of the 1960s returned as fetishes and souvenirs. They are associated with the total and ideal body. However, they return rather as kitsch, in the form of discs, pictures, souvenirs, having lost the mysterious aura of their time.[29] For the protagonist of Irena Karpa's novel *50 Minutes of Weed*, this ideal body is represented by The Doors CDs. "'I'm not a fan of Balzac. All those Rastignacs, the ill-fated idols of our childhood. I want to kiss Jim Morrison on the lips,' she said, and kissed the transparent box from the 'Best of The Doors' CD."[30] Lyrics by The Doors are cited liberally throughout *50 Minutes of Weed*: Yevka, the novel's protagonist, quotes "Break on Through to the Other Side," "Riders on the Storm," and "My Wild Love," and drops casual mentions

---

28 Serhii Zhadan, *Big Mak* (Kyiv: Krytyka, 2003), 44.
29 The connection between pop culture and kitsch is most clearly demonstrated by Michael Jackson, who loved kitsch art and became an idol of kitsch himself. See: Michael Jackson. Kitsch Art [218].
30 Irena Karpa, *50 khvylyn travy* [50 minutes of grass] [*Koly pomre tvoia krasa* (When your beauty dies)] (Kharkiv: Folio, 2007), 33.

of Sartre, John Lennon, and Bob Marley. For Sashko Ushkalov, as well as for Zhadan, whom he also frequently quotes, the ideal body is that of Red Elvis and Depeche Mode. In Lyubko Deresh's novel, Yurko Banzai listens to Van der Graaf Generator (1960s), and the singer and guitarist Jimi Hendrix, whom he meets in Dartsia's trans-reality, becomes the embodiment of the canon. Ultimately, Hendrix visually transforms into a satirical guitar player, a "strange gentleman dressed in a light black three-piece suit;" "the gentleman had long, shoulder-length, salt-and-pepper hair, an elongated pale face, eyes hidden behind black glasses, and agile gray-tinged eyebrows that often jumped out from behind the shadows of his glasses."[31]

Both the sick body and the melancholic sublimations—bohemian and extravagant—allow us to speak of the emergence of a *new existentialism* in contemporary Ukrainian young people's literature. In the novels and short stories mentioned above, the central issue is the immersion into being, while the key issues are responsibility and irresponsibility. Sashko Ushkalov engages in a polemic with Kant and his categorical moral imperative, while Mykhailo Brynykh, in a short story that, according to the blurb, is indebted to "cyberpunk, trash culture, and pop criticism," proposes a "program of irresponsibility": "What was said is forgotten. What was written is crossed out. What was convincing is refuted. A chain of transformations, the law of connected services."[32]

Thus a new modern "burlesque world" is created, one that has stirred up burlesque thinking, where highbrow and lowbrow, serious and ironic, alien and familiar are blended together and bodies melt together like plasticine sculptures. Such multiplication is a discursive variation of the body-text without organs, since "in the plasticine world, the beginning and the end are erased; there is neither linearity nor conditionality."[33]

The Loser Phenomenon

The prevalence of the "sick body" symptom in Ukrainian literature of the early twenty-first century, particularly in the period between the Orange Revolution and Euromaidan, is no accident. The disappointment caused by the loss of

---

31 Liubko Deresh, *Kult* (Lviv: Kalvariia, 2004), 252.
32 Mykhailo Brynykh, *Elektronnyi plastylin* (Kyiv: Fakt, 2007), 59.
33 Alina Bazhal, "Mykhailo Brynykh, 'Elektronnyi plastylin', vydavnytstvo 'Fakt'," *Dzerkalo tyzhnia*, no. 13 (692) (April 2008).

aspirations born on the Maidan during the Orange Revolution, the unfulfilled hopes that Ukraine would become more modern under the presidency of Viktor Yushchenko, and Viktor Yanukovych's rise to power, along with growing corruption and anti-democratic processes, became the breeding ground for the loser symptom. Six years after the Orange Revolution, reflecting on what it had achieved, Yaroslav Hrytsak concluded that "the Orange Revolution may have made Ukraine a little more Ukrainian, but it did not make it significantly more modern. There is no less corruption in Ukraine, no mass trade unions have appeared, no Ukrainian university has become more independent, Ukrainian parties are still more like clans, and so on."[34]

The Orange Revolution was the culmination of the processes that defined the carnivalized 1990s. The euphoria of freedom, the emergence of a new public sphere, play as a means of shedding the mask of totalitarianism, language, aesthetics, and text as forms of individual self-affirmation and transgression of boundaries and hierarchies—all this was fully realized on the Maidan in 2004. However, the revolution itself, as Yuri Andrukhovych later claimed, ended in disappointment: "When we all talked about disappointment, we actually meant the growing critical rejection of what the people we had brought to power with our votes and actions were doing." The reason for the disappointment was a feeling of betrayal—the betrayal being what Andrukhovych calls the "backdoor deal": "Cynically speaking, it was a backdoor deal. Yes, we won. But the way things turned out . . . points to a backdoor deal, there's no other way to put it."[35]

Post-Maidan sentiments are vividly represented in an anthology of the 2000s generation titled *Two Tons of Young Ukrainian Poetry* (2007). The 2000s generation is the generation whose literary formation coincided with the turn of the millennium. "Why two tons?" one reviewer asked. "Because that's the combined weight of the more than thirty poets whose work is featured in this anthology, from 93-kg (205-lb) Serhiy Osoka to 46-kg (104-lb) Olesia Mamchych. The emphasis here is on weight rather than a literary manifesto: here we are in literature, and we can be measured in certain ways—age, weight, some even give their height. Ultimately, that's not a bad way to manifest ourselves: trying to prove

---

34 Yaroslav Hrytsak, "Shcho zalyshylosia pislia Pomaranchevoi revoliutsii?" [What remained after the Orange Revolution?], *Istorychna pravda*, last modified October 18, 2010, https://www.istpravda.com.ua/articles/2010/10/18/559/.
35 Yurii Andrukhovych, "Inodi ia sumuiu za Maidanom," *Zbruch*, November 21, 2021, https://zbruc.eu/node/108848.

the 'necessity' of poetry is futile; it exists, and that's it. And it exists as a physical phenomenon, not just a metaphysical one."[36]

The "wear and tear" on and dissociation of the body, provoked on the one hand by Soviet social engineering and on the other by these social disappointments, manifest themselves in post-Maidan literature through the rehabilitation of corporeality and the return of the body to the orbit of history, although the body shows symptoms of disease.

A sickly condition—physical pain, mental disorder, spiritual hypochondria—is characteristic of the vast majority of the protagonists in the novels and short stories that were published immediately after the Maidan. In a sense, the characters in Sashko Ushkalov's *Life Safety* (2007), Mykhailo Brynykh's *Electronic Plasticine* (2007), Irena Karpa's *50 Minutes of Weeds* [When Your Beauty Dies] (2008), and Lyubko Deresh's *Cult* (2002) can all be referred to as sick: they all exist along the borderline of the split internal self and external self, their own consciousness and someone else's, reality and illusion. At the same time, the body itself appears as an *affective body*: it prepares to shift, that is, to change, weakening or strengthening its capabilities in order to combine with other bodies and events, but this state is delayed, and the shift does not occur.

The affective body has no protective properties; the forces of the external flow penetrate it and destroy its boundaries, so that it no longer has clear organic forms and resembles a computer-generated hyperreality. In Brynykh's novel, this hyperreality is akin to a plasticine structure, whereas in Deresh's novel, it assumes the form of a monstrous body. In Ushkalov's novel, this hyperreality is easily imitated as a prosthetic body, for example, "an arm and a leg in military uniform" and "real innards." The affective body takes on a hypochondriacal nature when, as Deleuze and Guattari argue, the organs are destroyed, leaving neither the brain, nerves, chest, stomach, nor entrails intact; only skin and bones remain. This is precisely the state experienced by the protagonist of Irena Karpa's *50 Minutes of Weed*.

The post-Maidan generation of the 2000s invents its own hero, who is essentially a loser. That's how Dania, a character in Irena Karpa's *50 Minutes of Weed*, refers to himself when he says: "You let a loser into your life, and one day this bastard will sprout through your ears, nose, throat, and ass and bloom with lush purple flowers."[37] The loser exists as an "inorganic" and "non-hierarchical" body

---

36 Zhezhera, Vitalii. "'Dvotysiachnyky' miriaiut poeziiu kilohramamy ['Two-thousanders' measure poetry in kilograms]." *Hazeta po-ukrainsky*. Last modified February 19, 2008. http://gazeta.ua/index.php?id=209675&eid=555.

37 Irena Karpa, *50 khvylyn travy* [50 minutes of weed] [*Koly pomre tvoia krasa* (When your beauty dies)] (Kharkiv: Folio, 2007), 6.

without organs. In this immanent shell of bodily existence, clots of pain flare up, and organs such as the stomach are formed and transformed, poisoned by some shrimp that was past its prime (in Ushkalov's *Life Safety*). The task is further complicated by the fact that you have to be a "good loser" and smile like you're in an ad. That is why Karpa talks about this new imperative—"to be a good loser."

> "Only one thing is expected of you:
> Smile,
> Smile,
> Smile. All the time, and three times over."[38]

Ultimately, the most intimate pair for the loser is "thoughtlessness" and "powerlessness." "I'm thoughtless. You're strengthless," Karpa writes in her novel. Someone has written these words (in English) on a wall; Yevka, the novel's protagonist, draws a frame around them, and this conceptual painting becomes the leitmotif of a story about a love that can never be realized in this life, only *post mortem*.

Life, the body, the organism, and nature take on a perverse, sickly appearance. Baz in Ushkalov's *Life Safety* doesn't want to grow up. Yevka can't stand children crying because she finds the sound unbearable: "There was no point in looking for meaning in it. Just like in children in general. Yevka did not want to have children; she already hated everything that could come out of her nasty womb." Despite her own stories of triumph over men, including surviving rape, she herself is also a homeless child who longs for old age.[39]

The symptoms of this condition are primarily defined in terms of illness: "She suffered from six-month bouts of depression and scornful stares, tuberculosis and fungal diseases, paranoia (I love butterflies!) and fear of psychosis."[40] In one online review, Karpa's protagonist is described as "Yevka, a 19-20-21-year-old girl who is insecure, mired in permanent depression, obsessed with manic ideas about her own death, suffering from periodic schizophrenia, riddled with self-doubt, and an occasional drug user. She tries to hide all this behind the mask of a shrewish bitch, and proves her own 'worth' to herself by constantly changing, to put it mildly, her sexual partners, [...]."[41]

---

38 Karpa, *50 khvylyn travy*, 5.
39 It is worth noting that Irena Karpa, a mother of two, would later speak publicly about being a mother and encourage other women to have children.
40 Karpa, *50 khvylyn travy*, 17.
41 Liera Lauda, "'Irena Karpa—literaturoiu navit ne pakhne...'" ['Irena Karpa—doesn't even smell like literature...'], *Khai Vei*, last modified December 23, 2005, http://h.ua/content/about/.

"I am sick with loserdom," another author, Tanja Maljartschuk, admitted in an interview. "Even my husband told me that I am turning into a fan of losers, because all my latest stories are about seriously screwed-up people. All these people are real . . . If I ever publish this book of stories, I'll also include a map marked with the places where you can bump into one of these losers."[42]

'Loserdom' is the diagnosis that society, personified by adults, lecturers, and teachers, gives the teenagers in Ushkalov's *Life Safety*. "I remember," says Baz, the main character, "once, based on the results of a test, our university psychologist determined that Icarus and I were, well, outsiders, fucking losers . . . That's exactly what he said: 'You two are losers, got it?' And grinned."[43]

The diagnosis of loserdom may be indirect, but it is nevertheless obvious, as, for example, in the case of Ivan Hakkerel, who has pink teeth and of whom the narrator in Mikhailo Brynykh's *Electronic Plasticine* says: "He . . . lives such a boring, monotonous, and incomprehensible life that there are doubts about his mental health."[44] Brynykh's other characters do not seem all that healthy either: Sharnir ("One word—income") and Korova are obsessed with their desire for "suicide with a return ticket."[45]

The psychotype of the "loser" takes us back to the 1960s and evokes the famous Beatles song "I'm a Loser" (1964). "I'm a loser, and I'm not what I appear to be," is how the loser presents himself. "Although I laugh and I act like a clown, beneath this mask I am wearing a frown." As John Lennon later explained the semantics of this dichotomy, "Part of me suspects that I'm a loser, and the other part of me thinks I'm God Almighty." The characters in contemporary young people's fiction share the same ambivalent identity, but they are more deeply immersed in melancholy.

The "sick body" is born of a reluctance to grow up and enter the adult world, where the patriarchal social unconscious reigns, where survival is defined by victory over others, where you have to "reclaim your meters and cubic meters of air" from "some invisible enemy," as the protagonist in Ushkalov's *Life Safety* admits. Thus, a teenager's psychosomatic regression into a "sick body" helps them to avoid the violence and power of society—that omnipresent and alien unconscious that makes you feel "as if some hand with nicotine-stained nails has opened up the empty projector of your head and put black-and-white short

---

42 Iryna Slavinska, "Tania Maliarchuk: 'Ia peretvoriuiusia na fanatku luzeriv'" [Tania Maliarchuk: 'I am turning into a fan of losers'], *Ukrainska pravda*, last modified September 8, 2008, https://life.pravda.com.ua/society/2008/09/08/7802/.
43 Sashko Ushkalov, *BZhD. Crazynovel*, 2nd ed. (Kyiv: Fakt, 2008), 52.
44 Mykhailo Brynykh, *Elektronnyi plastylin* (Kyiv: Fakt, 2007), 18.
45 Brynykh, *Elektronnyi plastylin*, 11.

films into it, and while those films are playing, you're living your life—well, at least you think you are."[46]

Asociality becomes desirable; the mask of the loser is worn consciously, signaling the contradiction between the inner and outer self, as well as the uncommunicativeness and hypochondria it generates. Since ancient times, hypochondria has been identified with inflammation, which causes dysfunction in various parts of the body, resulting in the body's inability to connect its feelings with the object that causes those feelings. Thus, hypochondria is a symptom of uncommunicativeness, a broken encounter with *the other*, an unformed or lost ideal.

All these symptoms are elements of melancholy—a mental state caused by a sense of loss, particularly the loss of oneself, the ideal, adult, socialized self. In his work on hypochondria and melancholy, the well-known German psychiatrist Wilhelm Griesinger described melancholy as "anomalies of self-consciousness, of the desires, and the will."[47] Hypochondria is associated with excessive attention to one's own vulnerable body, with fear of illness, loss of organs, decay, and a special rebirth of the body. According to the Brockhaus and Efron Encyclopedic Dictionary, when melancholy takes on a hypochondriacal character, patients feel "that all their orifices have become overgrown, their intestines are rotting, their stomachs have collapsed, they have been turned into wood, glass, animals, etc."

Hypochondria and melancholy reveal an anomaly of will and a desire not to go heroically to the barricades, but to hide in the ruins of unfinished buildings and in the emptiness caused by the erasure of unwanted memories. At the same time, the loser turns into a shapeless and blind body, with tentacles that stretch in all directions like signals to others like him.

In young people's fiction, affective bodies serve as signs of the erasure of beginnings and endings, a rejection of references, a symbol of severing ties with reality and with other people, except for their narrow circle of peers. In a sense, all of these symptoms are *suicidal desires*. At the same time, through extravagance, losers sublimate their desires through dreams and hallucinations frozen in the present, swearing, sex, drugs, alcoholism, and death. Thus, reality becomes a negative onto which young people's fiction imposes its impressions, borrowed from marginal subcultures. Hidden beneath them is a body that is in pain.

The psychology of homelessness and parentlessness that permeates Serhiy Zhadan's early work becomes archetypal for the loser's consciousness. Zhadan's

---

46 Sashko Ushkalov, *BZhD. Crazynovel* [Life Safety], 2nd ed. (Kyiv: Fakt, 2008), 87.
47 Wilhelm Griesinger, "Hypochondriasis and Melancholia," in *The Nature of Melancholy: From Aristotle to Kristeva*, ed. Jennifer Radden (New York: Oxford University Press, 2000), 226.

characters are generally devoid of past history, and they recognize this. As one of his protagonists in *Depeche Mode* says: "This always irritates me, in the sense of seeing that someone already lived here before me and in contrast to me lived a real life—ate breakfasts, had sex, maybe even loved someone, visited the markets and stores."[48] Zhadan's homeless character is also "fatherless" and would like someone to adopt him, but at the same time sees that person as homosexual: "Why did no one adopt me, let's say, when I lived for several days at the bus station and slept on wooden chairs, or when I lived off boiled water for several days, come to think of it why doesn't anyone adopt me now, why doesn't this faggot adopt me?."[49]

The father is mostly absent from Zhadan's *Depeche Mode*; only somewhere far away, there is a shadow of a father—a stepfather whose funeral one of the characters is supposed to attend. The symbolic Father can only exist as part of a system, for instance, like Marusya's father, a general who provided his daughter with "all that minimal collection of artificial limbs and false jaws that has been made to transport you more comfortably through your life."[50] The mother is also absent in this world, profaned by popular love, almost identical to cannibalism: "They ate my mom," as one of Zhadanov's characters says. The mother's "slightly salty" eyes in the song "Mother's Eyes" by Stepan Haliabarda, an almost anonymous artist, are a metaphor for symbolic matricide. "'They ate my mom,' Vasia said, contented, as if his suspicions about this world had been confirmed.

> 'Who did?'
> 'Those guys—Stepan Haliabarda.'
> 'Come on. Don't take it literally.'
> 'But it's true. Did you hear what they said—"slightly salty"?.'"[51]

The absence of the Father, or the symbolic principle that provides a center, has become completely painless and not particularly traumatic for the 2000s generation. Not only that: an unnatural and hybrid creature—the monster—is assigned the functions of the symbolic paternal center. "Who is the monster of contemporary literature for you?" the youngest authors ask their fellow writers on LiveJournal, referring to an image of a leading contemporary writer. Various

---

48   Serhii Zhadan, *Depeche Mode*, trans. Reilly Costigan-Humes and Isaac Stackhouse Wheeler (London: Glagoslav Publications, 2018), e-book, 151.
49   Serhii Zhadan, *Depeche Mode*, trans. Reilly Costigan-Humes and Isaac Stackhouse Wheeler (London: Glagoslav Publications, 2018), e-book, 151.
50   Zhadan, *Depeche Mode*, 127.
51   Zhadan, *Depeche Mode*, 161.

figures are associated with the monster, from Yuri Andrukhovych to Bohdan-Ihor Antonych and Taras Shevchenko. In fact, in Yuri Andrukhovych's *Twelve Circles*, the bohemian Antonych also resembles a monster and can be perceived as an attempt to recreate (restore) the symbolic Father. However, this recreation takes the form of a simulacrum, so the "pseudo-Antonych" repeats and clones his descendants, that is, Andrukhovych himself.

For the generation that began writing in the early 2000s, the *fatherless child* becomes a central character. This new type of loser character was also diagnosed by Serhiy Zhadan in *Voroshilovgrad*. The loser is born in the last Soviet generation. As one of the novel's protagonists says, "We all wanted to become pilots. The majority of us became losers."[52] Unlike the active and radical losers of the 1990s, the losers of the 2000s see themselves as asocial nonconformists. They are not failures at all, as one might have expected. The position of outsider is a conscious choice, a way of regaining inner freedom from both official society and the influence of the media.

Losers resist various social and consumer roles: geeks (computer experts), Yuccies (successful young businesspeople), bohemians (fashionable creatives and partygoers), and macho men (hyper-masculine sexual supermen). In this sense, the loser represents an intermediate identity, situated between children and the elderly, without a clearly defined gender, social, or professional identity—a fluid, transient self-identity formed by rejecting both totalitarian and globalized models of consciousness. Losers are accused of inactivity, asocial behavior, and breaking with their parents. But losers no longer trust the maternal sphere that should have protected them—culture, nature, country, and homeland. After all, all these maternal roles have now been appropriated by the advertising industry, the media, and politicians, none of whom are trusted by present-day losers.

The Symptom of Matricide

The loser consciously accepts his identity in a world "without a Father," that is, without authority. In general, he lives in a virtual reality that gives him a sense of integrity and security, as he is acutely aware of the contradiction between his inner self and his outer surroundings. These contradictions should have been harmonized and reconciled, modern psychoanalysts say, by a "good enough mother" (as defined by Donald Winnicott). Yet the "good enough mother" is

---

52 Zhadan, *Voroshilovgrad*, 29.

also absent. One of the reasons for this is migration processes, changes in the sociocultural roles of mothers and women in modern post-industrial society, and so on. The loser's psychology is therefore fueled by aggression towards the maternal world, which has turned out to be different from what it (ideally) should have been.

According to Winnicott's theory, it is the mother as an object that is the basis for the meeting of all the child's needs, including imaginary and illusory ones. "Only with her help can the child be protected from an excessive feeling of helplessness, a feeling that could destroy its immature psyche. Through this relationship, the mother creates a sense of trust in the world in the child."[53] When the child grows up, the mother-object must gradually distance herself—she can no longer be the basis of illusions for the individual. This process of "psychological weaning" is quite painful for a person. As a mother says of her relationship with her child in one of Halyna Pahutyak's short stories, describing a marginal existence—childishness that separates a garbage dump from a pristine land—"I am almighty, but only in our time together, which is now torn in two, like the veil of the temple."[54]

But the "good enough mother" disappears, and the teenagers begin their adult life. In *Voroshilovgrad*, Zhadan buries not only the symbolic father, but also depicts the funeral of a mother (and a mother with mixed heritage at that!) who is buried with all the attributes of the extremely unbalanced contemporary world, including "a gray suit jacket, black skirt, and red, polished high heels," a coffee machine and a Japanese sound system, embroidered portraits of Taras Shevchenko and Jesus, a powder compact and a hairdryer, medals and tokens. This is actually the funeral of something bigger—"a strange country where the weather and utilities cause constant vexation." Meanwhile, a parody of the national anthem is sung ("Sing to the Motherland, home of the free [...] Sing to our celestial Jerusalem, bulwark of peoples in brotherhood strong"),[55] and the priest delivers a speech consisting of Soviet clichés, praising the "long and heroic life [of the mother—T. H.]," who doggedly fought for "the happiness of her people, her friends and family, and her colleagues." And the priest's words sound quite sarcastic when he says that "the principles of brotherhood, genuineness, honesty, and Romanipen, which she upheld consistently and

---

53 P. Fonda and E. Iogan, "Razvitie psikhoanaliza v poslednie desiatiletiia" [Development of psychoanalysis in recent decades], in *Psikhoanaliz v razvitii* [Psychoanalysis in development] (Ekaterinburg: Delovaia kniga, 1998), 137.
54 Halyna Pahutiak, *Zapysky Biloho Ptashka* [Notes of the White Bird] (Kyiv: Ukrainskyi pysmennyk, 1999), 32.
55 Zhadan, *Voroshilovgrad*, 206.

staunchly throughout her entire life, will serve as a timeless example for generations to come, as they take the baton from their parents in the eternal fight for a brighter future.."[56]

Ultimately, as they observe the moral and material devaluation of the values of their parents, who were raised under the Soviet system, the post-Maidan generation of children feels completely orphaned. By analogy, we can recall Ivan Franko's short story "Homeland" (1904), in which the word "homeland" for the main character, Opanas Marymukha, encompasses "not so much his relatives and in-laws as something impersonal, though not abstract,"[57] namely a feeling of emotional attachment. In the new, modern world of the early twentieth century that he was depicting, Franko uses the word "homeland" to denote both his love for the place where he was born and raised and a fatal attachment to a woman.

In the post-postmodern world, the connection with the "homeland," as well as the ethics of responsibility, is interrupted. One of the characters in Sashko Ushkalov's *Life Safety* notes that "for some reason it began to seem that we were superfluous on the entire planet, on the vast EARTH, which is swarming with so many bastards, but there is simply no place for us here [...]."[58] In this world, the word "homeland" loses its meaning, and the slogan "The Motherland is thinking of you" becomes an advertisement for beer.

In the processes of sociocultural individualization, Freudian psychoanalysis emphasizes above all the special role of the father and the "name of the Father" as a signifier that inscribes the subject into the symbolic order and prohibits incest. However, symbolic identification/separation from the mother plays an equally important role in the processes of sociocultural representation, and at certain periods these processes become decisive. The maternal archetype is one of the most important for the development of cultural imagery and imagination. It emphasizes the symbolic power of the mother and collective values, reflects the fear of death, and embodies ideal fantasies and entities, such as *mater patria*. However, since motherhood is a sociocultural construct, real biological motherhood is often replaced by social and cultural constructs and subordinated to ideological goals.

---

56   Zhadan, *Voroshilovgrad*, 209.
57   Ivan Franko, "Batkivshchyna" [Fatherland], in *Zibrani tvory: u 50 t* [Collected works: in 50 volumes], vol. 21, *Opovidannia (1898–1904)* [Stories (1898–1904)] (Kyiv: Naukova dumka, 1979), 395.
58   Sashko Ushkalov, *BZhD. Crazynovel* [Life Safety], 2nd ed. (Kyiv: Fakt, 2008), 205.

According to Julia Kristeva, the loss of the mother is a necessary link in the process of an individual's autonomization. She argues that "For man and for woman the loss of the mother is a biological and psychic necessity, the first step on the way to becoming autonomous. Matricide is our vital necessity, the *sine qua non* condition of our individuation."[59] The functions and content of motherphobia in post-Soviet Ukrainian literature largely reflect the *ressentiment* generated by the rethinking of totalitarian myths about the Soviet Motherland. The role of the maternal image is also significant in national discourse. For example, one iconic poem for the Sixtiers generation was Vasyl Symonenko's "The Swans of Motherhood," in which he portrays Ukraine as "mother, sanctuary, the one that gives wings and strength, profoundness of thought and imaginative colors, and in his devotion to her, the poet finds his filial happiness, strength, and honor."[60]

Since the 1990s, Ukrainian literature has witnessed a growing critique of the image of motherhood and related symbolism, reflecting a challenge to the ideological symbolism of socialist realism, which was based on the concept of the motherland. The postcolonial approach also reveals criticism in Ukrainian literature of the idealized image of the mother as the guardian of the family. The maternal body of culture is perceived as incomplete, and symbolic incest and matricide become signs of the post-totalitarian struggle for freedom and autonomy against traditional values. Often, the symbolic mother is blamed for colonial traumas. In general, the idealization of the mother and motherhood, which served an ideological purpose in Soviet times, is replaced by generational nihilism in the post-Soviet generation. This has resulted in the increasing popularity of themes related to the desacralization of the mother, female migration, and resentment that mothers are occupying the father's place in society, gaining independence and adapting more easily to the new market economy.

All this can be compared to the role of the mother in the colonial subconscious, represented, in particular, in the romantic vision of Taras Shevchenko. The latter is associated with the personification of Ukraine as an oppressed woman, a pokrytka, or an unmarried mother, and a mother. As George Grabowicz has noted, Shevchenko saw the world of Ukraine at that time as defined by the conflict between the female powerlessness of ideal community, serfs, raped and seduced women and illegitimate children, and the corrupt, degenerate male

---

59 Julia Kristeva, *Black Sun: Depression and Melancholia*, trans. Leon S. Roudiez (New York: Columbia University Press, 1989), 38.
60 Oles Honchar, "Vytiaz molodoi ukrainskoi poezii" [Knight of young Ukrainian poetry], in Vasyl Symonenko, *Poezii* [Poetry] (Kyiv: Radianskyi pysmennyk, 1984), 5.

order of hierarchy and authoritarianism.⁶¹ In general, Grabowicz believes that in Shevchenko's utopian world—restored and compensated after the reconciliation of the main oppositions, which were largely caused by colonization—"the male figure, the father, is notably absent."⁶² In other words, in Shevchenko's anti-colonial paradigm there is no father, because colonialism has destroyed him. Instead, a special role is given to the maternal archetype, which embodies the ideal image of Ukraine itself and becomes part of the poet's "superego."

Shevchenko gave the maternal archetype an anti-colonial meaning while simultaneously demonstrating its ambivalence. A notable manifestation of this is the poet's image of the *pokrytka*, or the unwed mother. The unmarried mother is on the cusp of good and evil, righteous and sinful. On the one hand, she is often a victim of violence and humiliation, such as Kateryna in the poem of the same name, who was dishonored and abandoned by a "Moskal"—a Russian officer stationed in a Ukrainian village. As feminist critics have pointed out, it is women who are the first victims in colonial discourse. A serf girl also becomes a victim of her master, who sexually abuses her or even commits incest, with the master usually coming from the capital. On the other hand, the unwed mother is a victim of her own passion who has transgressed against traditional patriarchal morality and is misunderstood by society ("evil people").

As a mother and a woman who has been wronged, the unwed mother suffers, loves her child, and goes mad with grief, but she is also capable of committing a crime against her own child. In Shevchenko's "Rusalka," the mother drowns her newborn daughter and makes love to the master who wronged her. The eponymous heroine of the poem "Tytarivna" wants to drown her child in a well. The poem "I Could Not Sleep, and the Night Was Like the Sea . . ." tells the story of a girl who "would go to the young master" until she had a child and "drowned her in the well." For Shevchenko, the image of the unwed mother becomes not only the embodiment of sinful transgression and the presence of evil in the world of that time, but also a tragic symbol of society's inability to protect its values, personified by maidenhood, family, and happy motherhood.

The excessive idealization of motherhood in past sociocultural discourses, particularly patriarchal ones, is contributing to the growth of criticism of

---

61 Hryhorii Hrabovych, *Shevchenko yak mifotvorets. Semantyka symvoliv u tvorchosti poeta* [Shevchenko as myth-maker. Semantics of symbols in the poet's work] (Kyiv: Radianskyi pysmennyk, 1991), 154.
62 George G. Grabowicz, *The Poet as Mythmaker: A Study of Symbolic Meaning in Taras Ševčenko* (Cambridge, MA: Harvard Ukrainian Research Institute, 1982), 164. Hundorova cites the Ukrainian translation, Shevchenko yak mifotvorets (Kyiv: Radianskyi pysmennyk, 1991).

maternalism—the public and ideological use of values associated with motherhood. In the twentieth century, motherphobia became part of anti-colonial consciousness in Ukrainian literature. In the 1930s, the poet Yevhen Malaniuk, surveying the conflicts of national history and, in particular, Ukraine's subordination to neighboring Turkey, Poland, and Russia, called women promiscuous "whores of khans and tsars" who are "Powerless, / Helpless, drunk and mute / With barren flesh, wretched body / To give to everyone they meet."[63]

In the wake of postcolonial criticism, Oleksandr Irvanets parodies Volodymyr Sosyura's famous poem "Love Ukraine," which was written in 1944 and reflects the national-patriotic pathos of World War II. The poem was banned during the Soviet era and became iconic for the Ukrainian Sixties generation and the national movement as a whole. In Irvanets' interpretation, the maternal archetype is transformed into a globalizing idea and acquires a multicultural meaning. The lyrical hero ironically calls for love not only for Ukraine, but also for Oklahoma, Indiana, North and South Dakota, Alabama, Iowa, California, Florida, Nevada, the District of Columbia, Georgia, Montana, Louisiana, Arizona, Alaska, Nebraska, and Virginia. As Myroslav Shkandrij emphasizes, "The list of states, all of which have feminine endings in Ukrainian, suggests a list of female lovers. The poem hints at the need to share one's affection generously, even to the point of promiscuity."[64]

It is no secret that the depersonalization of the individual in a world "without a Father" draws in the characters of postmodernist novels by Yuri Andrukhovych, Oksana Zabuzhko, and Yuri Izdryk. All of them recreate a situation where the symbolic totalitarian and authoritarian Father no longer exists as the center that determines not only the integrity and hierarchy of society, but also the imagination of the individual. Thus, the central character of the postmodernist novel becomes an eccentric adventurer who moves freely in time and space, living on fragments of memories and hallucinatory dreams, and escaping into virtuality. One of the dreams in *Wozzeck* explicitly shows a theatrical staging with a fake ship and the departure of the "expelled and cursed debauched son," punished by "you, the father."

Olekło II, the imaginary king of Ukraine to whom Otto von F. writes letters in *The Moskoviad*; the Swiss citizen Dr. Popel in his Chrysler Imperial in *Recreations*; the devilish Monsignor, who holds the threads of all destinies in his

---

63 Yevhen Malaniuk, *Poezii v odnomu tomi* [Poetry in one volume] (New York: NTSh and UVAN, 1954), 80.
64 Myroslav Shkandrij, "The Shifting Object of Desire: The Poetry of Oleksandr Irvanets," *Canadian-American Slavic Studies* 44, no. 1–2 (2010): 68.

hands in *Perversion*—none of these characters are suited to the role of symbolic father, and even when they do fulfill it, it is only temporarily. They all exist on the cusp of reality and virtuality, and their central place is rather attributed to the game reality in which they are placed. Therefore, they are unable to fulfill the role of a true father.

Real fathers lack authority too: the father of the heroine in *Fieldwork in Ukrainian Sex* is a semi-dissident, unemployed, plagued by fear. His right to control his "daddy's girl" extends only to watching over his daughter, but it also entrenches her "lifelong filial obedience." Ultimately, the writer discovers that the emancipated woman is no good, raised within a patriarchal parental culture infected with fear of arrest, who loses her sacred attitude towards her mother, who has been traumatized by the Holodomor. As the protagonist notes, "because Mother was quite beside the point in all this, Mother was, in fact, frigid, and obviously out of it."[65] All this becomes a sign of post-totalitarian trauma, as does the decolonial perception of the masculine weakness of Ukrainian men, "castrated" by the colonial past and by their powerlessness.

One symptom of trauma is the demasculinization of colonized men, who transfer the violence they have suffered from male colonizers to their own wives and (in racial terms) white women. The protagonist of Zabuzhko's novel *Fieldwork in Ukrainian Sex* offers the following diagnosis of colonized society: "[. . .] We were raised by men fucked from all ends every which way [. . .]." Then they humiliated their own women, doing to them what others had done to them. Despite this, "[. . .] we accepted them and loved them as they were, because not to accept them was to go over to the others, the other side." Because "our only choice" was and remains "between victim and executioner: between nonexistence and an existence that kills you."[66]

As Frantz Fanon has noted, the conflict between parents and children in colonial history is particularly painful and acute. A family with a colonial father and a colonial mother, the relationships between brothers and sisters, children and parents, and the self-awareness of teenage sons in the postcolonial world form a surprisingly diverse and internally contradictory picture. Fanon referred, in particular, to the change in roles, the weakening of the father's role during the anti-colonial struggle, which is especially traumatic for children whose experience is limited to the family. "It is important to show that the colonized father at the time of the fight for liberation gave his children the impression of being

---

65 Oksana S. Zabuzhko, *Fieldwork in Ukrainian Sex*, trans. Halyna Hryn (Seattle: Amazon Crossing, 2011), Kindle edition, 112.
66 Zabuzhko, *Fieldwork in Ukrainian Sex*, 140.

undecided, of avoiding the taking of sides, even of adopting an evasive and irresponsible attitude."[67]

It is significant that Fanon emphasized the traumatic nature of colonialism: he paid a great deal of attention to psychosomatic disorders caused by colonialism. He considered physical, mental, and psychosomatic disorders to be both symptoms and means of adaptation, as they testify to how the body gets used to the constant pressure it is under and to the changes that are inevitable. It should be noted that the late Sigmund Freud also spoke about the transgenerational transmission of trauma. In particular, he argued that the original traumas absorbed into human psychology largely determine the behavior of subsequent generations.

Sashko Ushkalov's landmark novel *Life Safety*, which continues the punk traditions started by Serhiy Zhadan, is the most vivid manifestation of the post-totalitarian consciousness of the loser, the archetypal hero of the 2000s generation. The title of the novel, *Life Safety*, refers to a subject introduced in Ukrainian schools and universities in the 1990s with the aim of quickly and easily socializing the younger generation. The epigraph to the novel is a quote from Ivan Vyrypaev: "It's strange, very strange, where would I be if I hadn't existed?"

The main situation portrayed in *Life Safety* is related to disappointment in society, which in the post-totalitarian era is identified not only with the loss of the symbolic father, but also with distrust of the maternal role. For, as already mentioned, the mother symbolically personifies the body of being itself; her role is to create an environment in which the child can develop an authentic sense of self and form their identity. The maternal image correlates with a real world in which wishes always come true and do so just at the right time. When it turns out that this world is different from what was expected, that dissatisfaction (*ressentiment* towards reality) is carried over to the image of the mother herself.

Thus, as Baz (who, like the other characters in *Life Safety*, does not have a name of his own and hides behind a nickname) notes, he began swearing at the age of six, and it was because of his mother. "I had terrible toothache," he recounts. His mother took him to a dentist who was still an intern and "explained what the matter was using phrases like 'to hell with it', 'that fucking tooth', and 'Be careful, you bastard, got that? Because I'll rip your guts out!', and then for some reason she added that I was a very nervous child, a very, very nervous child, and

---

67 Frantz Fanon, *A Dying Colonialism*, trans. Haakon Chevalier, intro. Adolfo Gilly (New York: Grove Press, 1965), 100.

sometimes even dangerous." The intern "took out his sadistic pliers" and pulled out a tooth, but not the bad one, but a healthy one—the one next to it.⁶⁸

This episode can be considered key to understanding childhood trauma—a kind of castration and disconnection from "normal" people, as well as resentment towards the mother. Baz's mother eventually left to work in a foreign country, "ran off abroad," as Baz says, leaving him at home with his father, who did not take very good care of him. In Baz's perception, the image of his father exists more as a background than as a reality.

Thus, mistakenly castrated at the age of six (since a pulled tooth can be associated with castration), Baz is an eternally immature teenager with a deep wound in his soul. He has no desire to grow up; for him, life is not a home, but a bestiary, a circus, a madhouse. As he admits, he was nervous that someone was constantly watching him, like that half-darkened disc of the sun which resembles "a squinty, sleepy red eye watching me."⁶⁹ Clearly this "eye" can be associated with Jeremy Bentham's "panopticon" (from the ancient Greek πᾶν—"all" and ὀπτικός—"seeing"), an ideal prison designed in such a way that the guard in the center can secretly watch the prisoners, giving them the impression that they are being watched constantly. The control and supervision that Baz wants to get rid of are associated with parental authority, a reference to the totalitarian past of his parents' generation from which the teenager is trying to escape. It is important to note, however, that in his world, his father's authority no longer holds sway, nor does his moral authority. So what feeds the teenager's subconscious is his hostility towards his mother, who should have protected him. The image of his mother is erased from his memory like the talisman his grandfather once gave him—an antique German medallion bearing the image of a monastery "of the mother [. . .] I don't know exactly which one, but some mother."⁷⁰ Over time, the surface of the medallion was rubbed away, and the monastery simply disappeared. "I often tried to make out at least its outlines, but all that blinked at me from the medallion was my own eye," Baz says.⁷¹

Using Jacques Lacan's psychoanalytic symbolism, we can say that the mirror stage of identification with maternal culture, the maternal body of society, turns into narcissistic self-contemplation by the hero. He fails to break through to reality beyond the maternal image (and the image imposed by his mother) and build a coherent and protective world of reality. Instead of the controlling "eye,"

---

68 Ushkalov, Sashko. *BZhD. Crazynovel* [Life Safety], 2nd ed. Kyiv: Fakt, 2008.
69 Ushkalov, *BZhD*, 27.
70 Ushkalov, *BZhD*, 74.
71 Ushkalov, *BZhD*, 74.

Baz sees his own reflection. From the point of view of society, he is a loser, an outsider, as his psychosocial type was determined back in school. But he himself admits: "I am lost in . . . in a word, I am lost in the world . . ."

The formula for existence that Baz consciously develops is an antisocial counterargument to the world of parents, teachers, and educators. Their society is built on the opposition of "enemies" and "friends" and on the struggle against an imaginary adversary. Such a world is controlled and divided into winners and losers. But the world the teenager wants to live in is a space of freedom, where there is no struggle, no need to defend or conquer inches and cubic feet, and no need to think about an imaginary enemy.

In general, Baz's antisocial escapist mood is identified with the postcolonial state of infantilism. One might, of course, think that the authoritarian world from which Baz flees into infantilism and loserdom is the world of the totalitarian past, which is now behind us. However, the novel is generally about moral authority, even Kant's moral imperative, against which the loser rebels.

There is another motif in the novel that significantly complicates the state of post-totalitarian infantilism. Although the paternal authoritarian world has been completely discredited, the maternal world, with which the new globalized reality could be associated, is just as unhelpful, as Ushkalov shows. In his novel, the image of the mother is transferred to the maternal body of the *motherland*, which can no longer protect the post-totalitarian individual. After all, in the new era, in the society of spectacle, the "homeland" is featured in a commercial for officers' beer, in which Baz is destined to play a certain role. Against a backdrop of trenches, war, and Italian soldiers, the words "The motherland is thinking of you" appear in an advertisement for Italian beer. The computer-generated effect makes it look "as if someone was firing a machine gun at the TV screen so that it spelled out the words 'OFFICER'S BEER—THE MOTHERLAND IS THINKING OF YOU!!!'"[72] "THE MOTHERLAND IS THINKING OF YOU!!!" becomes a magic phrase and is repeated in different variations and different situations in *Life Safety*, but with profane words "motherfucker" and "your motherfucking cock"—as a counterpoint.[73]

Mothers, grandmothers, ordinary women—all of them pass before Baz like "border guards of some state, not an ordinary state that appears on all geographical maps, but some kind of state of their own—an internal one whose paths and passages they carefully guarded against smuggling, illegal immigrants, and other

---

72 Ushkalov, *BZhD*, 21.
73 Ushkalov, *BZhD*, 74.

misfortunes."⁷⁴ But these guardians of the "internal state" turn out to be not only weak, but also traumatized: in the perception of a teenager whose mother abandoned him in childhood to seek work abroad, they become defective representatives of the female gender.

Baz's resentment towards his mother is reflected in violence against the female body. In his view, the overwhelming majority of women (all except for one, Ket, who is as lonely as he is) personify sexual degradation: there are "old hags," a female security guard, an "old whore" with sagging breasts, a call-girl, a "nice-looking harlot," and other "sluts." Even his impressions of school are associated with the word "bitches," which covers his impressions of both a slow teacher from one of the Baltic states and his classmates—"bitchy nerds." A skinny female bartender, a drunk nurse in a hospital, a fat woman on a bus—all of them are worthy objects of the teenager's contempt.

So Baz lives in a world without a mother ("I last saw her fifteen years ago. And now she's somewhere in Portugal . . . or so they say"⁷⁵). The last scene in the novel, when Baz is sitting on the beach and the sun "was BIG and at the same time very far away, so FAR that if it bothered to look at me, it would see nothing but the empty seashore . . . ,"⁷⁶ is the apotheosis of escape from society and his father's "eye." But at the same time, the ending can also be seen as a suicidal regression to the primordial maternal womb, traditionally associated with the element of water.

The search for the mother and a kind of regression to mother-child unity are important themes in *Life Safety*. The return to the primordial mother's body, where protection and salvation can be found, takes on a melancholic and fetishistic dimension in the novel. "No, I wasn't a fetishist," Baz admits, "but I had things that meant a lot to me. It had been that way since I was a child, when I always wore clothes with large pockets that I could put all my favorite trinkets in."⁷⁷ Large pockets where you can hide yourself, a car, a bus—all these are objects that can replace a lost mother. After all, the eternal teenager Baz did not survive the separation from his mother and therefore seeks substitutes for her at least in things and objects.

One episode is particularly noteworthy. Baz's friend Yatsyk has a "crazy mother." After her death, Yatsyk, who used to sell himself for money to buy her medicine, buys himself a trailer, a "sort of house on wheels." This house is perceived as a

---

74   Ushkalov, *BZhD*, 54.
75   Ushkalov, *BZhD*, 150.
76   Ushkalov, *BZhD*, 239.
77   Ushkalov, *BZhD*, 146.

green planet where all losers can escape—the Hare Krishna Yatsyk, Icarus, Baz, and Signal, a paralyzed French bulldog. Baz also associates the bus with childhood, as it brings back memories of how he used to run around the bus, sitting down in a new seat as soon as it became available, and feeling "how warm and soft it was."[78] He also recalls the candy that a stranger gave him and his mother confiscating it, teaching him not to accept gifts from strangers.

Why is the loser so disappointed in mothers? It would seem that Ukraine had gained independence and the Motherland had taken on new—real and familiar—contours for citizens of all ages. Why, then, does Baz perceive the slogan "The Motherland is thinking of you!!!" so negatively? And the Kantian moral imperative is by no means to blame for the fact that the global world is not at all based on ethical principles of respect for the freedom of others. Ushkalov's *Life Safety*, published in 2007, can be viewed in the context of the disappointments that arose after the Orange Revolution and became fertile ground for the emergence of the loser-outsider.

Interestingly, the post-revolutionary reflections of another writer from the Sixtiers generation, Lina Kostenko, also laid bare the existence of the loser. In *Diary of a Ukrainian Madman*, published in 2009, two years after Ushkalov's novel, the main character, a programmer who narrates the story, is depicted as a loser. Dissatisfaction, self-doubt, disappointment in society, and misunderstandings with his wife, father, and son—all these characteristics mark out his loser mentality at the beginning of the 2000s. However, all these loser sentiments are overcome by the Orange Revolution, which unites three generations—parents, children, and grandchildren—in a single burst of freedom on the Maidan. Behind this act of unity is the novel's author, who orchestrates the entire narrative and conveys her thoughts to the main character. In this way, Lina Kostenko fulfills her protective role as a mother—as the mother of her children, the mother of the nation she protects, and the mother–author of the work itself.

The novel concludes with the last of many catastrophes: the betrayal by Ukraine's political leaders and the resulting disappointment with the outcome of the Maidan. What next? For adults like Lina Kostenko, who portrayed in *Diary of a Ukrainian Madman* the collapse of the ideal Ukraine created by the Sixtiers generation to which she belongs, this collapse is apocalyptic, universal. After all, it affects not only the fate of the country but also the purpose of the entire existence dedicated to the ideal of Ukraine. Moreover, this collapse threatens the very existence of the 1960s generation, which is passing away. For Ushkalov

---

78 Ushkalov, *BZhD*, 156.

and the generation that is just coming of age, disappointment in Maidan and in the motherland does not carry such a catastrophic connotation. Therefore, by accepting the mask of a loser, young people are simply stepping aside, outside the world of adult society, only to return to it again.

Quite unexpectedly, Baz recalls Shevchenko and even identifies the poet with his non-conformist generation. "[. . .] If Taras Shevchenko had been born, say, in 1983, not as a serf, but, say, a homeless kid in a Soviet orphanage, he would have become a pretty good rapper, performing hard-hitting social rap to the whole country [. . .]. And what would have stopped our genius, born in 1983, from remaking his famous line "To every man his destiny, his path before him lies"[79] into the more dramatic and poetic "To every man his karma, and his Jeep Cherokee"? [. . .] Then he would have come on stage in baggy jeans and a hockey jersey and recited "To every man his karma, and fuck that Jeep Cherokee" . . . — and I'd have been under the stage at that moment saying: Yo, big daddy TARAS, you rock!!!"[80]

Shevchenko emerges from icons, frees himself from banknotes, and appears in a form similar to that of vulnerable teenagers such as Baz, the main character in Ushkalov's novel. Baz grows up without a mother because his mother is working somewhere in Portugal, and he identifies as a loser. Vulnerability and resentment towards society, including the Motherland and his real mother, who abandoned her son as an illegitimate child, feed on the resentment of the teenage son. Here we have an example of a symbolic inversion of the image of the bastard child, a key image in Shevchenko's poetry, as well as the actualization of a motherless world. In Ushkalov's novel, the abandoned son (who in Shevchenko's work "cries under the window") feels like both a loser and God at the same time, and also seeks fetishes as substitutes for the maternal world in which he could have felt protected. One of the fetishes with which Baz identifies is Shevchenko, whom, like a toy, he could have put in the big pocket where he used to put his favorite things as a child. True, it would have been a Shevchenko in rapper jeans and not his traditional sheepskin coat. Thus, "pop Shevchenko" becomes a self-projection of the traumatized generation of the post-totalitarian era, and in a broader sense, a living, rather than museumified, cultural memory, actualized by contemporary Ukrainian authors.

---

79 Translated from Ukrainian by Vera Rich.
80 Ushkalov, *BZhD*, 126-27.

CHAPTER 6

After The Trauma: Chornobyl and Catastrophism

Chornobyl as a Catastrophe

How has Chornobyl influenced thinking, what new forms of consciousness did it give rise to, and in what form did it enter the postmodern and post-postmodern world? From the perspective of time, Chornobyl is seen as an event that shaped the preconditions for contemporary catastrophic consciousness. This is demonstrated rather symbolically by the popular Italian singer Adriano Celentano in his song "Sognando Chernobyl" (2008), in which the accident is depicted as a demonic ghost that casts its shadow over the whole world. In the music video of the same name, a succession of images flash before our eyes against the backdrop of the Chornobyl skyline: melting glaciers, Venice being flooded, the collapse of the Twin Towers on September 11, 2001, floods, nuclear explosions, cloning, the appearance of mutants, and other fears of contemporary time. The tentacles of radiation-induced cancer have spread from Chornobyl across the world to poison everything, says the song, with its refrain: "We will all be blown up."

It is no coincidence that the French philosopher Paul Virilio asks: "Why does the experience of Chornobyl call our worldview into question?" Indeed, the worldview has changed significantly since Chornobyl. Philosophers in the West have been seeking an explanation for the changes that the Chornobyl disaster has brought about. Frédérick Lemarchand has noted that we seem to be facing "the emergence of *a new world*. [. . .] The world that emerged with Chornobyl marks the beginning of a new era, an era of a shrinking inhabited world, an era of a regressing world, a world shaped by technical 'progress,' first nuclear, and a little later, genetic, and by the manipulation of living beings."[1] Jean Baudrillard attributes a global significance to the Chornobyl accident in the new configuration of Europe: "After Chornobyl, the Berlin Wall no longer existed."[2] He also notes that the reality of Chornobyl proved to be more powerful and impressive than the most fantastical virtual wars, so in a sense, Chornobyl marks the end of the naive belief in virtuality, a place where one can painlessly escape.

Scholars generally emphasize the special role Chornobyl played in the cultural formation that has come to be known as nuclear culture. In his examination of how late twentieth-century culture and art responded to the atomic bomb,

---

1 Frederik Lemarshand, *Topos Chornobylia* [Topos of Chernobyl] (Kyiv: Dukh i Litera, 2001), 374.
2 Jean Baudrillard, *The Illusion of the End*, trans. Chris Turner (Stanford: Stanford University Press, 1994), 45.

Spencer Weart argues: "The history of our current period, a new and distinct era of nuclear culture, begins with the 1986 Chornobyl disaster."[3]

We have long associated the traumatic events of twentieth-century history with catastrophe and, accordingly, endowed them with a certain symbolic meaning. Thus, Theodor Adorno appeals to the symbolic meaning of Auschwitz, noting the crisis of "the positivity of existence" and the failure of enlightened humanism, since the suffering "in the camps, without any consolation, burned every soothing feature out of the mind, and out of culture, the mind's objectification."[4] Later, the concept of "Auschwitz" became for Jean-François Lyotard a sign for legitimizing a general distrust of progress and, accordingly, an impetus for justifying the new postmodern situation. "To show how far our most recent Western history diverges from the 'modern' project of liberating humanity," Lyotard argued, "I have followed Theodor Adorno in using the symbolic word 'Auschwitz'. What kind of thinking is capable of 'removing'—in the sense of *aufheben*—this 'Auschwitz', by including it in some general empirical or even mental process oriented towards universal liberation?"[5]

Lyotard's last question is a starting point for reflections on "postmodernity," in which trust in some kind of "appropriate" and "complete" reality has been lost. "There is a sort of grief in the Zeitgeist," Lyotard argues. "It can find expression in reactive, even reactionary, attitudes or in utopias—but not in a positive orientation that would open up a new perspective."[6] Thus, based on the symbolic word "Auschwitz," Lyotard justifies the absence of a "positive orientation" toward progress.

"Chornobyl" has also long since become a symbolic word that calls into question the notion of a "positive orientation" toward progress. Precisely because it has evolved from a real historical event into a symbolic category, Chornobyl is associated with various contexts. First, the Chornobyl explosion signified an explosion within the Soviet system itself: it undermined faith in the socialist modernization that for more than half a century had been carried out through the excessive exploitation of human intellect and physical strength, as well as violence against individual freedom, ethnic groups, genders, social classes, and

---

3   Spencer R. Weart, "Nuclear Fear 1987–2007: Has Anything Changed? Has Everything Changed?," in *Filling the Hole in the Nuclear Future: Art and Popular Culture Respond to the Bomb*, ed. Robert Jacobs (Lanham, MD: Lexington Books, 2010), 233.
4   Theodor W. Adorno, "Posle Osventsima" [After Auschwitz], in *Negativnaia dialektika* [Negative dialectics], trans. E. Petrenko (Moscow: Nauchnyi mir, 2003), 365.
5   Jean-François Lyotard, "Zametka o smyslakh 'post'" [Note on the meanings of 'post'], *Inostrannaia literatura* [Foreign literature], no. 1 (1994): 48–49.
6   Lyotard, "Zametka o smyslakh 'post'," 48–49.

culture. Second, the Chornobyl accident highlighted the value of human life, suggesting that the most significant aspect was not the investigation into the causes of the disaster, but the experience of survival after the disaster. For this reason, stories about everyday life are particularly interesting: about the first responders (known in Ukraine as "liquidators") and their families, about how Kyiv residents took their children away to escape radiation, about the health and survival of those who were evacuated from areas close to the disaster zone. And thirdly, the Chornobyl disaster ushered in the era of post-truth, in which information, symbolic signs, and virtuality become more real than reality itself.

The nuclear accident brought the effect of fake news and information trauma to the fore. Thus, Chornobyl immediately became an informative precedent. When the Politburo of the Central Committee of the Communist Party of the Soviet Union met three days after the accident (on April 29, 1986), one of the issues they discussed was "how to present information." It was decided to prepare "three statements: one for our own people, one for socialist countries, and also one for Europe, the United States, and Canada."[7] Another fascinating sociolinguistic phenomenon was the emergence of Chornobyl jokes, which mocked the official statements and undermined trust in them, parodied patriotic songs in the genre of "sadistic poems," and constructed a new paradoxical mythology.

Virtual beryllium and roentgen, and the radiation that covered a vast area while remaining invisible and imperceptible, destroyed the immutability of the real world and undermined trust in nature. This stimulated an increase in catastrophic thinking, driving consciousness into a state of fear of the terrible— apocalyptic visions of nuclear war, terrorist attacks, global wars with aliens, and so on. The real became ominous and unknowable.

The turn of the twenty-first century saw the role of *catastrophic consciousness* continue to grow.[8] Catastrophism also permeates the perception of Chornobyl as a national and humanitarian tragedy. This is quite a remarkable circumstance, since until recently, the closely related but distinct metaphors of *"human tragedy"*

---

7   Alla Iaroshinskaia, *Prestuplenie bez nakazaniia. Chernobyl' 20 let spustia* [Crime without punishment. Chernobyl 20 years later] (Moscow: Vremia, 2006), 170.
8   It is quite telling that on September 11, 2001, at a seminar at the National University of Kyiv-Mohyla Academy dedicated to discussing the situation of postmodernism in Ukraine, Oksana Pakhlovska argued that "in much of Eastern Europe, and in Ukraine in particular, Catastrophe can stop Culture, if Culture does not attempt to stop Catastrophe." Oksana Pakhlovska, quoted in "Sytuatsiia postmodernizmu v Ukraini. Kruhlyi stil" [The situation of postmodernism in Ukraine. Round table], n.d., http://www.ktm.ukma.kiev.ua/2001/6/postmodern.html.

and *"manmade disaster"* coexisted equally in the perception of Chornobyl.⁹ It is telling that, as the makers of the documentary *Chornobyl: Chronicle of Difficult Weeks* (directed by Volodymyr Shevchenko, 1986) attest, in the early days after the accident, officials avoided using the word "catastrophe" and even banned its use in the media, preferring tragic, humanitarian-sounding concepts such as "accident," "misfortune," and "tragedy." In the early twenty-first century, the perception of Chornobyl takes on a distinctly catastrophic tone associated with "a catastrophe in the ecology of our souls," "a catastrophe of morality," and generally becomes a sign of "the extinction of the nation."¹⁰

Over time, the Chornobyl disaster became associated with the collapse of the entire Soviet system. Twenty years after the explosion at the nuclear power plant, Mikhail Gorbachev admitted in an interview that "the Chernobyl catastrophe was a historical turning point: there was an era before the disaster, and there is the very different era that has followed."¹¹ The former architect of *perestroika* acknowledged that Chornobyl had turned from a technogenic event into a political and social one, since, as he put it, "the Chernobyl disaster, more than anything else, opened the possibility of much greater freedom of expression in the Soviet Union, to the point that the system as we knew it became untenable." According to the former General Secretary of the Communist Party, this event was the factor that stimulated a reassessment of the by then completely rotten socialist system, since it "made starkly apparent how important it was to continue the policy of *glasnost*. Personally, I began to perceive time in terms of pre-Chernobyl and post-Chernobyl."¹² Of course, Gorbachev's reflections should be considered in the context of the creation of the myth surrounding the Chornobyl catastrophe, but it is essential to emphasize that the disaster was, in fact, the catalyst that revolutionized the entire so-called "Soviet people" in the mid-1980s, from the center to the periphery.

---

9   See, in particular, the commentary on the 2006 web guide *Chornobyl: rana i bil planety (Do 20-richchia avarii na Chornobylskii AES). Veb-bibliohrafichnyi pokazhchyk* [Chernobyl: the wound and pain of the planet (On the 20th anniversary of the Chernobyl NPP accident). Web-bibliographic index], 2006, http://webcache.googleusercontent.com.

10 Mykhailo Kuryk, "Chornobyl dushi nashoi. Ukraintsiam potribna ekolohiia svidomosti" [Chornobyl of our soul. Ukrainians need an ecology of consciousness], *Den*, no. 75 (April 2009), http://www.day.kiev.ua/273696/.

11 Ultimately, the feeling that time is divided between the "pre-atomic age" and the "unknown age which demands a fundamental restructuring of our thought" is actually a new discovery brought about by Chornobyl. (See: Iurii Shcherbak, *Chernobyl: A Documentary Story*, trans. Ian Press (Edmonton: CIUS, 1989), 2.) Mykhailo Horbachov, "Chornobylskyi perelom" [The Chernobyl turning point], *Den*, no. 65 (April 2006), 1.

12 Horbachov, "Chornobylskyi perelom," 1.

Chornobyl also became an important anti-colonial factor, contributing to the emergence of the Narodnyi Rukh Ukrainy (People's Movement of Ukraine) party and intensifying the fight for Ukrainian independence. The explosion at a nuclear power plant located in close proximity to Kyiv, in the protected Polissia region, was perceived as a deliberate act of colonization aimed at destroying the ancient Polissian culture and the Ukrainian people. The nationalization of disasters—traumatic events—plays a significant role in modern history, particularly in postcolonial history. For example, Central American literature features extensive discussion of volcanic identity—volcanic imagery thus becomes a trope through which to describe the emotional trauma of "threatened subjects" living "in the shadow of government repression, social alienation, and individual anxiety." [13]

Overall, we can agree with Mark Anderson, who emphasized that "disasters force the renegotiation and modification of the individual, collective local, and national narratives that endow social and political life with meaning."[14] After all, each of the victims tells their story, their traumatic experience, and these stories intersect, connect with similar past experiences, help people survive, and undermine the current political and social order. It is precisely this kind of nationally consolidating role that Chornobyl has played in Ukraine and Belarus. Svetlana Alexievich later noted, for example, that "for tiny Belarus (population: 10 million), it was a national disaster."[15]

The Chornobyl disaster simultaneously contributed to the emergence of a special Chornobyl "environmental identity" shared by the different peoples and countries that were affected by radiation and for whom life was divided into "before 1986 and after 1986."[16] The range of such people is quite broad: in addition to Belarusians, Ukrainians, Russians, Poles, and others, it also includes residents of remote regions in Northern or Eastern Europe who were affected by radiation dispersed by the radioactive cloud from Chornobyl, as well as liquidators and miners from other Soviet republics who participated in the cleanup after the accident, and workers from Kazakhstan and Tajikistan who were affected by

---

13 For more information, see Mark D. Anderson, *Disaster Writing: The Cultural Politics of Catastrophe in Latin America* (Charlottesville: University of Virginia Press, 2011), 130.
14 Mark D. Anderson, *Disaster Writing: The Cultural Politics of Catastrophe in Latin America* (Charlottesville: University of Virginia Press, 2011), 191.
15 Svetlana Alexievich, *Voices from Chernobyl: The Oral History of a Nuclear Disaster*, trans. Keith Gessen (New York: Picador, 2006), 1.
16 See, for example: J. Brummond, "Liquidators, Chornobylets, and the Masonic Ekologists: Ukrainian Environmental Identities," *Oral History*, no. 61 (Spring 2000): 53–65.

interethnic conflicts after being offered housing and work in the contaminated Chornobyl zone.

Meanwhile, for more than 20 years, the reflection on what Chornobyl meant for the post-Soviet future was limited mainly to the paradigm of victimization. Thus, the theme of a new world war, popular in Soviet times, also entered into the Chornobyl narrative. Iurii Shcherbak quotes Anelia Perkovska, one of the people featured in his documentary account, as saying that she perceives the Chornobyl disaster as a "reminiscence of war." Film director Rollan Serhiienko, who made several documentaries about Chornobyl (*The Bells of Chornobyl*, 1986; *Approaching the Apocalypse. Chornobyl is Near*, 1991; *Chornobyl. A Trinity*, 1993; *Chornobyl-2001. A Testament*, 2001), stated that his objective was "[…] to record and preserve the state of people who had directly encountered a rehearsal for a future war," since for him, Chornobyl was associated with the war that had begun "which was talked about throughout my childhood — nuclear war."[17] For generations of Soviet people, accustomed to talk about nuclear war on civil defense training courses, Chornobyl was the embodiment of their worst fears. However, the first and most common associations were comparisons with the experience of World War II.

Now, in the early twenty-first century, the military aspects in the perception of Chornobyl are losing their relevance, and the topic of *illness* is emerging as a key focus in post-Chornobyl perception. In reports, presentations, and at the everyday level, Chornobyl is consistently associated with illnesses caused by the spread of radiation. In addition to the real consequences of radiation on health, a significant role is played by the mental and psychosomatic syndromes that are also associated with the impact of Chornobyl. This is reflected in the general depressive mood of people who experience a catastrophic fear of life. "Many people have been affected. To a large extent, those who had not yet been born. Constant visits to hospitals. Day after day, year after year. Round and round. First the children. Then their children. Then their children's children": this is how it feels for the significant section of the Ukrainian population that has been affected by radiation.[18]

In 2005, the translator of the US edition of Svitlana Alexievich's *Voices from Chernobyl* noted in the preface that one of the biggest problems currently facing

---

17 Oleksandr-Nestor Naumenko, "Vozvrashchenie v ad. Chernobyl: kinodokumenty epokhi glazami rezhissera i operatora" [Return to hell. Chernobyl: film documents of the era through the eyes of director and cameraman], *Zerkalo nedeli* [Mirror of the week], no. 15 (April 2009), http://zn.ua/SOCIETY/vozvraschenie_v_ad__chernobyl_kinodokumenty_epohi_glazami_rezhissera_i_operatora-56740.html.
18 "Klip uchastnika (Obraz)" [Participant clip (Image)], n.d., http://pripyat.com/video.

the residents of the Chornobyl region is "an excess of pessimism."[19] Sociologist Yuri Saienko stated that "the victims continue to perceive the Chornobyl disaster as a personal tragedy, a complete collapse of their worldview, way of life, and life plans," noting the emergence of a special "community of the doomed" almost ten years on from the accident. "For 90% of these people, their sole focus is their own health and the health of their children and loved ones."[20]

According to research conducted by the Institute of Sociology at the National Academy of Sciences of Ukraine, by 1998, the group of Chornobyl victims in Ukraine with a "victim mentality" had doubled compared to 1992–1997, when the figure was 20%. It is important to note that 80% of this group are internally displaced people; only 20% live in contaminated areas. The main characteristics of people with this mentality are the following: they cannot forget the disaster, they are convinced that they suffered greatly from it and that they feel its consequences now and will feel them in the future, they are highly anxious about the possibility of a repeat of the Chornobyl disaster, they are deeply disappointed in people, they are inactive, and they are systematically ill.[21]

According to the 2004 monitoring conducted in contaminated areas of Belarus and Russia (four oblasts), 32% of the citizens living in these areas (about 440,000 people) were at risk in terms of the degree of psycho-emotional stress caused by radiation. A joint program to remedy the consequences of the Chornobyl disaster in Belarus and Russia aimed to reduce the percentage of people with signs of psycho-emotional anxiety to 24–15% (330,000–206,000 people) by 2010.[22]

Notably, the nationalization process following the Chornobyl disaster, observed in both Ukraine and Belarus, gave rise to different narratives. In Belarus, the theme of childhood affected by Chornobyl, a traditional aspect of the Soviet paradigm, took on special significance, retransmitting mass

---

19 Svetlana Alexievich, *Voices from Chernobyl: The Oral History of a Nuclear Disaster*, trans. Keith Gessen (New York: Picador, 2006), xiii.
20 Yurii Saienko, "Sotsialno-psykholohichnyi slid Chornobylia" [Social-psychological trace of Chernobyl], in *Sotsialni naslidky Chornobylskoi katastrofy. Rezultaty sotsiolohichnykh doslidzhen 1986–1995 rr* [Social consequences of the Chernobyl disaster. Results of sociological research 1986–1995] (Kharkiv: Folio, 1996), 60–61.
21 G. I. Mimandusova, Iu. A. Privalov, and Iu. I. Saenko, "Sotsialnyi monitoring postchernobylskoi situatsii" [Social monitoring of the post-Chernobyl situation], *Sotsiologiia katastrof* [Sociology of catastrophes], 1999, 119, http://ecsocman.hse.ru/data/414/669/1216/013_Sotsiologiya_katastrof.pdf.
22 *Programma sovmestnoi deiatelnosti po provedeniiu posledstvii chernobylskoi katastrofy v ramkakh Soiuznogo gosudarstva na 2006–2010 gody* [Program of joint activities to address the consequences of the Chernobyl disaster within the framework of the Union State for 2006–2010] (Minsk, 2007), 27, 92.

sentiments in the most emotional and accessible form, directing them through the official channel.

Apocalyptic, anti-colonial symbolism became part of the national narrative in Ukrainian literature, while in Belarusian literature, a tragic perception of the accident and its human dimension has vividly unfolded, as evidenced, in particular, by Svetlana Alexievich's *Voices from Chernobyl*.[23] In Ukraine, on the other hand, the national narrative is gaining widespread acceptance, and the concept of "*spiritual Chornobyl*" is becoming popular. This concept emerged in the 1980s among the national intelligentsia, affiliated with the Sixties generation, as a symbol of the devastating catastrophe and spread to other aspects of life at that time—language, culture, ecology, spirituality, politics. The topos of "spiritual Chornobyl" has acquired a particularly broad interpretation, signifying global spiritual, religious, ecological, and national threats.

This is fairly symptomatic, since, according to sociologists who studied the values of people living in contaminated areas and displaced persons, "catastrophic and extreme living conditions affect the semantic field of individual experiences in such a way that higher-order values such as 'God', 'conscience', 'freedom', 'honor', etc., are becoming increasingly rare, and more and more often, people begin to perceive their physiological survival as the only and greatest value."[24] This perception has been confirmed by the results of surveys of Chornobyl victims, for whom health, caring for their children, and rising prices are priorities.[25]

Another notable post-Chornobyl receptive model is the growth of *post-apocalyptic consciousness*, which is widely used in mass literature and digital culture. Computer games such as S.T.A.L.K.E.R., which appeared shortly after the Chornobyl disaster, reflected a shift from the apocalyptic thinking that

---

23   I would like to note that the US title of the book is different from the original one. In Ukrainian, the book came out as *Chornobylska Molytva: Khronika Maibutnioho* (Chornobyl Prayer: A Chronicle of the Future), but the English translation published in the US was titled *Voices from Chernobyl: The Oral History of a Nuclear Disaster*, dialing down the tragic pathos and emphasizing the role of oral history as testimony of the Chornobyl disaster instead. In the translator's preface, Chornobyl is also compared to the terrorist attack on the World Trade Center in New York on September 11, 2001.

24   Yurii Saienko and Yurii Privalov, "Zhyttievi tsinnosti naselennia, poterpiloho vid avarii na ChAES, ta otsinka shansiv yikh realizatsii u postchornobylskyi period" [Life values of the population affected by the ChNPP accident and assessment of chances for their realization in the post-Chernobyl period], in *Sotsialni naslidky Chornobylskoi katastrofy. Rezultaty sotsiolohichnykh doslidzhen 1986–1995 rr* [Social consequences of the Chernobyl disaster. Results of sociological research 1986–1995] (Kharkiv: Folio, 1996), 93.

25   O. Donchenko, O. Zlobina, and V. Tykhonovych, "Chornobylskyi syndrom: sotsialno-psykholohichnyi analiz," *Sotsialni naslidky Chornobylskoi katastrofy: Rezult. sotsioloh. doslidzhen 1986–1995 rr*, 1996, 68–69.

permeated the perception of the Chornobyl disaster in the first decade after the explosion to post-apocalyptic thinking, where the main plot is *survival in the post-atomic era.*

It is essential to note that the apocalyptic symbolism of Chornobyl which emerged immediately after the accident in a sense opposed the official Chornobyl discourse, which focused on the themes of heroic deeds and friendship among the Soviet peoples. In the mass consciousness, the nuclear accident, on the contrary, was associated primarily with the Apocalypse of St. John and the symbolism of the star named Wormwood (another name for the mugwort plant), which fell from the sky and turned a third of the waters into bitter wormwood—"and many people died from the waters that had become bitter" (Rev. 8:11). The waters of the Prypiat River, the sky slashed by the pipe reaching beyond the limits of Earth's gravity and piercing the heavens, the gaping hole in the place of Reactor 4 that resembled a dragon that had to be imprisoned, the conflagration and the firefighters like angels striving to tame it—all this read like an apocalyptic story. The post-apocalyptic symbols of Chornobyl are dominated by technological and planetary symbols: mutants, zombies, aliens, industrial infrastructure in ruins, and nature reclaiming what used to be people's homes and destroying all traces of human presence.

Apocalyptic symbolism became particularly popular in Ukrainian literature (Lina Kostenko's poem "A Terrible Kaleidoscope..." (1987), Ivan Drach's poem "The Chornobyl Madonna" (1988), Volodymyr Iavorivskyi's novel *Maria and Wormwood at the End of the Century* (1988), etc.) and took on an anti-colonial tone, as, for example, in the poem "U RA NA (A Thousand Years of Solitude)" (1989) by the Ukrainian-American writer Yuriy Tarnawsky:

> *A sarcophagus*
> *(a coffin)*
> *of Ukraine*
> *stands*
> *in the city of Chornobyl*
> *It's a gift*
> *from its older sister*
> *Russia*
> *[...]*
> *Ukraine*
> *rolls on the ground,*
> *holding Chornobyl*
> *with its hands,*

like a cut-up gut,
radioactivity,
like intestines,
slips through its fingers.[26]

Ultimately, it is the rise of catastrophism that determines the evolution of the perception of Chornobyl. It is also noteworthy that *technogenic* catastrophism, which dominates in the West, is replaced by *spiritual* catastrophism and takes on a national character in Ukraine. Catastrophic sentiments in Ukraine are generally quite strong. The Russian sociologists V. Ivanova and V. Shubkin provide an interesting comparison between catastrophic thinking in Ukraine and Russia at the end of the twentieth century. "First of all, it should be noted once again," they argue, "that the level of fear in Ukraine is higher than in Russia in all respects. Compared to Russians, Ukrainians are particularly fearful of mass epidemics, the spread of Aids and other deadly diseases (78.1% in Ukraine versus 18.4% in Russia), catastrophic crop failures (66.8% in Ukraine versus 37.4% in Russia), natural disasters (60.6% in Ukraine versus 37.3% in Russia), dictatorship and mass repression (37.1% in Ukraine versus 14.6% in Russia), genocide and mass repression (28.1% in Ukraine versus 8.7% in Russia), complete lawlessness (79.2% in Ukraine versus 61.0% in Russia), disbelief in God, crude materialism, and lack of spirituality (40.0% in Ukraine versus 18.4% in Russia), dangerous overpopulation of cities (20.1% in Ukraine versus 5.8% in Russia), and the end of the world (28.0% in Ukraine versus 9% in Russia)."[27]

It is noteworthy that, according to the results of a national monthly Omnibus survey conducted in July 2011 (1,200 respondents aged 16 to 75 were interviewed), Ukrainians feared: rising prices (74.7%), unemployment (71.9%), not being paid their salaries and pensions (56.8%), rising crime (42%), and hunger (33.6%); they were afraid of contracting incurable infections such as Aids and tuberculosis (26.6%), mass street protests (19.4%), and cold apartments (19.3%). 16.1% feared the possible collapse of Ukraine, 5.9% the consequences of the Chornobyl disaster, 13.8% the imposition of a dictatorship,

---

26 Yurii Tarnavskyi, "U ra na (tysiacha rokiv samotnosti)" [U ra na (a thousand years of loneliness)], in *Yikh nemaie. Poezii 1970–1999* [They are not there. Poetry 1970–1999] (Kyiv: Rodovid, 1999), 222, 225.
27 V. A. Ivanova and V. N. Shubkin, "Struktura strakhov i trevog v Rossii i na Ukraine" [Structure of fears and anxieties in Russia and Ukraine], *Mir Rossii* [The world of Russia], no. 1–2 (1998): 151–66, http://ecsocman.hse.ru/data/532/989/1219/1999_n1x2c2_p151-166.pdf.

12.1% interethnic conflicts, and 11.5% a return to the period of stagnation. 8.9% feared an influx of refugees, migrants, and internally displaced people, and 6.5% an external attack on Ukraine. Only 2.3% of respondents claimed that they were "not afraid of anything."[28] Regarding the Chornobyl disaster, the level of fear has decreased significantly compared to 1998. However, according to a survey conducted by the Gorshenin Institute in March 2011, approximately 70% of the Ukrainian population feared that accidents could occur at Ukrainian nuclear power plants, while 21% of respondents said they were not afraid of such disasters.[29]

These statistics suggest a susceptibility to catastrophic thinking in post-Soviet Ukrainian society, where memories of the traumatic events of the twentieth century (collectivization, the Holodomor, war, Chornobyl) overlap with the current unstable political and economic situation. Yet the Chornobyl disaster, combined with the post-Soviet crisis, is one of the central agents in the development of catastrophic consciousness in Ukraine at the turn of the twenty-first century.

Francis Fukuyama's essay "The End of History?" (1989) famously had a significant impact on the formation of a catastrophic mentality at the end of the twentieth century. Later, clarifying his position, Fukuyama emphasized that one of the impulses for the emergence of the "end of history" formula was the collapse of totalitarian dictatorships, since the life experience of the victims of political violence in the twentieth century—from Hitlerism to Stalinism and the Pol Pot regime—contradicts the idea that progress as such exists at all. And, of course, our mentality, which is geared toward expectations of "post-," plays a significant role in this: when it comes to health, security, and fair, liberal, and democratic political practices, we are expecting only bad news, so it is difficult for us to recognize good news when it appears. "Our own experience has taught us, seemingly, that the future is more likely than not to contain new and unimagined evils," Fukuyama claimed, "from fanatical dictatorships and bloody genocides to the banalization of life through modern consumerism, and that unprecedented disasters await us from nuclear winter to global warming."[30]

---

28 "Ukraintsy ne strashchatsya ustanovleniia diktatury i opasaiutsia bezrabotitsy" [Ukrainians are not afraid of the establishment of dictatorship and fear unemployment], *Podrobnosti* [Details], last modified August 19, 2011, http://podrobnosti.ua/society/2011/08/19/786773.html.

29 Review of materials: "Chego boiatsia ukraintsy? Rosta tsen, bezrabotitsy, zadolzhennosti" [What are Ukrainians afraid of? Rising prices, unemployment, debt], http://www.trust.ua/news/48801.html; "Ukraintsy obespokoeny rabotoi AES" [Ukrainians are concerned about the operation of nuclear power plants], http://www.novostimira.com.ua/news_4843.html..

30 Francis Fukuyama, *The End of History and the Last Man* (New York: Harper Perennial, 2006), 3–4.

It should be noted that Fukuyama tends to associate catastrophic thinking with a way of perceiving phenomena that *categorizes historical events as global and exceptional*. Often, in the perception of catastrophes, historicity is completely reduced, and the prevailing idea is that they arise out of nowhere, without any historical causes, and reproduce themselves indefinitely. Another extreme of catastrophic thinking is believing that catastrophes are a form of retribution for human sins. In general, as Pitirim A. Sorokin said, "in eras when aspirations and goals have not been fully realized, motifs of fatalism always stand out more or less clearly from the symphony of various theories and views."[31]

As already noted, two metaphors coexist in the perception of the Chornobyl disaster: "tragedy" and "catastrophe," although they have different symbolic connotations and program different types of discourse. The concept of the "Chornobyl tragedy" dominated in Soviet times, but it still occurs today in the titles of many a school essay, and in journalistic discourse (*Ukrainska Pravda*, for example, speaks of "the tragedy that upended the country's history and took and continues to take hundreds of lives"), and in common use, as in this excerpt from an article titled "The Chornobyl Tragedy—Forever in the Memory of the People": "This *tragedy* took the lives of many people and compromised the health of millions of Ukrainians. Its consequences will continue to be felt by future generations. It is considered the most terrible *catastrophe* in human history. Its name: Chornobyl [italics mine—T. H.]."[32]

In the West, however, the Chornobyl disaster tends to be compared with a catastrophe, and it is in this guise that Chornobyl enters European cultural memory. This perception is also widespread in contemporary Ukraine. For many Western philosophers, such as the eminent French philosopher Paul Virilio, Chornobyl is primarily associated with catastrophe, and in terms of its symbolic significance, it is comparable to other traumatic events of the twentieth century, including Auschwitz and Hiroshima.

For Virilio, Chornobyl, like Auschwitz and Hiroshima, is primarily a catastrophe of consciousness. Moreover, as Virilio argues, "we are dealing with three catastrophes in one, a kind of triptych catastrophe: a catastrophe of substance (the explosion in the reactor), a catastrophe of knowledge (a catastrophe that somehow goes beyond the knowledge of astrophysicists), and, finally,

---

31   P. A. Sorokin, *Chelovek. Tsivilizatsiia. Obshchestvo* [Man. Civilization. Society], ed. and pref. A. Yu. Soiumonov, trans. from English (Moscow: Politizdat, 1992), 513.
32   M. Hutsuliak, "Chornobylska trahediia—navichno v pamiati narodu" [The Chernobyl tragedy—forever in the memory of the people], *Kosiv*, last modified December 25, 2008, http://kosivart.if.ua/2008/12/25/821.

a catastrophe of consciousness—that is, there is no understanding of this event, since it transcends the capabilities of consciousness. Three catastrophes in one [...]."[33]

Paul Virilio speaks of the transformation of Chornobyl from a temporal event into a timeless one and says that, as such, Chornobyl will outlive contemporary generations. In his search for a philosophical and ethical explanation for the Chornobyl disaster, Virilio considers it a symbolic event. In this regard, he states that Chornobyl will last more than a century and, in a sense, the Chornobyl disaster is prophetic. According to Virilio, it is not apocalyptic (in the sense that the Apocalypse speaks of the possibility of salvation), but rather belongs to the category of finitude. It forces us to "look Medusa in the face," that is, to face the possible destruction of our species—not just the death of particular individuals, but the possible end of the (biological) species called "humans." For the contemporary philosopher, Chornobyl marks a new philosophy of death and a new heroism unlike the heroism of war. It also marks the birth of new prophets, such as the liquidators, and further attests to the distinction between catastrophe and war, on the one hand, and the threatening convergence of catastrophe and terrorism strategies on the other. For Virilio, Chornobyl is evidence of the onset of "catastrophic history."

The Nuclear Sublime

What unites the tragic and catastrophic types of Chornobyl perception is the appeal to *the sublime*. The *tragic* Chornobyl discourse, firstly, attests to the power of aesthetic and cultural forms such as tragedy in understanding human history and, secondly, speaks to the popularity of tragic rhetoric, which views a particular event as a profoundly psychological act for humans, caused by the clash of powerful conflicts that are ultimately resolved, dissolving into some higher, cathartic harmony. In general, tragedy emphasizes the human aspect of the event that has occurred.

Tragedy introduces us to the realm of the aesthetically *sublime*, and language based on the sublime possesses extraordinary power and authority, capable of subjugating and evoking a state of ecstasy or enthusiasm. Longinus, widely

---

33 "Radioaktivnyi ogon'. Pochemu opyt Chernobylia stavit pod somnenie nashu kartinu mira" [Radioactive fire. Why the Chernobyl experience calls into question our picture of the world], *Lettre international*, no. 60 (2003), https://alexievich.info/wp-content/uploads/articlesDialog.pdf.

regarded as the author of the treatise *On the Sublime*, maintains that the warrior is the protagonist of the sublime,[34] and therefore, tragic discourse is addressed to *heroes* and *victims*, as well as to the phenomenon of heroization itself. At the same time, it is important to remember that some researchers say the two greatest, as yet unresolved tragedies of our time are the "growing threat of nuclear death," which is looking increasingly realistic, and the "collapse of 'real socialism,'" which put an end to the age-old dream of a happy future for all.[35]

Philosophers and artists have repeatedly emphasized the special role of aestheticization and narrativization in representing tragic events. When discussing sublimity in the context of tragedy, it is worth noting that the very meaning of the tragic, particularly in its Hegelian sense, is perceived in different ways in contemporary culture. Some argue that tragedy releases emotions that help us to know ourselves in the modern world. Others support Bertolt Brecht's distrust of the tragic, arguing that tragedy, which is built on a dramatic narrative about a character's individual guilt, only evokes sympathy for suffering and does not teach us to critically reflect on the causes of actual human suffering.[36]

The tragic nuclear apocalypse took on a special tone after the Chornobyl disaster. But even before that, in 1984, Frances Ferguson had demonstrated that nuclear discourse, like other major projects of modernity—art, beauty, and progress—is based on sublimity. An atomic explosion is something "unthinkable," and it has become the latest version of *the sublime* precisely because it is so incredibly terrifying. "For when in the eighteenth century an aesthetics of sublimity emerges as a means of providing testimony to the uniqueness of individual consciousness, it portrays a world in which the status of objects is progressively attenuated so as to suggest that it is subjectivity rather than the mere fact of the existence of objects that gives things their force," Ferguson argues.[37]

Thus, sublimity becomes a way of affirming subjectivity, which is concerned with the future world, humanity, the planet, and the "unborn" descendants who must be preserved. The nuclear sublime, according to Ferguson, is similar to

---

34 Winfried Menninghaus, "Mezhdu podchineniem i soprotivleniem: Sila i nasilie v teoriiakh vozvyshennogo" [Between submission and resistance: Force and violence in theories of the sublime], in *Nemetskoe filosofskoe literaturovedenie nashikh dnei. Antologiia* [German philosophical literary studies of our days. Anthology], trans. Marina Bobrik (St. Petersburg: Izdatelstvo S.-Peterburskogo universiteta, 2001), 272.

35 Pavel Toper, "Tragicheskoe v iskusstve XX veka" [The tragic in twentieth-century art], *Voprosy literatury* [Questions of literature], no. 2 (2000), http://magazines.russ.ru/voplit/2000/2/toper.html.

36 For more on this, see: Angela Curran, "Brecht's Criticisms of Aristotle's Aesthetics of Tragedy," *Journal of Aesthetics & Art Criticism* 59, no. 2 (2001): 190.

37 Frances Ferguson, "Nuclear Sublime," *Diacritics* 14, no. 2 (1984): 4–10.

other forms of sublimity in that it is based on the idea that human freedom, particularly the infinite freedom of self-realization, is threatened by some power, which causes a special, subjective psycho-emotional tension. "One must understand this: that the sublime offering is the act—or the motion or emotion—of freedom," Jean-Luc Nancy argues.[38]

Edmund Burke, who in the eighteenth century adapted the concept of the sublime to modern ethics and aesthetics, noted that the source of the sublime is "whatever is fitted in any sort to excite the ideas of pain, and danger, that is to say, whatever is in any sort terrible, or is conversant about terrible objects, or operates in a manner analogous to terror, is a source of the sublime."[39] It is worth noting, however, that, apart from the terrible object of *the sublime* itself, sublimity shows the limits of representation as such. Sublimity is not a meaning, a totality, or an idea that is endowed with a certain aesthetic form. Nor is it a means of presentation or a premonition of a scheme (formula) of representation.

In modern times, the sublime is characterized by the rupture and distancing of the subject from the object, and sublimity is a means of aestheticizing the terrifying, which brings suffering and threatens life. After all, a person experiences the feeling of the sublime while they are in a safe place, at a distance sufficient for their own salvation—this is how they fall under the power of imagery and emotionally experience an encounter with the terrible. The dangerous object, the terrifying *other*, exists in reality, but in the imagination, the person gripped by fear must overcome it emotionally and morally. Thus, the aesthetic means of identification allows one not to succumb to the powerful force of extraordinary natural phenomena, such as earthquakes, floods, mountain heights, and so on.

But the sublime also helps one to escape from a state of blindness and paralysis in the face of the terrible, and most importantly, it allows one to identify with those who suffer, whose torments are caused not by nature but by human actions. This is the formative function of beauty, as taught by Enlightenment thinkers: according to Friedrich Schiller, this *contemplative-sublime* frees us from the power of the other, which is perceived as terrible, while the *pathetic-sublime* inspires empathy for all other suffering and generates compassion not only for heroic victors, but also for the victims of terrible events—accidents, floods, acts of terrorism. This is how the terrible is overcome, according to Schiller, who divides the sublime moment into three parts: "(1) an objective, physical

---

38 Jean-Luc Nancy, "The Sublime Offering," in *Of the Sublime: Presence in Question*, trans. Jeffrey S. Librett (Albany: State University of New York Press, 1993), 48.
39 Edmund Burke, *A Philosophical Enquiry into the Origin of Our Ideas of the Sublime and Beautiful* (London: Routledge and Kegan Paul, 1958), 39.

power, (2) our subjective, physical impotence, and (3) our subjective, moral superiority."[40]

In recent times, however, ethical perception has increasingly remained at the aesthetic stage. Structurally, sublimity becomes similar to *staging*. This theatrical representation involves a "rudimentary typology of heroic and tragic protagonists," as well as a discontinuity between the first-person spectator and the third-person protagonist.[41] However, the meaning of the sublime lies not in the heroic overcoming of terrifyingly sublime phenomena that go beyond human limits and conceal an ancient fear of the incomprehensible world, nor in the sublime objects themselves (natural or man-made), but in *the imagination*. On the one hand, it can allow one to identify with ordinary people and protect against fear of the mystical and incomprehensible, and on the other hand, it can linger at the stage of emotional satisfaction or suspense.

Aesthetic empathy helps one identify with the suffering subject, but when such identification becomes too strong and turns into an almost physical experience of pain, the *pathetic-sublime* helps to distinguish between suffering and pain, between what is being imitated and what is the imitation, and to distance oneself from overly close identification. The nuclear sublime, which offers images of universal destruction, of an atomic holocaust, plunges us into a terrible experience. However, the possibility of sublimity lies in the fact that in an extreme situation, bringing us to the edge, to the limit of imagery itself, it gives us the opportunity to free ourselves from the terrible rather than remain stuck in it. The difference between the tragic and catastrophic perceptions of the nuclear holocaust is that tragedy helps a person to free themselves from the horrific through catharsis whereas catastrophism plunges them into an endless reproduction of the horrific. Contemporary culture makes extensive use of the possibilities offered by catastrophic sublimity in genres such as horror, survival horror, horror punk, suspense, and thriller.

The Chornobyl Apocalyptic Discourse

The scene depicting the catastrophe and the meaning it conveys are most often associated with the apocalypse, that is, the destruction of the entire world and the rebirth of a new, fair world, and the survival of humankind (humanity,

---

40   Quoted from: Charles H. Hinnant, "Schiller and the Political Sublime: Two Perspectives," *Criticism* 44, no. 2 (2002): 201.
41   Hinnant, "Schiller and the Political Sublime," 201.

country, planet). As M. H. Abrams argues, the biblical paradigm of the Apocalypse has an author and assumes that earthly history has a plot with a beginning, a catastrophe (the fall of man), a crisis (the Incarnation and Resurrection of Christ), and a coming end (the abrupt Second Advent of Christ as King and the replacement of the old world with "a new heaven and a new earth"), which transforms the tragedy of human history into a cosmic comedy.[42] It is with the apocalypse, the mother of all catastrophes, that the Chornobyl disaster is associated in contemporary culture. At the same time, the tragic sublime undergoes important transformations in the Chornobyl sublimity. And most importantly, the real tragedy and death of 28 firefighters, who were the first to take on the nuclear blaze, saving the world from the most terrible consequences of the accident, gradually fades into the background of the *imagined* apocalyptic catastrophe that Chornobyl is turning into.

Catastrophes become stand-ins for real events. At the same time, on the one hand, catastrophes introduce the sublime and effectively appropriate an ironic attitude towards reality, taking away the irony from the subject, who thus turns from a player into a victim. As Douglas Kellner notes, catastrophes not only "confirm the power of the object over the subject, and delight people in their spectacular excess," but also test the imagination and act as humor, "which subverts the order of language and produces pleasure."[43] On the other hand, catastrophes seem (at least they did until 2001) to be safeguards against real tragic events, as they create the impression that "we live in the shadow of all kinds of 'bombs' that don't go off—virtual catastrophes that never take place."[44]

After all, since the 1930s, the atomic theme has had its favorite topoi. By the end of the 1930s, as Spencer Weart argues, "any mention of atomic energy could remind people of loss of self-control and horrific victimization, along with hopes for domination and rebirth. Talk of radioactive rays reproduced old ideas about life force, sexual or otherwise, leading to monstrosity or immortality; talk of the mysterious nucleus of the atom reminded people of the problem of hidden secrets; talk of atomic energy was associated with fantasies of enormous power, apocalypse, and a Golden Age ."[45]

---

42   M. H. Abrams, "Apocalypse: Theme and Variations," in *The Apocalypse in English Renaissance Thought and Literature: Patterns, Antecedents and Repercussions*, ed. C. A. Patrides and J. Wittreich (Manchester: Manchester University Press, 1984), 342–68.

43   Douglas Kellner, *Jean Baudrillard: From Marxism to Postmodernism and Beyond* (Stanford: Stanford University Press, 1989), 161.

44   Jean Baudrillard, *The Transparency of Evil: Essays on Extreme Phenomena* (Brooklyn: Verso, 1993), 26.

45   Spencer R. Weart, *Nuclear Fear: A History of Images* (Cambridge: Harvard University Press, 1988), 72–73.

However, apocalyptic narratives become a matrix not only for virtual games, but also for political discourses. As Alexander Sosland notes, apocalyptic tragic discourse is a certain type of message that becomes relevant in situations of social upheaval. It has its author and its addressee, it has a goal, most often related to the demand for a minority to change their worldview and/or behavior patterns, and it gives a certain satisfaction (orgasm) to those who apocalyptize. "Thus," Sosland concludes, "the three main elements of such discourse are the instigation of fear, blackmail, and recruitment."[46]

The apocalypse also has powerful narrative and imaginative potential. In particular, the apocalypse is one of the most powerful matrices of fictional narrative in modern literature. Frank Kermode's *The Sense of an Ending: Studies in the Theory of Fiction* (1967) has become instrumental in understanding the nature of apocalyptic narrative. The eminent British critic draws an analogy between the apocalypse and artistic form, assigning a key role to the idea of the "end" of the narrative.

Kermode emphasizes that every story should be viewed existentially, from the perspective of beginning and end. He considers the naive idea of the end of the world, as reflected in the Apocalypse, to be fundamental to the self-awareness of modern man. Moreover, in his opinion, the idea of the end of the world is present in every work of art, and it constitutes the plot of the work, allowing the reader to become immersed in the story as a narrative. The inevitability of the story's end is similar to death. Just as death is inevitable and a person's entire life extends between the beginning and the end, the story in a work of art also unfolds between the beginning and the end, and the reader's expectations are directed toward the end of the story, which gives meaning to everything that has been depicted.

Affirming the role of the apocalyptic model in the development of modern literature, Kermode emphasizes not only the orientation of plot toward the finale, but also the significance of "peripeteia" (twists and turns), which perform ironic functions, undermining expectations and naive belief in the ending. Peripeteia show readers' expectations to have been false and provide an opportunity to learn about reality beyond the boundaries of the work. Thus, "the paradigms of apocalypse continue to lie under our ways of making sense of the world."[47]

---

46 Aleksandr Sosland, "Udovol'stvie ot apokalipsisa" [Pleasure from the apocalypse], http://www.ruthenia.ru/logos/number/2000_3/07.htm.
47 Frank Kermode, *The Sense of an Ending: Studies in the Theory of Fiction* (Oxford: Oxford University Press, 1968), 28.

All apocalyptic discourse about Chornobyl is brought to the fore by so-called *nuclear discourse*. Since the Hiroshima and Nagasaki bombings, the threat of nuclear holocaust has become an important topic of our time: it is widely used by politicians and the media, and it fuels creative imagination. During the Cold War, it served to consolidate nations divided into two military blocs. At the same time, it has shaped global planetary thinking, as it has brought the human world to the very brink of survival. Nuclear discourse also plays a significant role in philosophy, stimulating the development of existential and futuristic thinking. Overall, it can be stated that the nuclear narrative became an integral part of the culture of the second half of the twentieth century, when nuclear catastrophe was identified as a real threat. The fact that this threat is perceived as likely is evidenced by the now-published "Emergency Plans Book," developed by the US government and turned over to the National Archives only in 1998.[48]

The Chornobyl Witness: From Madman to Stalker and Archaeologist

How can one describe something for which there are no words and no culturally appropriate forms of expression? Chornobyl has become a place of the inexpressible in culture, similar to other disasters—Auschwitz, Hiroshima, the Holocaust. What makes traumatic events so hard to talk about is that they're impossible to describe. According to Giorgio Agamben, the figure of the witness has a special role to play in overcoming the traumatic past: the one who testifies does so without coercion, and his story is an arbitrary and self-determined act. But this is not simply someone who survived Auschwitz, but rather a "Muslim" (the name used in a concentration camp to refer to a sickly prisoner) who has been driven to the point of losing human dignity, and who, as a "non-human," is no longer even capable of speaking, that is, of testifying. Yet he is the one that Agamben calls the "embodiment of the witness," because such a silent witness is a true witness. Language, in particular, plays a special role in testimony. As Agamben argues, such a witness "in its very possibility of speech, bears witness to an impossibility of speech. This is why subjectivity appears as witness; this is why it can speak for those who cannot speak. Testimony is a potentiality that

---

48 Jonathon Keats, "Apocalypse Made Easy," http://dir.salon.com/story/books/feature/2002/02/07/doomsday/index.html.

becomes actual through an impotentiality of speech; it is, moreover, an impossibility that gives itself existence through a possibility of speaking."[49]

Chornobyl also produced its own witness. Svitlana Alexievich collected the voices of ordinary people in a book originally titled *Chernobyl Prayer: A Chronicle of the Future*. The author has repeatedly emphasized that while recording the stories of the terminally ill, she had the impression that they were talking not about the past, but about the future, and that they were speaking precisely through their inability to speak. The terminally ill liquidators were aware that they had knowledge that needed to be passed on, even though they themselves no longer needed it. "At first, people sacrificed their lives; they died without understanding what was happening," Alexievich said. "But later, I met many seriously ill liquidators who were about to die. (I spoke with at least a hundred of them.) Some called me and asked me to come see them. These soldiers of fire [. . .] realized that they were the first to gain new knowledge, and they didn't want that knowledge to be lost when they died. They did not talk to me about their imminent death—at 25, you don't want to die!—but about the knowledge they wanted to pass on. They said: Write down what we saw. They said: We didn't understand it, and maybe you won't understand it either, but write it down."[50]

However, over time, the nature and role of the Chornobyl witness changed. From the perspective of the 2000s, the very image of the liquidator began to fade, and their testimonies began to blur. People falsely claiming to be liquidators had bred mistrust, and the names of the real heroes, the firefighters, were forgotten. It is noteworthy that after the Chornobyl disaster, a search began for the most powerful and universal witness. In keeping with the Soviet tradition of grandiose heroization of the sublime, that witness was ultimately found in the children. School essays on the topic of Chornobyl multiplied in both Ukraine and Belarus. As the editor of a collection of essays written by Belarusian schoolchildren stated, "It is these children who now speak with a pained, measured, and wise voice [. . .]. The works of the authors in our collection reveal their documentary basis and in fact are documents themselves, because they vividly attest to the feelings and thoughts of the participants and witnesses of the events."[51]

---

49 Giorgio Agamben, *Remnants of Auschwitz: The Witness and the Archive* (New York: Zone Books, 1999), 146.
50 "Radioaktivnyi ogon'. Pochemu opyt Chernobylia stavit pod somnenie nashu kartinu mira" [Radioactive fire. Why the Chernobyl experience calls into question our picture of the world], *Lettre international*, no. 60 (2003), https://alexievich.info/wp-content/uploads/articlesDialog.pdf.
51 *Sled chornogo vetru. Vachima dziatsei* [Trail of the black wind. Through children's eyes] (Minsk: Beloruski sotsial'no-ekologichny soiuz "Charnobyl'," 1996), 327.

The humanization and desacralization (de-apocalyptization) of Chornobyl go hand in hand with the removal of catastrophism. Atomic (or nuclear) literature significantly expands its field when it goes beyond the apocalyptic genre. Such literature covers ecological issues, the regeneration of nature, the fate of people, animals, and birds, and, in general, the preservation of the ecosystem disrupted by the accident. The post-apocalyptic paradigm includes stories about the lives of people who had moved to the affected area and the fates of those who fell ill from radiation. Similarly, post-apocalyptic Chornobyl literature tells the stories of people who are not directly connected to Chornobyl and are spatially and temporally separated from it, but who are somehow intertwined with the traces of Chornobyl radiation (not only in Ukraine or Belarus, but also in Sweden, France, and Lapland). It tells of the Ukrainian children who received medical treatment in Cuba, of the transcultural and transethnic conflicts witnessed by those who fled the radiation zone and radioactive Kyiv for Moscow, Georgia, Poltava Oblast, the Carpathians, and elsewhere.

This approach uproots the witness from their usual ontological place and shifts the focus of their narrative, since their usual purpose is to attest to and document the nuclear apocalypse. In fact, it cannot be attested to; one can only say that it is "inevitable" and "uncontrollable," and moreover, it is total and as such destroys even our imagination: there will be no survivors, no monsters—nothing.

Jacques Derrida said in 1985 that nuclear war can only be "imaginary." Yet in today's world, the nuclear threat is becoming increasingly real. Kyoko Matsunaga argues that "'fictionalizing' nuclear war undermines the connection between nuclear/atomic issues and human agents."[52] If we accept her post-apocalyptic perspective, we can give a broader meaning to the concept of "hibakusha"— the traditional name for those who survived the bombing of Hiroshima and Nagasaki.[53] "The term *hibakusha*—as I invoke it—includes not only those who have experienced the bombings in Hiroshima and Nagasaki, but also the 'downwinders' and other residents affected by nuclear weapons testing and radioactive fallout," Matsunaga explains.[54] This approach enables us to go beyond the

---

52 Taras Prokhasko, "Kozhnomu svoie" [To each his own], in *Yevromaidan. Khronika vidchuttiv* [Euromaidan. Chronicle of feelings] (Brusturiv: Dyskursus, 2014), 9.
53 The Atomic Bomb Survivors Law defines *hibakusha* as those who fall into one of the following categories: those who were within a few kilometers of the epicenter of the explosion; those who were within a two-kilometer radius of the epicenter for two weeks after the bombing; those who were exposed to radiation; or those who did not experience the bombing but were carried by pregnant women who belong to any of these categories.
54 Kyoko Matsunaga, *Post-Apocalyptic Vision and Survivance: Nuclear Writings in Native America and Japan* (Lincoln: University of Nebraska Press, 2006), 11.

sublime, which often sanctions the *heroization* of the nuclear apocalypse, while simultaneously setting limits on the *fictionalizing* of nuclear catastrophe. After all, when Derrida reduces the atomic bombings of Nagasaki and Hiroshima to "non-events," or fictions separated from historical events, he theoretically removes the "real" impact of these factors on human existence. Apocalyptic sublimity confines perception within the realm of imagination, whereas post-apocalyptic representation seeks to go beyond its limits into reality.

In fact, these issues are addressed by econuclear criticism, which focuses on the problems of nuclear explosion, nuclear colonization, nuclear representation of the state of survival, cross-cultural consequences of atomic explosions, nuclear writing, as well as ecological, cultural, and informational aspects related to atomic explosions. The concept of "nuclear criticism" as a new avant-garde direction in cultural studies was introduced in the mid-1980s and announced in a special issue of the "Diacritics" journal. Today, there are increasingly vocal calls for a new wave of nuclear criticism. At its core is an analysis of atomic imagery and the fear generated by nuclear explosions, and an analysis of terrorist and traumatic literature. Ecocriticism and nuclear criticism open up new perspectives for interpreting the Chornobyl explosion, freeing us from both *tragic paralysis* and *catastrophic numbness*.

Lina Kostenko: "Ukrainian Madman"

The present-day perception of Chornobyl is markedly different from how it was immediately following the accident. Our sense of connection has shifted, we have become uncomfortable with tragic and apocalyptic dramatizing, and the motivation for visiting the Chornobyl exclusion zone has changed (and become increasingly tourism-related). In 2007, one visitor explained his connection to Chornobyl by saying that he'd grown up with memories and conversations about the disaster and therefore felt a sense of connection to it. "I tried for a long time to figure out why I needed to go on this trip [to the Chornobyl exclusion zone.—T. H.], I can't quite refer to myself as a tourist, and I can't bring myself to call a trip to the Chornobyl exclusion zone tourism . . . ," he writes in his diary. "I should say right away that I am not a liquidator, and there were no liquidators in my family. Back in 1986, I was four years old, but for some reason I remembered the strange and scary word 'Chornobyl' for the rest of my life."[55] Thus, not only

---

55 Dolgoprudnyĭ, "Moskva—Kyiv—Chornobyl—Pripiat—Moskva," n.d., http://pripyat.com/people-and-fates/dolgoprudnyi-moskva-kiev-chernobyl-pripyat-moskva.html.

parents, but also children who grew up with memories of Chornobyl have the right to bear witness. After all, parents and children remember things differently.

The parents' generation can be roughly identified with the Sixties. For representatives of this generation, Chornobyl was not merely a literary theme (the disaster immediately found literary reflection in works by Ivan Drach, Borys Oliynyk, Yevhen Sverstiuk, and Lina Kostenko), but also an embodiment of the global post-Soviet humanitarian crisis. Lina Kostenko, who worked extensively in the exclusion zone as a member of an expedition to preserve Chornobyl cultural sites and was herself born in an area close to Chornobyl, was perhaps the writer who most consistently developed the tragic rhetoric of Chornobyl, which evolved into a form of catastrophism. At the same time, on the one hand Kostenko seeks to replace the technogenic perception with a humanitarian-catastrophic one, and on the other hand, the concept of "tragedy" in her statements is increasingly replaced by the word "catastrophe." "Let the specialists study the technogenic aspects of the *catastrophe*," Kostenko claimed in 2005. "Let us turn to a theme that focuses on people. Even today, Ukraine cannot imagine the consequences of the *catastrophe* of this 'patch' of land covering 4,000 square kilometers (about 1,545 square miles) in *the very center of the Slavic world*. The entire area of the ancient culture of the Polissia people is disappearing before our eyes (the same can be said of their neighbors in the southernmost parts of Belarus), and an irreparable blow has been dealt to everything that we have so often grandly referred to as 'culture and spirituality'"[56](italics mine—T. H.).

On the whole, Kostenko sees Chornobyl as the place where "Ukraine died." And that is how the protagonist of her novel *Diary of a Ukrainian Madman* (2010) views the closure of the Chornobyl Nuclear Power Plant as well. "Today I heard a strange sound on the Maidan," he says, "as if a coffin lid was being hammered shut."[57] The consistent perception of Chornobyl as a catastrophic phenomenon is also characteristic of Kostenko's journalistic writing. In her article "Ukraine as a Victim and Factor of Globalization of Catastrophes" (2003), she maintained: "It is not only the economy or the universal conditioning of interests that is globalizing, but also conflicts and the preconditions for ecological, technogenic, and moral catastrophes."[58]

---

56 Serhii Makhun, "Lina Kostenko: 'Poidte tudy, de vmerla Ukraina'" [Lina Kostenko: 'Go there where Ukraine died'], *Dzerkalo tyzhnia*, no. 44 (2005), http://dt.ua/SOCIETY/lina_kostenko_poyidte_tudi,_de_vmerla_ukrayina-45094.htm.

57 Lina Kostenko, *Zapysky ukrainskoho samashedsheho* [Notes of a Ukrainian madman] (Kyiv: A-ba-ba-ha-la-ma-ha, 2010), 32.

58 Lina Kostenko, "Ukraina yak zhertva i chynnyk hlobalizatsii katastrof" [Ukraine as victim and factor of globalization of catastrophes], *Den*, no. 76 (April 2003), http://ukrlife.org/main/evshan/kostenko_l.htm.

This perception of Chornobyl is based on *catastrophism* as a model of humanitarian thinking that became widespread at the beginning of the twenty-first century and signals global processes in the modern world, particularly those intensified by the terrorist attacks of September 11, 2001. This model of thinking is associated with crisis processes in society, as well as the anxiety and fear brought about by the threat of terrorism, natural disasters, nuclear threats, etc.

Catastrophism is on the rise in the modern world, influenced by factors such as the media, the spread of technologies related to simulating real events, and the visualization of various kinds of threats—terrorist attacks, star wars, nuclear war, and techno-ecological disasters. In this representation, real disasters are transformed into simulacra spectacles, similar to real ones, yet different and fictitious. After all, in hyperreality, the difference between man and machine, the physical self and the avatar, disappears; here, "real" and "simulated" deaths are indistinguishable; humans are polymorphic and can be reborn in infinite forms, and real pain does not hurt. Hyperreal images, in one way or another, evoke emotional responses characteristic of humans and lock them into a circle of total plausibility.

This is how the media works, too, transforming a certain fact that could potentially be considered relevant into a "major event." This is achieved through a series of strategies designed to transform and re-embody viewers into witnesses and participants in the event. The main mechanism for unfolding such catastrophic thinking is the transformation of *catastrophe into spectacle* and the perceiver into a *witness*.[59] By perceiving the terrorist attacks of September 11, 2001 in the discourse of television news, we become "participants in a brilliantly staged television show that turned the event into a *myth*."[60]

Lina Kostenko's novel *Diary of a Ukrainian Madman* helps us understand how such catastrophism works. The catastrophization of reality in the novel occurs in several ways:

1) by transforming an event, specifically Maidan, into the "main event";
2) by using the technique of media reporting of events;
3) by employing autothematicism, that is, a monological, self-referential narrative in which the author's voice is recognizable.

---

59 Oleksandr Sarna, "Katastrofa kak zrelishche: reprezentatsiia sobytii 11 sentiabria 2001 g. v diskurse telenov estei" [Catastrophe as spectacle: representation of the events of September 11, 2001 in television news discourse], in *Vizual'noe (kak) nasilie* [Visual (as) violence] (Vilnius: EGU, 2007), 336.
60 Sarna, "Katastrofa kak zrelishche," 339.

The tastes and preferences that Kostenko gives the protagonist in the novel are autobiographical and easily recognizable as the author's own. The protagonist frequently references facts and events from the media (including "main events"), to which he adds lesser-known, local details, thereby engaging all readers in the process of emotional immersion in media news. The technique of manipulation through recollection is important because the protagonist's comments do not allow the reader to perceive the news independently; the news is presented as if on a screen, with an authoritative, *direct speech* somewhere behind it. Thus, despite the supposed reference to a chronicle, the novel is dominated by *a single overarching author's voice*.

Kostenko consistently unfolds a catastrophic mentality in the novel. It is no coincidence that the prototype for this mentality is the Chornobyl disaster. *Diary of a Ukrainian Madman* is the apotheosis of catastrophism as a discourse superimposed on the history of the early twenty-first century. Take away the plot about a nameless thirty-five-year-old programmer and the novel becomes nothing more than a list of catastrophes, meticulously selected from television news, rumors, and newspapers. Essentially, we are presented with one mega-catastrophe, starting in 2000: "We welcomed 2000 with a bang. A neighbor jumped from the eighth floor. An acquaintance drowned in the bathtub. A new president came to power in Russia and started a new Chechen war. We got an unusual prime minister who set about implementing reforms."[61] It seems that by listing these news items, the protagonist is trying to be ironic, to rise above events and history, but this liberation is fictitious. In fact, he finds himself completely in the power of virtual reality, including media reality. His own judgments are nothing more than a broadcast of catastrophic consciousness into which the author has totally immersed him, leaving no room for his own "self." The author's perspective, which she has passed on to him, is characterized solely by catastrophic thinking. Thus, he turns out to be only a focus through which the social unconscious, formed by catastrophic media news items that fall into place as in a kaleidoscope, voices itself: "Shake it—and you get a new picture. Shake it—and there's another one. Only now the pictures are getting scarier."[62]

The kaleidoscope of life is composed of news, in which the characters play the role of extras, serving as "empty signifiers" of the author's consciousness,

---

61 Lina Kostenko, *Zapysky ukrainskoho samashedsheho* [Notes of a Ukrainian madman] (Kyiv: A-ba-ba-ha-la-ma-ha, 2010), 10.
62 Kostenko, *Zapysky ukrainskoho samashedsheho*, 10.

permeated with apocalyptic anxiety. What the protagonist "sees" coincides exactly with what is "shown" to him. He is given no inner world, despite all the hints at the special mentality of the protagonist, his wife, or his son. Their purpose is to voice the ideas that the demiurge-author is holding by strings. More precisely, she scrolls through a kaleidoscope, holding it in front of the protagonist's eyes so that he sees nothing but what he is supposed to see.

Thus, the hero becomes a screen displaying a single story, and, importantly, this overarching story is identical to the media representation. The "images" it creates replace the whole reality, turning it into a perpetual reality show. The world as a whole becomes a permanent disaster: "There's a disaster here, a terrorist attack there, a methane explosion here, a military plane accidentally dropping a bomb there. Some maniac shot some passers-by. An unknown infection broke out. A bus full of children was taken hostage. A cable car crashed in the Alps. A sect poisoned people with gas in the Tokyo subway. Some schoolkids trampled each other to death on the stairs in Chervonohrad after watching 'Armageddon.' [...] This is no longer a chronicle of events, it's a horror documentary."[63]

This "horror documentary" not only captures the new role of the media in public consciousness, it also becomes "public consciousness" itself, drawing in viewers and readers, and the title of this horror film is "The Catastrophic Death of Ukraine." In Kostenko's novel, reminders of catastrophes become, in fact, their duplication, driving the reader, as a witness, into the sublime world of the horrific, which is evoked by the return of the same thing. At the same time, repressed historical and personal traumas resurface through a catastrophic perception of the world, undermining the rational understanding of events and giving the character a sense of his supposed "normality" against the backdrop of a supposedly "abnormal" existence.

For the early twentieth-century Viennese psychoanalyst Sigmund Freud, "the uncanny is the hidden, the familiar, which has withstood repression and returns from it." In particular, it arises "from repressed infantile complexes, from the castration complex, womb-phantasies, etc.."[64] For the late twentieth-century cultural theorist Slavoj Žižek, the terrible becomes an inevitable element of the perception of the Other, as well as a manifestation of the Real, to which the subject aspires. In culture, the terrible becomes one of the hallmarks of post-Soviet aesthetics. At the same time, the post-Soviet terrible comes to the surface

---

63   Kostenko, *Zapysky ukrainskoho samashedsheho*, 10.
64   Sigmund Freud, "Zhutkoe" [The uncanny], in *Khudozhnik i fantazirovanie* [The artist and fantasy], trans. G. Baryshnikova and E. Smirnova (Moscow: Respublika, 1995), 248.

sublimated, that is, elevated, and disappointment in reality is compensated for by aesthetics and virtuality.⁶⁵

In *Diary of a Ukrainian Madman*, Lina Kostenko identified three important factors of the new post-Chornobyl reality: reducing history to catastrophes, the role of the media in broadcasting catastrophic reality, and reducing the human witness to the role of a mediating screen. All these factors become important in post-Soviet Chornobyl discourse, where the real event has long since turned into a *media event*, and *the hot atomic explosion* has become *a cold information explosion*.

After all, as Jean Baudrillard said, "The nuclearization of bodies began at Hiroshima, but it continues endemically, incessantly, in irradiation by the media, by images, signs, programs and networks."⁶⁶ Thus begins the "long, cold catastrophe" of the global system of allotropy,⁶⁷ i.e., the production of hyper-real simulacra images. These images arise from the neutralization and cooling (or freezing) of emotions, experiences, relationships, and events. Moreover, the *catastrophe* becomes the central figure of so-called fateful events, which affect not only individuals, institutions, and states, but also "transversal structures" (such as sex, money, information, and communication).

This freezing function is performed by spectacular *catastrophism*, which cannot exist without aestheticism, sublimation, and the visualization of what is depicted. The media representation of a catastrophic event often transforms it into a *melodrama*, equating the sublime with the everyday and offering simple, easily consumable emotions. This is how "trauma kitsch" is created: "As the mass media moreover rely on melodrama's plot formula for representing victimization and suffering, the trauma kitsch ubiquitously generated in popular culture conveys a sense of comfort, because it asserts that no matter what happens— whether genocide or child abuse or lesser evils—good always wins over evil, and the world is predictable and safe."⁶⁸

This vision of the world also has a melodramatic effect: terrible events most often unfold against the backdrop of a stark contrast between good and evil,

---

65 Mark Lipovetsky and Aleksandr Etkind, "Novoe literaturnoe obozrenie" [New literary review], *NLO [Novoe literaturnoe obozrenie]*, no. 4 (2008): 291–300, http://magazines.russ.ru/nlo/2008/94/li17.html.
66 Jean Baudrillard, *The Transparency of Evil: Essays on Extreme Phenomena* (Brooklyn: Verso, 1993), 14.
67 Zhan Bodriiar [Jean Baudrillard], "Kytaiskyi syndrom" [Chinese syndrome], in *Symuliakry i symuliatsiia* [Simulacra and simulation], trans. V. Khovkhun (Kyiv: Osnovy, 2004), 53.
68 Anne Rothe, *Popular Trauma Culture: Selling the Pain of Others in the Mass Media* (New Brunswick, NJ: Rutgers University Press, 2011), 45.

often involving a couple in love or the fate of future children, the human race, or the entire planet; the viewer (player), while actually at a distance, in a safe place (sitting in a movie theater or in their own room), identifies with the winners (more often) and victims (less often) and feels excitement. Thus, media catastrophism tends to lock the imagination into a circle of imaginary and easily perceived similarities—simulacra. When catastrophism transfers to the perception of reality, a total mirror effect occurs, which, according to Freudianism, signals a regression to primitive narcissism, where the object and subject merge.

It was no coincidence that at a press conference on the occasion of the novel's release, Kostenko spoke about the role of the media in the process of her work on the manuscript. "When I was working on the book, I entered your journalistic territory," she noted. "I needed a lot of information—about local, global, and worldwide events—I needed you. [...] I saw that without journalists, this society is doomed," she emphasized.[69]

Thus, the journalism in this novel is there for a reason. How does the author use it, and what does it signal? Journalism is known to have had a significant impact on literature, and vice versa—literature has influenced journalism. At the very least, this union has introduced forms of reporting, live experimentation, documentation, and quasi-documentation, as well as advertising and staging. We can speak in general terms about the media as a condition and means of existence for contemporary culture, particularly in Ukraine. If nothing else, the most recent novels by Oksana Zabuzhko and Yuri Andrukhovych demonstrate that media is becoming not only a theme, but also a tool and setting for novelistic action. So it is no accident that Kostenko turned to journalism. The media becomes perhaps the main agent in her *Diary of a Ukrainian Madman*—not the programmer, his wife, father, son, friend, or anyone else. All of them—except perhaps the programmer's wife, who plays the role of a traditional *raisonneur*—are screen characters: their identities and characters are one-dimensional and reflect media patterns.

The media form of representation of "reality" is catastrophism, which in the novel becomes absolute and forms a mirror image of the world. "Gangster TV shows gradually become our reality. There is a kind of transfer of ideas, plots, and storylines," the narrator of *Diary of a Ukrainian Madman* points out.[70] But

---

69 Valentyna Klymenko, "Hirkyi 'mykolaichyk' vid Liny Kostenko" [Bitter 'little Nicholas' from Lina Kostenko], *Ukraina moloda*, no. 238 (December 2010), http://www.umoloda.kiev.ua/number/1805/164/64070/.
70 Lina Kostenko, *Zapysky ukrainskoho samashedsheho* [Notes of a Ukrainian madman] (Kyiv: A-ba-ba-ha-la-ma-ha, 2010), 285.

the problem is much broader: it is not the transfer of media images to reality, but the lack of any difference between them. The tragedy that *Diary of a Ukrainian Madman* invokes disappears when it contrasts "abnormal" and "sick" reality with "normal" reality. In Gogol, this contrast is deeply tragic; in Kostenko it is catastrophic. After all, both "normality" and "abnormality" are merely functions of screen reality.

The main character of *Diary of a Ukrainian Madman* is melancholic. He is physically and morally weakened, suffering, as he admits, from phantom pains. In short, he is "samashedshyi," or "mad," as Kostenko ironically rephrases Gogol's formula [from *Zapiski sumasshedshego* to *Zapysky ukrainskoho samashedshoho*], clearly alluding not only to the Ukrainian linguistic phenomenon of *surzhyk*, but also the ontological-existential "self" of the protagonist, who admits that he "has always been normal."[71] On the contrary, the author emphatically stresses that it is modern Ukraine that is sick, with the "mark of an imbecile" on its face.[72]

In the novel, it is not the protagonist but the author herself who speaks about the Orange Revolution, the long-awaited cleansing of the country, the unity of the nation that was rising up, and the Maidan, where people come together—parents and children, people in good health and people with disabilities. The image of Maidan is quite elevated, aestheticized, like an image on a TV screen in the news about the "main event." On this media screen, even a father in a wheelchair on the Maidan is presented as a "noble figure, with an orange scarf around his neck that goes really well with the wintry color of his graying hair."[73] Thus, a real fact is transformed into a media aestheticized object, the sublime obscures reality, replacing it with a glamorous image, where a person with a disability is transformed into a fashionista, and the poisoned Yushchenko—a presidential candidate—is associated with a pop star: "Bronson or Raf Vallone can't measure up to him."[74]

At first glance, the protagonist's melancholic state is caused by the feeling that he has lost a beloved object—*a healthy full-fledged Ukraine*. The melancholic tone of the work stems from the fact that this loss already exists, and no compensation, not even Maidan, can restore it. This loss (and the catastrophic thinking it causes) presumably also applies to the generational vision of Ukraine. "My father's generation is passing away. The Ocean of Time is carrying away the last unforgettable people of the twentieth century" is a constant refrain

---

71 Kostenko, *Zapysky ukrainskoho samashedsheho*, 5.
72 Kostenko, *Zapysky ukrainskoho samashedsheho*, 6.
73 Kostenko, *Zapysky ukrainskoho samashedsheho*, 412.
74 Kostenko, *Zapysky ukrainskoho samashedsheho*, 409

in Kostenko's novel.⁷⁵ In a sense, the catastrophic perception of Ukraine's fate conveyed in the work reflects the vision of the Sixties generation. We do not hear the voice of the protagonist himself (he is only a means of relaying the author's ideas). It is he who visits the graves of the "murdered poets and heroes" of the past generation and identifies with that past generation: "And Stus. And Svitlychnyi. And Mykolaichuk. And Chornovil. And further back in time, Alla Horska and Symonenko."⁷⁶

It turns out that the tragic perception of reality by the author, who belongs to the Sixties generation, overlaps with the thinking of the modern generation, since the protagonist is a young computer programmer. Interestingly, Kostenko's son is a programmer, too, and the writer has admitted that he served as the prototype for the novel's main character. Thus, in a sense, *Diary of a Ukrainian Madman* is primarily the author's voice. The young narrator himself is deprived of the right to speak on his own behalf, and in conceptual terms, to have his own generational vision of Ukraine.

Generational issues are quite prominent in the novel. The main character consciously considers himself part of a "damaged generation" that has taken something from its ancestors but has nothing to pass on to its descendants. He also speaks of certain misunderstanding with his father, a former member of the Sixties generation, regarding the "wasted life" of his own generation, and the incomprehensibility and hermeticism of that of his teenage children. At the same time, great hopes are pinned on the fact that a new generation will be born on Maidan—the "generation of the Orange Revolution": "And only these will come out as winners. This is no longer something between a riot and a drinking bout that came in the meantime, that hung out in cafés and could not shake its apathy when the voice of a generation was needed—this is the NEXT generation we have been waiting for, and it has arrived."⁷⁷

The novel also mentions a discussion about the "death of the Sixties generation" raised by the 1990s generation at the beginning of the twenty-first century. The main character finds the very idea of his father's death quite painful. This obviously refers not only to his real biographical father, but also to the symbolic role of his father's generation. "My father had put down the newspaper and was asking me about my family, and I looked at him and thought: 'God, he could die! Not the Sixties generation, no, that phenomenon has already come to pass. But he, my father, he could die, and then what about my

---

75   Kostenko, *Zapysky ukrainskoho samashedsheho*, 194.
76   Kostenko, *Zapysky ukrainskoho samashedsheho*, 351.
77   Kostenko, *Zapysky ukrainskoho samashedsheho*, 407.

compassion for him, and my jealousy, yes, admit it, it's jealousy—what about all that when he's gone?."[78] In fact, this sharp generational shift is one of the factors exacerbating the drama of contemporary Ukrainian history. It could even be said that in modern Ukraine, national catastrophism is clearly colored by generational tones and is largely a result of the departure of the Sixtiers generation from the public arena.

The student hunger strike of the 1990s was perceived by its participants as the birth of a new generation—the "velvet revolution generation."[79] "For me, October 1990 is the birth of a new creative generation, which is still at the forefront today," Taras Batenko says.[80] He defines the milestones of this new generation, which managed to make the *"rebellion"* a *"fait accompli."* Batenko also finds new heroes and symbolic fathers of the cultural movement among the representatives of this new generation. There is even an attempt to replace the symbolic "fathers" with his peers and include them in the pantheon of "classics." "This generation has cultural figures who, even during their lifetimes, could match the level of the classics," he argues, "Yuri Andrukhovych, Viktor Neborak, Volodymyr Tsybulko, Oksana Zabuzhko, and others. It has politically engaged 'fathers' in eternal creative fervor—Markiyan Ivashchyshyn, Oles Donii. It had and still has intellectual products—the Vyvykh festival of alternative culture, the *Young Wine* poetry anthology, the Association 500 writers' union, the New Degeneration literary group, etc.."[81]

In 2001, Oles Donii announced "the death of the Sixtiers generation." "The Sixtiers generation was a myth. A myth about the intelligentsia. And the degradation of the Sixtiers generation contributes to the final degradation of the intelligentsia in the old sense," he said. "The Sixtiers generation has died—as a myth about a generation of intellectuals fighting for democracy. The old myths that everyone who fought for Ukraine's independence and everyone who speaks perfect Ukrainian is a democrat are dying."[82] Although the generational discussion remained hidden, it echoes in various forms in the works of different authors and becomes an important part of the cultural landscape in *Diary of a Ukrainian Madman.*

---

78 Kostenko, *Zapysky ukrainskoho samashedsheho*, 52.
79 See, in particular: Oles Donii, *Pokolinnia oksamytovoi revoliutsii* (Kyiv: Smoloskyp, 1999).
80 Taras Batenko, "Bunt i my. Nasha epokha" [Revolt and us. Our epoch], *Postup*, n.d., accessed August 19, 2025, http://postup.brama.com/001005/164_1_1.html.
81 Batenko, "Bunt i my. Nasha epokha."
82 Oles Donii, "Smert shistdesiatnykiv," *Postup*, n.d., http://postup.brama.com/010209/23_2_3.html.

Markiyan Kamysh: "Stalker"

The younger generation have responded to the catastrophe in their own way, and this is especially true of the children of Chornobyl liquidators. First and foremost, it is important to note that a new type of Chornobyl witness has emerged. Many of those who were four or five years old at the time of the Chornobyl disaster have spoken out about their connection to Chornobyl. They maintain that they grew up in an atmosphere of memories of the Chornobyl disaster and that (in one way or another) it has affected their lives or the lives of their family members. They want to see Chornobyl as a place to which they have a right. Moreover, they themselves want to bear witness to Chornobyl. As one of them says, "Yes, there was a catastrophe, and no one knows the exact death toll, and in a sense, this catastrophe is still ongoing. But. To go mad, wringing your hands, beating your chest and those around you, writing useless treatises on Grief and Memory (yes, yes, this is a jab at Alexievich, the Chornobyl Nienna, and she deserves it) or—what's even worse—about the Wormwood star, aliens, and black energy emissions—is twice as stupid and offensive. For those who died, and for us who are still alive, it would be much better if we learned our lesson, supported the sick and orphans, and set up a nature reserve in Prypiat. Where else can you see a lynx living in an apartment?."[83]

In fact, it is from this generation and the emergence of a new witness ("a stalker") that a new Chornobyl literature arises, represented in particular by Markiyan Kamysh in his novel *Stalking the Atomic City: Life Among the Decadent and the Depraved of Chornobyl* (2015). "Literature of real experience" is what Kamysh calls it. Born after Chornobyl, but connected to it through family memories, as his father was one of the liquidators and suffered seriously from radiation, which led to his early death, Markiyan recreates the experience of an illegal stalker in the Chornobyl exclusion zone. He effectively destroys the apocalyptic vision of Chornobyl, exploring the Zone (with a capital Z) like a *new land*. In his description of a single day in the Zone, Kamysh documents its reality: "I slept on bare concrete, wrapped in oilcloth. It was 4°C (ca. 39°F). A flask of vodka for breakfast, a bonfire lit with a book, and a road north, into the wilderness of the Belarusian borderlands to villages that are on the map but never appear on photos. A road through fog, across broken bridges with frozen icicles that you slip on, struggling to walk. Fatigue, strands of hair covered with frost, and forty

---

83 Dzhud, "O gore, radosti i razumnykh liudiakh" [About grief, joy and reasonable people], *S.T.A.L.K.E.R. Shadow of Chernobyl*, last modified July 27, 2007, http://stalker-portal.ru/page.php?al=alias2274.

kilometers further on—the warmest wood stove on the planet, a village with old imperial cobblestones, just a stone's throw away from the border. And real exclusion, pounding with fists of silence, darkens the windows of your peace only in those places where there are no tourist routes, where no excursion buses go. Where people only come once a year. For a memorial service. And not even every year."[84]

And although the story about the Zone is aimed at recreating its current realities, the most important thing in *Stalking the Atomic City* is "my personal map of impressions, geographies, locations, and myself," as Kamysh admits.[85] In fact, despite the names of towns and villages (Kamianka, Hornostaipil, Hubyn, Kopachi, Krasno, the village of Olshanka, Vilcha station, Buriakovka, the Rossokha equipment storage facility, Dytiatky, the wood stove in Novoshepelychi) and the peculiar cartography of the landscapes, the author focuses on his own impressions: "But I found a new destination each time I went there. At first, Prypiat and Chornobyl-2, then villages, villages, villages, pioneer camps, recreation camps, antiaircraft installations, warehouses, hangars, railroad tracks, cooling towers, churches. I wanted to sniff and touch every patch of this dump, every fragment of the past. And every time I came back, I swore that it would be my last, my very last visit."[86] In a sense, this is also an escapist perspective—memories of the people the narrator meets remain on the margins; they, like communication, interaction, and settlement in the Zone, are not the goal of the journey at all. The author brings his own exclusion and loneliness to the Exclusion Zone: "I'm sitting like this with the balcony doors open, listening to raindrops pattering, wild boars padding around, listening to the rain, silence, distant metal banging, and the screams of illegal tourists."[87]

This is how the Zone becomes fetishized. The narrator transforms it into a place of desire, even erotic desire. The Zone also serves as a parallel reality to the city, civilization, and everyday life. On a symbolic level, this kind of perception of Chornobyl, devoid of catastrophism, can be correlated with the voice of the programmer in Kostenko's novel who was overshadowed by the author's voice.

---

84 Markiian Kamysh, "Plavannia sered chornobylskykh bolit bulo chymos na zrazok kolumbovoi mandrivky" [Swimming among Chernobyl swamps was something like Columbus's journey], *Vikna*, December 2015, http://vikna.if.ua/news/category/culture/2015/12/21/46336/view.
85 Kamysh, "Plavannia sered chornobylskykh bolit bulo chymos na zrazok kolumbovoi mandrivky."
86 Markiian Kamysh, *Oformliandiia, abo Prohulianka v Zonu* [Stalkerland, or A walk in the Zone] (Kyiv: Nora-Druk, 2015), 89.
87 Kamysh, *Oformliandiia, abo Prohulianka v Zonu*, 84.

Stalking and the term "stalker" acquired a special non-conformist meaning back in Soviet times thanks to Andrei Tarkovsky's film *Stalker* (1979), based on the Strugatsky brothers' novel *Roadside Picnic*. In the film, the Zone is depicted as an abnormal and fantastical reality that exists alongside the ordinary world. This reality symbolizes a subconscious desire that must be fulfilled in the Zone. The film is permeated with sensuality and a peculiar existential suspension of being, while the Stalker resembles both a messiah and a weak, intelligent outsider-intellectual, superfluous in society and his own family, and disenchanted with life. After the film, the image of the stalker became associated with nonconformity and escapism, as well as post-industrial melancholy and the search for new spiritual practices based on irrationalism.

In Kamysh's novel, the Zone is depicted primarily as real, not abnormal. The stalker loses his messianic traits and becomes a tourist, although the motives for his travels to the Zone remain escapist. After visiting the Chornobyl exclusion zone, the witness/tourist decides to change the meaning of Chornobyl itself from apocalyptic to aesthetic. He refutes the widespread notions about the horror of Chornobyl and admits honestly that he finds it "really BEAUTIFUL" there. One such tourist explains: "You see, if I say what I really think, I'll immediately get a dressing-down from those for whom Chornobyl is a symbol of disaster, grief, death, sickness, forced resettlement . . . What could be good here? But it's hard for me to look for compromises, and I don't want to. [. . .] Who am I? Just a tourist who wants to have a good time, 'see some good stuff' and hear some urban legends. In April 1986, I was seven years old, what can I remember?."[88] And yet he admits, removing the mask of "tragic omniscience": "People, it's really BEAUTIFUL there. It's incredible. There is such peace, such silence, such . . . goddamn harmony. There is no death."[89]

It is noteworthy that a purely documentary book about the Zone appeared almost at the same time—*Notes of a Chornobyl Illegal* by Kyryl Stepanets (2014). It describes the same places and similar experiences of stalking as Kamysh. Both authors draw on real experiences and talk about real places, and both share the same attitude towards the Zone as an object of desire: "My first encounter with the coveted Zone awaited me," Stepanets confesses. In essence, the touristification of the Zone brings back the reality of Chornobyl, which had been suppressed by trauma. By objectively documenting it, Stepanets helps the Chornobyl Zone regain the reality of places, dates, stories, and routes that had

---

88 Dzhud, "O gore, radosti i razumnykh liudiakh" [About grief, joy and reasonable people], S.T.A.L.K.E.R. *Shadow of Chernobyl*, last modified July 27, 2007, http://stalker-portal.ru/page.php?al=alias2274.

89 Dzhud, "O gore, radosti i razumnykh liudiakh."

been lost and washed away by phantasms. "This book is the story of an illegal Chornobyl stalker," he admits. "And at the same time, it is a historical reference book about the settlements of Ukrainian Polissia that were abandoned after the Chornobyl disaster. At the same time, it is a guidebook written by someone who has walked here secretly," he warns.

Kamysh's *reality* is both violent and melancholic, threatening and desirable, exotic and familiar, life-giving and deadly dangerous. It manifests itself as a *repeated presence*, or post-presence, in a world that exists without humans. Reality for the stalker-narrator is in the repetitions of intrusions and returns; in other words, it is born of the endless retracing of the path between life and death, the constant falling into oblivion. Repeated returns to the City and everyday life and new returns to the Zone—yes, through repetitions and the weaving of traces of his presence in the Zone, a post-traumatic reality is created in *Stalking the Atomic City*. It is a circling around the routes of the Zone, its incarnation, filling it with details of lost time, obscene language, Zen meditations. The core of the *reality* in Kamysh's story is the expulsion of the traumatic symbolic (social) from the subject, and in particular, the death of the Father, which is connected to Chornobyl.

Thus, the perception of Chornobyl is a powerful figurative mechanism in the culture and literature of the early twenty-first century, and Chornobyl remains a relevant signifier of the present, capable of producing new artistic forms. Atomic unreality is a fantasy reality, like Susan Sontag's "imagination of disaster." However, nuclear imagery is not limited to depicting catastrophe and its consequences. It also has a therapeutic dimension—as a non-event, as an omission, as a return to reality. After all, as Christopher Norris writes, "to think the possibility of nuclear war—a very real and present possibility—is to think beyond the limits of reason itself."[90] It is not limited to depicting catastrophe and its consequences. It also has a therapeutic dimension, speaking not only of catastrophe but also of risk and the possibility of a different reality. And intergenerational attraction and repulsion are among the important agents on this path.

Chornobyldorf: "Archeologist"

Chornobyldorf (2020), an archeological opera by Roman Grygoriv and Illia Razumeiko, offers another contemporary post-apocalyptic version of the Chornobyl disaster and the Chornobyl exclusion zone. Billed as an "archeological

---

90 Christopher Norris, "Versions of Apocalypse: Kant, Derrida, Foucault," in *Apocalypse Theory and the Ends of the World*, ed. Malcolm Bull (Oxford: Blackwell, 1995), 245.

opera in seven novellas," it tells the story of a post-society in which the "descendants of humanity" find themselves living "after the death of capitalism, opera, and philosophy." The metaphor of an "anthropological museum" is perhaps the best way of describing the nature of this "archeological opera," which tells of how those who settled on the site of the former Chornobyl after the disaster attempted to regenerate the lost civilization through a series of performances—ancient pagan chants, imitations of classical opera, prayers to Chornobyl, and worship of a golden calf through the means of digital civilization. One fascinating and eerie scene in the ritual performance shows them worshiping the Rhea, an algorithmic piano invented by the Austrian Winfried Ritsch which automatically generates music, like a new God replacing man.

Grygoriv, Razumeiko and their team collected a wide variety of instruments from different periods and ethnic groups to illustrate the deep polyphony/polymorphism of sounds and tones of the post-modern world. The instruments include the microtonal bandura and cymbals, the Alpine zither, the gusli, the kantele, and the morin khuur (a traditional Mongolian two-stringed cello). All of them, and each one separately, convey the agony of giving birth to tones and composing harmony out of the fragments, quotations, and artifacts left behind on the burial mound of culture. These attempts to revive human culture are painful, raw, and tactile.

Thus, *Chornobyldorf* presents another version of a nuclear post-apocalypse, not in the form of an encounter with monsters and mutants in a theater of horrors, but through a situation where information entropy has to be overcome amid cultural chaos, silence, and soundlessness. It is an attempt at creating a world, not starting from a blank slate, but using snippets and scraps of civilization, following the traces of other people's letters and memories of the world as it was before the explosion, before "the end." All that remains of that world are fragments of memory, a few artifacts, snatches of melodies, echoes of myths. In the post-historical era, these fragments of the past are assembled into a new mosaic and fused into a new amalgam. The post-apocalyptic human "will attempt to reconstruct fragments of once-great music and philosophy, transforming the formulas of radioactive decay into microtonal harmonies, turning ancient folk instruments into sonic generators and laboratory instruments, mixing fragments of Christian masses with pantheistic rituals and polyphonic folk songs," says Ilya Razumeiko, one of the creators of *Chornobyldorf*, referring to eco-critical thinking about Chornobyl.[91] In this way, Chornobyl is transformed into a hyperobject.

---

91 "'Chornobuildorf': startuvav novyi mizhnarodnyi opernyi proekt" ['Chornobuildorf': a new international opera project has started], Art Arsenal, https://artarsenal.in.ua/povidomlennya/chornobyldorf-startuvav-novyj-mizhnarodnyjopernyj-proyekt/.

This new way of speaking, as demonstrated by the creators of *Chornobyldorf*, is reminiscent of Walter Benjamin's angel of history, who charges forward, but with a terrified face turned toward the past. In fact, the memory of the past, which is also a call to the future, is the central idea of the opera. The opera as a whole clearly refers to the already bygone era of postmodernism and its artistic practices, from which it has carried over the ironic replaying of the "end of history," pastiche as a form of total quotation, fragmentation, the multilayeredness of cultural styles that are peeled away layer by layer like archeological strata, as well as the impossibility of ending—an open finale.

The lyrics were written by Yuri Izdryk (with a little help from Ivan Kotliarevsky and Ovid), whose works (*Wozzeck, Double Leon*, "Chetver" magazine) are perhaps the best representation of post-apocalyptic writing in Ukrainian literature with its virtual dreams—transformations of reality, the disintegration of words and messages, parallel grammatical forms and meanings, hybrid bodies. It is noteworthy that Izdryk plays one of the main roles, Orpheus, that is, the man who sought to lead Eurydice out of oblivion and who, after being torn to pieces by the Maenads, became the prototype of the Orphic author who assembles a world out of fragments and multiplied splits of his own self. Thus, we have a situation where postmodernism itself becomes a quotation, a replica in a new action proposed by the "new opera."

Chornobyldorf is a "flower of despair and delight," as Orpheus calls it. The opera conveys the indivisibility of horror and pleasure, something chthonic, something that lies at the bottom of the archives of the subconscious. Hence the images born at the intersection of *arche* and *techne*, a combination of barbarism, cultural myths, and digital technologies, a Chornobyl mash-up of ethno-folk-techno-classical-punk. Fragments of techno civilization are everywhere in this "post-explosion" world, and the world itself is post-functional—all the old habits have been destroyed, everything is beginning anew and being readapted from the relics of the past. Here, people have chips embedded in their bodies; instead of flower crowns, necklaces, and embroidery, they wear wires and plastic headdresses. They pray to ancient gods who appear in the form of computer disks. The most ancient folk melodies ring out in an improvised church where the walls are hung with huge circuit boards instead of icons and the ruins of Reactor 4 can be seen from the door.

What is *Chornobyldorf* telling us? It tells of a post-explosion world in which civilization, culture, and music have fallen apart into fragments and shards and everything has to start over again. The purpose of all things has been forgotten; for example, no one knows what an accordion is for. It is an object from which sounds can be extracted, but in a different way from what we are used to, or it can be worn on the head like a crown. In this environment of primal touches, sounds, and movements, people must learn to speak, sing, dance, and love. An important aspect of the "archeological opera" is the emphasis on the corporeality of everything that happens in the post-human world, and in particular the innocence of physicality and the nakedness of existence itself. The rebuilding of the world is connected with the ability to move, to walk. Hence the spasmodic movements, convulsions, somnambulistic plasticity, and the focus on the landscape as an extension of the body.

Music is a metaphor for human life. Thus, the opera includes stunning moments when tones and sounds are born out of the deformed objects and material remnants of the human world, and the embodiment of the voice through throat singing, growling, screaming, whispering, and recitative. Ritual restorations of the world before the "explosion" are carried out through the search for melody, its inception, unfolding, repetition—and its disappearance, erasure, disintegration. Melodies emerge and fade away; sounds are born, arranged in a row, and disintegrate. Woven into this pulsation of moments of birth and disappearance are snatches of Bach, songs of ancient Polissian Rusalia, and melodies from the Ukrainian folk song "The Sun is Low, Evening is Near" arranged by Mykola Lysenko. The whirlings of Ulysses the Radiation Supervisor and his headlong rush "in search of tonality" are stunning, desperate, and terrifying in their automatism.

Maurice Blanchot said that it is not just us who write about disasters—disasters also write about us (and through us). In *Chornobyldorf*, the disaster is writing about us. The disaster speaks of the illusory nature of rebuilding harmony (civilization) out of chaos and the remnants of culture; of ritualistic repetition (going as far as a new Saturnalia—the beginning of a new world and the worship of the golden Taurus-Lenin); of the danger of forgetting and destroying the cultural code. All attempts to revive life in this settlement on the site of Chornobyl fail, just like the information that appears and then disappears, turning into noise. It is not stored anywhere—everything starts all over again, with no archive.

As landscape and as object, Chornobyl becomes a full-fledged character and a real participant in the story—in the form of the power lines that extend from the nuclear plant; a graveyard of contaminated equipment, the arm of an excavator sticking out like the arm of some giant; the almost cosmic "Arc" that cuts through the entire space; the Red Forest, along which not only the villagers but also we, the audience, walk for an agonizingly long time; the doors of the church, through which Reactor 4 can be seen; and photographs documenting the construction of the Chornobyl nuclear power plant. The visual and auditory violence—looking at naked bodies, listening to gibberish instead of words and convulsive attempts to speak and move—turns into a receptive focus, and we are inextricably involved in everything that is happening on stage. Moreover, we all fit into the maternal landscapes of the Chornobyl exclusion zone, like the helpless little naked person curled up like a newborn baby on the screen. This constant visual integration into the space of Chornobyl and the reminders of it render the opera distinctly Chornobyl-like, drawing the audience into the story.

What does *Chornobyldorf* symbolize? That Chornobyl is a metaphor for global catastrophe. Here, Orpheus, doomed, convulsively follows Eurydice—into Nothingness, into Horror. In fact, as Orpheus ironically remarks in the finale, there is no Eurydice; it is all just an illusion, a non-novel, an unwritten letter, a new opera of the old world. You can continue to live in a world of illusions, praying to the television and CDs. All new attempts to start over are futile. Orpheus reassures us, but we don't really believe him. Because Chornobyl is writing about us and through us once more.

CHAPTER 7

Verka Serduchka: Kitsch Therapy in Transit

The character of Verka Serduchka, a car attendant on the Poltava train, created by entertainer Andriy Danylko, has been a fixture in the variety scene since 1993, although Danylko performed the first two skits, "The Canteen" and "The Train Attendant," in 1991. Verka Serduchka has undergone various transformations over time, but has always remained recognizable (*The SV (Sleeping Car) Show*, *The Verka Serduchka Show*, *Verka Serduchka's House of Fun*). As Oleksandr Hrytsenko notes, "Serduchka's visual image was created with the help of a train attendant's usual attire—a navy uniform jacket with 'hammer' patches on the lapels; a beret pulled down over the forehead; and a signal flag wound around a stick. The substantial 'inflatable' bust, gesticulations, and unforgiving *surzhyk* helped achieve a grotesque effect."[1] Hrytsenko details the milestones in Serduchka's evolution: later, "instead of the usual uniform jacket, a seemingly elegant suit jacket appeared, covered with glitter; the beret is now also covered with sequins, but the gray-colored skirt hasn't changed, while the tights underneath now feature a hole in a conspicuous place. The inflatable bust has grown even larger, and the audience knows from numerous TV and press interviews with Andriy Danylko that the bust is made of two inflated condoms [...]."[2]

In 2001, Verka Serduchka was transformed from a burlesque train attendant to an outrageous, quasi-glamorous "star." In 2007, Serduchka represented Ukraine at the Eurovision Song Contest in Helsinki, where she took second place. At the same time, Serduchka underwent another transformation—she became associated with punk, favoring shiny metallic outfits, and turned into a kind of cyborg. The next stage in Serduchka's evolution began when she formed a double act with her "mama" and started wearing the Ukrainian national Olympic team tracksuit. This personification is explicitly associated with the image of Ukrainian migrants scattered around the world—the tracksuit is often a telltale characteristic of Ukrainian migrant workers abroad. Thus, Serduchka's transformations capture the various stages of sociocultural change in Ukrainian society as a whole. Playfulness, a key attribute of the character, shifts perception from ideological coordinates to entertainment. And yet the sociocultural context is important.

Serhy Yekelchyk suggests considering Serduchka "as a jester, who, perhaps unwittingly but very much in line with the Ukrainian cultural tradition, makes

---

1   Oleksandr Hrytsenko, "Vierka Serdiuchka yak dzerkalo kulturnoi transformatsii [Vierka Serdiuchka as a Mirror of Cultural Transformation]," Izbornyk, n.d., accessed November 24, 2025, http://litopys.org.ua/heroes/hero15.htm.
2   Hrytsenko, "Vierka Serdiuchka yak dzerkalo kulturnoi transformatsii."

audiences laugh at their own cultural stereotypes and prejudices."[3] Oleksandr Hrytsenko believes that "today's Verka Serduchka is a parody of the newly minted post-Soviet 'showbiz stars' who try to look like Hollywood celebrities but still end up resembling provincial train attendants or saleswomen."[4] Thus, both critics note the parodic and predominantly entertaining nature of Serduchka's persona. However, in addition to the parodic subtext, her persona also has significant sociocultural implications, so it would be incorrect to reduce her clowning to mere parody.

The Verka Serduchka character personifies the *migrant mindset* and is linked to the perception of Ukraine as a transit country. From a semiotic point of view, Serduchka acts as an intermediary, a mediator, connecting the center and the periphery, thereby removing the boundaries between highbrow and lowbrow, global and local, humorous and serious. She also symbolizes the feminization of post-Soviet society, traumatized by "shock therapy." From a practical point of view, she also demonstrates how popular culture assumes therapeutic functions in a world in transit.

It is also worth emphasizing the almost postcolonial implications embodied by Verka Serduchka. Danylko uses dual coding in the line "Russia Goodbye / Lasha Tumbai" in the song "Dancing," Ukraine's 2007 Eurovision entry. The song drew considerable criticism from the Russian audience. Danylko also has not shied away from the topic of deconstructing the traditional kitsch image of Ukraine in the rest of the world, often associated with *Sharovarshchyna*. "People thought Ukraine was just *salo* [pork fat], *samohonka* [moonshine], and flower crowns with *sharovary* [wide Cossack pants]," he notes. Serduchka's goal was to present a completely different image of Ukraine at Eurovision—one that was fun, peaceful, and ultimately even technogenic, as Serduchka's metallic silver sparkle at the contest transformed her from a Ukrainian doll into an alien cyborg.

Danylko describes his new, parodic persona as "a whole new genre, sarcastic and upbeat" and agrees that at its core is a cultural and linguistic insanity taken to the point of grotesqueness, but in essence, this "insanity" is very positive, a kind of "happy pill" that brings people together. On the whole, unlike the Ukrainian kitsch with Cossacks and *hopak*, which is characterized by its attachment to

---

3   Serhy Yekelchyk, "What Is Ukrainian about Ukraine's Pop Culture?: The Strange Case of Verka Serduchka," *Canadian–American Slavic Studies* 44 (2010): 217–232.
4   Oleksandr Hrytsenko, "Vierka Serdiuchka yak dzerkalo kulturnoi transformatsii [Vierka Serdiuchka as a Mirror of Cultural Transformation]," Izbornyk, n.d., accessed November 24, 2025, http://litopys.org.ua/heroes/hero15.htm.

the past, the "starry Serduchka"—and with her, the whole image of Ukraine—looked like a futuristic project at the Eurovision Song Contest.

And yet interpretations of this persona have rarely gone beyond critical assessments. As Serhiy Hrabovskyi notes, Serduchka represents "the Little Russian identity as a component of authentic Ukrainian culture in its real, colonial, and postcolonial existence. And if there is a joke or mockery here, it is only within the limits of this cultural paradigm, which knows nothing else in Ukrainian existence than the object of such jokes or parodies, this peasant, or rather, collective farm/commuter mentality with its never-ending alcohol-fueled celebrations."[5]

The post-Soviet relevance of the Serduchka character is rarely emphasized, although Ilya Khineyko does call Serduchka "the true vox populi of the silent majority" and associates her with the new types of work that it fell to women to do in the 1990s: "shuttle trading"—trips to wholesale markets in Ukraine, Poland, and Turkey, market trading, reselling, migrant work, and migration. "After the collapse of the Soviet Union and its economy," Khineyko notes, "thousands of such women could be found traveling on trains to sell goods in open-air markets in provincial Russian and Ukrainian cities; hence Serduchka became the true vox populi of a silent majority. She can be simultaneously laughed at and with, delivering a message of unbridled optimism, reflected in the title of one of her most famous songs, "Vsyo budet khorosho" (Everything will be fine)."[6] In other words, as Volodymyr Beglov noted, "She was, pardon me, just like us."[7]

What is it like, this *transit train attendant-mediator*, born in the post-Soviet era? As an image of a certain identity, Verka Serduchka was born in the early 1990s at a time when Ukraine was going through a particularly abrupt change in social roles and functions, the old moral and ideological categories and values that had been shaped during the totalitarian period were changing, and the whole of post-Soviet society was experiencing a kind of trauma. It is important to note that when trauma remains psychologically and culturally "unprocessed," that is, when consciousness "gets stuck" on the trauma, it is perpetually reproduced. So it is no coincidence that the 1990s saw the proliferation of various (quasi) psychotherapeutic practices, including pastors and preachers who could fill stadiums, and psychics of the likes of Anatoly Kashpirovsky and Allan

---

5 Serhii Hrabovskyi, "'Skysle moloko' Andriia Danylka ['Sour Milk' of Andrii Danylko]," Detektor Media, May 15, 2007, https://detector.media/kritika/article/8871/2007-05-15-skysle-moloko-andriya-danylka/.
6 Ilya Khineyko, "The Little Russian: Verka Serduchka," Ukraine Analysis (blog), May 22, 2007, http://ukraineanalysis.wordpress.com/2007/05/22/the-little-russian-verka-serduchka/.
7 Volodymyr Biehlov, "Chy mozhna pyshatysia Serdiuchkoiu? [Can One Be Proud of Serdiuchka?]," JeyArt, n.d., accessed August 19, 2025, http://jeyart.com.ua/people/sub158/.

Chumak, whose followers flocked to their TV sets, waiting to be healed with "charged water."

Having emerged by accident, Serduchka the clown quickly turned into a feel-good "happy pill." Endowed with unwavering optimism and a comical appearance, she was the antithesis of officialdom and the voice of "grassroots" society. Her meaningless tall tales, told in *surzhyk*, cheered people up, and she evolved as a popular culture project rather than an ideological one. However, as we know, popular culture also plays an important constructive role in modern society. In the early 1990s, new forms of identity—based on ethnicity, class, gender—were emerging. Serduchka's burlesque persona, which combined high and low culture, served as a conductor from the provinces to the metropolitan area, aiming not to be realistic, but above all to bring people together and fill them with optimism. The character provided a form of emergency psychotherapy during a period of catastrophe.

The persona was the mask of a young performer, Andriy Danylko, who himself came from a low-income background and in fact epitomized the "little man" or marginalized person. According to the facts outlined in a local Poltavshchyna news outlet, Danylko was born into a poor family; his mother was a painter and decorator, his father was a driver who suffered from alcoholism and died early; the family lived in a post-war barracks on the outskirts of Poltava. Danylko's membership in the "lower," marginalized stratum is thus marked both at the social level (broken home, poor family) and at the level of topos (the outskirts of the city, the barracks). Danylko has constantly emphasized his solidarity with disadvantaged people in his interviews. "You know, I achieved everything myself, I had no rich patrons, not a penny to my name," he admits. "And I'm proud of that, although I'm often dissatisfied with some of my creations—how they were produced, their quality."[8] In a conversation with Oleksandr Tkachenko, he recalls his childhood and talks about the "annex" where he lived, as well as waking up with "frost on his face" before going to school in the morning. "The wallpaper was peeling. We built it ourselves, painted it ourselves," the actor explains.[9]

The feeling of nostalgia for the happy moments of childhood serves as a form of escapism from the instability and pragmatism of the post-Soviet era.

---

[8] Andrii Danilko, "'V detstve ia khotel byt vrachom ili sviashchennikom' ['In Childhood I Wanted to Be a Doctor or a Priest']," Internet-vydannia "Poltavshchyna," December 13, 2009, http://www.poltava.pl.ua/news/236.

[9] "Ia duzhe zakompleksovana liudyna [I Am a Very Complexed Person]," TSN, July 20, 2011, https://tsn.ua/analitika/ya-duzhe-zakompleksovana-lyudina.html.

However, it was only in this new era, which stimulated entrepreneurship, that the project called "Verka Serduchka" could have originated and been successfully implemented. "People still don't know who Serduchka is. One moment she makes everyone laugh until they cry, the next she can make them burst into tears," Danylko commented, not without respect for his character.[10] On the whole, Serduchka has grown into a separate, independent persona, about whom Danylko speaks in the third person. The character has become Danylko's public persona, and his relationship with Serduchka is similar to that of a mother and child. After all, the maternal functions in this character are obvious. Later, Serduchka's "mama" appears as a character and they perform as a double act.

This marginalized and somewhat aggressive female train attendant served as a mediator between people divided by social, gender, and class differences. A train compartment is a unique microcosm where people who might never meet in other parts of their lives come together. It is also a place where strangers talk, dramas unfold, and the most extraordinary desires can be fulfilled as if by magic. In short, it is a space of transition, transience, and initiation. Born as a train attendant character, Serduchka the clown serves as a transporter between different worlds—high and low, provincial and metropolitan, Soviet and post-Soviet. The character both evoked the demise of the Soviet era and was deeply rooted in that era. It is characteristic that Danylko makes this belonging to the Soviet past iconic, as symbolized by the silver five-pointed star on Serduchka's hat, which transforms her into an emblem of post-Soviet transit.

Serduchka as a Doll

Verka Serduchka, as a provincial car attendant on the Poltava–Kyiv train, wearing an official jacket with a badge, with a large padded bust and skinny legs in torn tights, speaking in a mixture of Ukrainian and Russian, seemed to be transporting the entire country to the other side of *perestroika*. At the same time, her image—lowbrow, vulgar, kitschy—parodied the typical attributes of "femininity," presenting them in a mirror of exaggerated, even monstrous imagery. With her exaggerated bust made of inflated condoms, Serduchka is both asexual and phallic, and the flag in her hands is a symbol of this.

---

10 Andrii Danilko, "'V detstve ia khotel byt vrachom ili sviashchennikom' ['In Childhood I Wanted to Be a Doctor or a Priest']," Internet-vydannia "Poltavshchyna," December 13, 2009, http://www.poltava.pl.ua/news/236.

Verka symbolizes desire and at the same time engenders fear, like an archaic "phallic mother" who exists in an ancient, sexually undifferentiated world. Psychoanalytically, the "phallic mother" is an object of fear for the "ego" and at the same time its deepest desire. She represents the absolute power of a woman, autonomous and self-sufficient; she is neither human nor monster, but both fantastic and caricatured.[11]

By capturing the fear of the "lowbrow" feminine, in particular female sexuality, Serduchka, like a litmus test, reveals the fluidity and instability of social, ethnic, class, and gender boundaries in a transitional society. At the same time, like a phallic mother, she heals and generates the desire to be *different*, that is, she aims to help people define themselves and gain social, ethnic, class, and gender identity. It is no coincidence that Danylko links the inner story of Verka Serduchka's character with the fairy tale of Cinderella. She goes from train attendant to star, and—we might add—just like Danylko himself, she moves from a post-war barrack to a prestigious apartment building favored by celebrities in the center of Kyiv, on Khreshchatyk Street.

With the unfolding of new sociocultural realities in the 2000s, Serduchka's masquerade persona became increasingly associated for Danylko with a "cute, cheerful character," "not evil," but "simple-minded," who "symbolizes success." Thus, the sociocultural models of the character are replaced by psycho-emotional ones, the parody element diminishes, and the entertainment value increases. Verka's headwear attests to the evolution of the character: the train attendant's beret she wore on the *SV Show* is replaced by a bouquet of flowers, signifying Ukrainization and doll-like qualities. The image acquires therapeutic functions, and the symbolism of the frightening "phallic mother" is replaced by the symbolism of an infantile puppet character—rather like Masyanya, who helps wishes come true. "She's not a doll," Danylko explains. "But a mask. A cartoon, a character, Masyanya...."[12]

A mask, a doll, clowning—these are the sources of Serduchka's persona, whose purpose is to entertain the audience, chatter, and turn everything into a celebration. That is why Serhiy Rakhmanin said in an interview with Danylko on Radio Svoboda (Radio Liberty): "... When you said that, in your opinion, Verka Serduchka is not a trashy woman, but rather a child, a celebration, or Cinderella,

---

11 See: Marcia Ian, *Remembering the Phallic Mother: Psychoanalysis, Modernism, and the Fetish* (Ithaca: Cornell University Press, 1993), 8–9.
12 "Andrei Danilko: 'Serdiuchka'—simvol potentsii!," NEWSmuz.com, March 17, 2008, http://www.newsmusic.ru/news_3_10126.htm.

I think that's exactly how a lot of people see Verka."[13] Indeed, Serduchka is like a doll that entertains the entire country. The surprisingly significant visual elements of Serduchka's image, in particular her high bust and skinny legs, make her resemble a *motanka* doll, a traditional Ukrainian toy. This oversized doll named Verka Serduchka is both a mother and a child, an adult woman and an asexual teenager from the lower social classes.

It was no accident when, in 2004, Serduchka was joined by her "mama," played by actress Inna Bilokon. The "Serduchka & Mama" double act is a hybrid persona, revealing the hidden maternal associations of Serduchka the train attendant on the one hand, and objectifying the childish implications of this persona on the other. Serduchka served as an amulet for all those who found themselves struggling in the 1990s—those who lost their homes and jobs, those who were forced to leave professional jobs in sectors like engineering to sell goods in the markets, and the migrant workers who dispersed across the world from Ukraine. Over time, Serduchka also became an advocate for those provincial girls who wear knock-offs of Dolce & Gabbana, live off the emotions cultivated by popular culture, and dream of success in a big city. It is with them that Serduchka identifies, and it is to them that most of her messages that "Everything will be fine" are addressed:

> "And I walk around in Dolce & Gabbana,
> I walk around with a wound in my heart.
> I'm choking back tears, held captive by deception,
> But I walk around in Dolce & Gabbana."
>
> ("Dolce & Gabbana")

On the whole, Verka Serduchka can be seen as a kind of totem image of post-totalitarian Ukraine, captured through kitsch. In this sense, she appears as an archetypal post-Soviet and at the same time post-catastrophic image, which creates the illusion of happiness in a society undergoing a period of global transformation that, although deeply traumatized by the past, retains a nostalgic attachment to it. As Danylko said in an interview, "The only thing that's interesting is what happens to you. Everyone likes to laugh at someone else while seeing

---

13 Serhii Rakhmanin, "Vona superzirka, ale yoho malo khto znaie. Providnytsia Vierka Serdiuchka maizhe zatmaruje sutnist samoho avtora. Khto vin naspravdi? [She Is a Superstar, but Few People Know Him. The Leading Lady Vierka Serdiuchka Almost Overshadows the Essence of the Author Himself. Who Is He Really?]," Radio Svoboda, June 23, 2007, http://www.radiosvoboda.org/content/article/965700.html.

their own reflection. Everyone understands that they've had the same experience and felt the same way." The ideal sociocultural meaning of such a burlesque image, immersed in folk humor culture, is to consolidate and personify social, ethnic, and gender complexes in one flamboyant character and, by exposing them to public ridicule, break free from them.

Serduchka as Lady Surzhyk

Oleksandr Hrytsenko argues that "Verka Serduchka was created by television. Created in both a direct, factual sense and in a much deeper sense—it was the rapid formation of post-Soviet media culture that made Verka possible as a cultural phenomenon."[14] Indeed, without TV shows and without her unique visual clowning, Verka Serduchka would not have been possible. Hrytsenko also links the phenomenon of Verka Serduchka with "loser television," in which the main characters are marginalized or even lumpen representatives of the underclass. In Hrytsenko's opinion, Verka is "a kind of cross-section of the mentality of a disillusioned, internally confused ordinary resident of Ukraine, who, while parting (willingly or unwillingly, but almost always painfully) with his own past, can at least enjoy the opportunity to 'relax and enjoy himself,' if only by watching Verka and other similar shows."[15]

It seems that the parodic transgressions personified by Serduchka are not limited to "common people," "new Europeans," and "showbiz stars." It is also difficult to reduce Serduchka to a distraught "loser," since her entire image is aimed at "success." Verka Serduchka breaks down many stereotypes and builds bridges to new identities. First of all, she performs gender inversion, demonstrating the relativity of gender and confirming Judith Butler's thesis that gender identity is based on masquerade. As a travesti character, Danylko shows the relativity of gender labeling, although he does not identify with queer sexuality. The semiotic basis of Serduchka's persona (her last name derives from a somewhat playful and almost intimate nickname for women who often get angry—"serdiatsia" in Ukrainian) is built on the tension that arises at the intersection of various transgressive strategies—gender, sociocultural, linguistic—and has explicitly masquerade forms that refer us to the technique of drag.

---

14 Oleksandr Hrytsenko, "Vierka Serduchka yak dzerkalo kulturnoi transformatsii [Vierka Serdiuchka as a Mirror of Cultural Transformation]," Izbornyk, n.d., http://litopys.org.ua/heroes/hero15.htm.
15 Hrytsenko, "Vierka Serdiuchka yak dzerkalo kulturnoi transformatsii."

We have a costume performance—a situation where a young man is dressed in women's clothing, that is, made to resemble a woman—reminiscent of drag, a technique that involves personifying the opposite sex by dressing in women's or men's clothing. Such dressing up—grotesque, with exaggerated characteristics of the opposite sex—is mainly done for the purposes of entertainment, but drag queens have become particularly popular in gay and lesbian communities. A hallmark of drag is the "costumes": they are "excessive, garish and 'glamorous' and are constituted by large fake breasts, high heels, revealing dresses, wigs, fake nails and thick make-up."[16] This form developed under the influence of "melodrama, a 'camp' sensibility, comedy, musical theater and cabaret."[17] However, despite her external attributes of sexuality, the oversized doll that is Verka Serduchka is entirely asexual—and in this way, she counters the exaggerated sexualization of women in contemporary pop culture.

After all, men dressing in women's clothes is a popular theatrical technique that has been around since Shakespeare's time. Women have been documented as dressing in men's clothes since at least the seventeenth century as members of the "weaker sex" sought to present as soldiers or sailors in order to participate in dangerous ventures. In modern times, such cross-dressing is aimed at inverting traditional roles in a largely male-dominated society.

It is important to note right away that in making use of drag as a technique, Andriy Danylko does not associate his stage image with a travesti sexual identity. He insists he is tolerant of gay people, but says he "doesn't like it when men wear eye make-up, get manicures, and wear women's clothing."[18] For him, Serduchka is primarily an art character, "not artistic or entertaining. It's a feelgood character, a showstopper." Commenting on the ambivalence of his gender image, Danylko has said: "My stage persona as Verka Serduchka is completely incompatible with the category of 'Performer', but at the same time, Serduchka cannot compete with the divas of the Ukrainian stage in the category of 'Performer.'"[19] Rather, Andriy Danylko's use of drag costumes has clownish and circus motifs.

Serduchka is one of the most interesting products of late twentieth-century pop culture. She not only reflects obvious stereotypes and clichés, but also

---

16 Georgie Bousher and Sarah French, "Postfeminist Pleasure and Politics: Moira Finucane and The Burlesque Hour," *Australasian Drama Studies* 58 (2011): 198.
17 Bousher and French, "Postfeminist Pleasure and Politics," 198.
18 "Danilko Andrii Mykhailovych," Internet-vydannia "Poltavshchyna," November 3, 2010, https://poltava.to/dossier/31/.
19 "Danylko: Serdiuchka ne maie analohiv [Danylko: Serdiuchka Has No Analogues]," Tabloid, January 16, 2012, https://tabloid.pravda.com.ua/news/4f13fb152d96d/.

subverts them. The source of this persona is her belonging to the fringe—
the migrants and marginalized people who occupy the intermediate territory
between the center and the periphery, between the bottom and the top, between
urbanism and rusticity. As an intermediate type and the personification of bad
taste, Verka Serduchka is the classic embodiment of the kitsch that Clement
Greenberg, in his essay "Avant-Garde and Kitsch," attributed to the culture of
"migrants," whose tastes reflect an extravagant combination of traditional rural
(provincial, colonial) culture and urban (metropolitan) culture.

Serduchka, by her origins, personifies the type of low-culture provincial
woman of low social status and represents the marginal context that is usually
associated with stereotypes of so-called common people. The so-called Little
Russian theater of the nineteenth century played a particularly active role in
shaping this image, with its operettas and vaudevilles, in which Ukrainianness
was primarily presented through popular "repertoires with *paysans*" (Dmytro
Antonovych). One of the primary modes of such "quasi-folklore" is the fair, and
its presentation is largely centered on "music and dancing with *horilka*." Kyrylo
Topolia, in his preface to "Spells, or Several Scenes from Ukrainian Folk Tales
and Stories," published in Moscow in 1837, introduced the exoticism of Ukraine
as a province of the empire and explained that in Ukraine "you will hardly find
a single village without music played on the violin, cymbals, cello, or tambou-
rine." He also turned Ukrainian performances into colonial kitsch: "in the evenings they walk on some rural square called a street."[20] Since the time of Mykola
Gogol, the unchanging stock characters of such "quasi-folklore" have been a
young man and a girl, as well as a quarrelsome woman. Mykola Yanchuk, in his
vaudeville "At the Fair" (1887), introduces one such character—a mother who
"is willing to give her daughter to a bald-headed devil in exchange for a glass of
honey."[21] Verka Serduchka recreates the image of "ordinary people" in a parodic
form, thus imitating the principles of colonial theater. Danylko tries to explain
this: "Sometimes people see me through the lens of a stereotype. Some people
think that I still say, 'What's that stinky smell?' [...] I haven't used that phrase
for five years, but everyone still associates me with it."[22] The stereotypical image

---

20 *Ukrainska dramaturhiia pershoi polovyny XIX st.: Malovidomi piesy* [*Ukrainian Drama of the First Half of the 19th Century: Little-Known Plays*] (Kyiv: Derzhavne vydavnytstvo khudozh-noi literatury, 1958), 177.
21 Mykola Ianchuk, "Po yarmarku. Ukrainskyi vodevil na odnu diiu [At the Fair. Ukrainian Vaudeville in One Act]," in *Ukrainskyi vodevil. XIX st* [*Ukrainian Vaudeville. 19th Century*] (Kyiv: Mystetstvo, 1965), 140.
22 Dmitrii Gordon, "Esli by Pugacheva predlozhila mne, kak Galkinu: 'Davai v reklamnykh tseliakh razduem istoriiu', ia by v etom ne uchastvoval, ne smog. Ia ne takoi, mne stydno!

of a provincial and somewhat vulgar train attendant who speaks *surzhyk*, however, has a specific historical reference—the late twentieth and early twenty-first centuries.

Verka's language—the *surzhyk* spoken by a large part of the population in Ukraine—is also marked. This is an important element of Verka Serduchka's transgression, which has often been and still remains the subject of academic research.[23] Serduchka is Lady Surzhyk. Verka, as a hybrid figure, personifies *surzhyk*—a hybrid language practice popular in Ukraine that arises when Ukrainian is combined with Russian elements. On the one hand, *surzhyk* is a consequence of the policy of Russification, and on the other, it is a feature of colloquial spoken language in Ukraine's eastern regions. Like *surzhyk* itself, Serduchka straddles the border between the normative and non-normative, the official and unofficial worlds. Her persona also straddles the border between the real and virtual worlds, because Serduchka is, on the one hand, a very recognizable character of the modern Ukrainian province, which, according to the laws of postmodernism, has long since become the center, and on the other hand, a kind of reincarnation of the virtual Baba Paraska and Baba Palazhka from the works of Ivan Nechui-Levytsky.

Verka Serduchka is frequently associated with the image of colonial Ukraine also known as "Little Russianness." She has been called "a Ukrainian woman whose national consciousness is close to zero, but has not yet become zero," as well as "a simple-minded, helpless *khokhlushka*" whose function is "to entertain the 'older brother,'" which she does successfully by resorting to buffoonery.[24] Singer and politician Oksana Bilozir has remarked that "this genre" is not "the kind of spirit that animates our people—either now or in the future."[25] Some are of the opinion that the clown Verka Serduchka is "a new symbol of Ukraine alongside *salo*, *borshch*, *horilka*, and the book *Kobzar*," that she is "the embodiment

---

[If Pugacheva Had Offered Me, like to Galkin: 'Let's Blow Up a Story for Advertising Purposes', I Would Not Have Participated, I Could Not. I'm Not like That, I'm Ashamed!]," Gordon: Geroi smutnogo vremeni [Gordon: Heroes of Troubled Times], 2002, https://www.gordon.com.ua/books/heroes/danilko/.

23 Interest in Verka Serduchka has so far been limited mainly to the linguistic aspects. See these interesting studies: Lada Bilaniuk, *Contested Tongues: Language Politics and Cultural Correction in Ukraine* (Ithaca, NY: Cornell University Press, 2005); Serhy Yekelchyk, "What Is Ukrainian about Ukraine's Pop Culture?: The Strange Case of Verka Serduchka," *Canadian–American Slavic Studies* 44 (2010): 217–232.

24 Petro Kraliuk, "Bez 'kulturnykh kompleksiv' [Without 'Cultural Complexes']," *Den*, no. 16 (2004).

25 Oksana Bilozir, "Virka Serdiuchka—tse ne dukh nashoho narodu," ForUm, March 15, 2007, http://ua.for-ua.com/interview/2007/03/15/090549.html.

of the post-imperial complex of Little Russianness" that haunts Ukrainians and should not be displayed to the whole world.[26] Ultimately, the range of assessments of Serduchka's persona is quite wide—from claims that "Serduchka represents everything that is most uneducated and banal" in Ukrainians[27] and is a caricature of Ukrainian women, to the recognition that Serduchka is a "child, a celebration, or Cinderella."[28] At the same time, Serhy Yekelchyk has spoken of Serduchka's "ambiguous" identity, the embodiment of "a national mass culture in a bilingual country with an ambiguous national identity."[29]

Incidentally, it is worth comparing Verka Serduchka with the "singing rector" Mykhailo Poplavsky to better understand the nature of colonial kitsch. Poplavsky built his image by resorting to stylizing "Little Russian" stereotypes. The lyrics, dances, and stylized Ukrainian folk costumes help to make Poplavsky's performances entertaining. At the same time, the youthfulness, vibrancy, and mass appeal of his shows, in which he is joined by students from the Institute of Culture, give a vitality to the type of exotic "Ukrainianness" that he represents.

Using stereotypical clichés of Ukrainian identity such as "varenyky," "salo," and "borshch," Poplavsky's show conjures up a stylized and exotically colored *tourist* image of the Ukrainian world, transforming it into a sensual and culinary Eden. The performer plays a crucial role in such a performance: in Poplavsky's case, there is no question of detachment, irony, or transgression—be it ethnic, social, or gender—as demonstrated by Verka Serduchka. His characters refer to traditional *sharovarshchyna* and also create a new culinary kitsch. National symbols are identified not with the folkloric images of a young man and a girl, as in the days of romanticism, but with a fetish, which is Ukrainian borshch. As Poplavsky sings,

---

26 Viktoriia Yehorova, "Andrii Danylko vidmovyvsia vid premii YUNA," tochka.net, January 16, 2012.
27 Afric_Dymon, "Manifest anty-Vierka Serdiuchka [Manifesto Anti-Vierka Serdiuchka]," LiveJournal (blog), March 20, 2007, http://afric-dymon.livejournal.com/28455.html?thread=35623.
28 Serhii Rakhmanin, "Vona superzirka, ale yoho malo khto znaie. Providnytsia Vierka Serdiuchka maizhe zatmaruje sutnist samoho avtora. Khto vin naspravdi? [She Is a Superstar, but Few People Know Him. The Leading Lady Vierka Serdiuchka Almost Overshadows the Essence of the Author Himself. Who Is He Really?]," Radio Svoboda, June 23, 2007, http://www.radiosvoboda.org/content/article/965700.html.
29 Markiian Kamysh, "Plavannia sered chornobylskykh bolit bulo chymos na zrazok kolumbovoi mandrivky [Swimming among Chernobyl Swamps Was Something like Columbus's Journey]," *Vikna*, December 2015, http://vikna.if.ua/news/category/culture/2015/12/21/46336/view.

> "In the afternoon, it calls everyone home,
> And our souls are poured out onto the bowl.
> We can't be torn away from the borshch,
> When it's poured like a song from the ladle."

In Poplavsky's culinary paradise, *varenyky*, Ukrainian dumplings, become an object of love ("my beloved varenyky"), and the Cossack's love for a girl is transformed into love for a *makitra*, a large clay bowl for serving *varenyky*: "and my heart belongs to the *makitra*." *Salo* acts as a sweet Ukrainian talisman:

> "I eat salo, I sleep on salo,
> Because I love it so much,
> If only I could cover myself with salo,
> I would be the happiest person alive."

Essentially, Poplavsky trivializes the "Little Russian" image of Ukraine as a "tribe of dancers and singers" and makes it an exotic object of tourist entertainment rather than transgression. In this way, he re-exoticizes modern Ukraine. And this is the essential difference between him and Verka Serduchka, who, for her part, while transmitting the feminine image of Ukraine traditional in colonial consciousness, embodies its subjectivity and polymorphous performativity. Serduchka is a social and gender, linguistic, and ethno-national symbol. Through various transgressions, she also transforms the feminine image of Ukraine into a character that has different modes of expressing identity—highbrow and lowbrow, glamorous and burlesque, negative and positive.

By inventing Verka Serduchka, Danylko has embodied his image of society, assembled from fragments of the past and present, an image which was, in fact, a fragment of a hybrid post-totalitarian reality. As a trickster and grotesque character, Serduchka illustrates life in Ukrainian society as it transitions from socialism to a market economy and privatization. And she does this in a playful—carnivalesque and burlesque—manner, modifying the character traits, physical features, clothing, and behavior patterns. The Verka Serduchka project has proved to be one of the most innovative media products of the postmodern era in Ukraine. As a member of the last Soviet generation, Danylko has modeled the persona of a "doll-mother" which, thanks to its playful kitschy nature, performed therapeutic functions during the post-Soviet transit.

Instead of an Epilogue

From Inside the Transit

I never imagined that in March 2022 I would become "a displaced person"—"a refugee." Not that I find this term offensive, not at all, but the concept seemed too far removed from my reality. I had a fulfilling job, a home where I felt comfortable and cozy, family and friends nearby, and my beloved Kyiv. I love traveling and I always have, but my umbilical cord was always tied to my doorstep and stretched tight like a thread. So I always knew that at some point, whenever a fellowship or conference came to an end, I would come back home. Like a hermit crab, I carried my shell with me, a place I could always hide in.

And suddenly, one March morning in 2022, I was forced to leave my home, lock the door, and leave, not knowing where I was going or when I would return. Two weeks later, I found myself in Munich. Everything happened rapidly and unexpectedly—both the invitation itself and the speed with which my colleagues from the Ludwig Maximilian University took care of all the formalities, even finding me somewhere to live. I had visited Munich many times, but this time I was arriving as a different person and in a different way: I was stepping into the river that we know as the history of migrants and displaced persons. For me, Munich in March 2022 overlapped with Munich in the late 1940s.

I had recently become fascinated by the history of the Ukrainian Art Movement of 1946–1948, a powerful and still largely unexplored phenomenon that unfolded in the displaced persons camps of post-war Germany, dubbed "Planet DP" by Ulas Samchuk. Munich was one of the symbolic centers of this planet. While working on the biography of Yuri Shevelov (also known as Sherekh), I delved into his discussion with Arnold Toynbee on Occidentalism, explored magazines and newspapers published in DP camps, and immersed myself in the atmosphere of that time, so that Munich became, for me, a city of Ukrainian emigrants. The image of Munich in my mind was a partly documented but mostly fictionalized picture of a postwar Bavarian city ravaged by war. My mental map was filled with literary impressions: the green Isar as a river of memory from Yuri Kosach's novel *Aeneas and the Lives of Others*, the anonymous antiquarian wandering through the labyrinths of the city from Emma

Andijewska's *Herostratus*, grotesque tales about losing one's name and identity from the short stories of Ihor Kostetsky, and so on.

Intellectually, it was important for me to understand that the DP camps became the birthplace of the idea of a new Ukraine and a new Ukrainian culture. It was this Ukrainian emigration that was to determine the cultural progress of Ukrainians in the years to come, leading up to independence. The idea of migration as rootlessness was one of the key concepts that emerged here. Up until then, the topic of migration had not been a central concern in Ukrainian emigrant circles—the Prague emigration was more concerned with the past than with the future. Yuri Shevelov developed the concept of rootlessness as a defining characteristic of the twentieth century, thereby inscribing his own experience and that of post-war Ukrainian migration into contemporary history.

"The problem of rootlessness is perhaps the most characteristic problem of the twentieth century [...]. All the historical processes of our time seem to be specifically aimed at depriving people of their roots," he wrote in Lund, Sweden, in 1950, having just moved there from Planet DP. He discussed how this problem connects the mood and theme of Mykhailo Kotsiubinsky's brilliant novella *On the Stone* (1902) with Roberto Rossellini's film *Stromboli, Land of God* (1950), a vivid example of Italian neorealism that had just appeared in cinemas. For Shevelov, both works touched on the same theme, a concern central to his time: the "experience of uprooting" of individuals and entire nations caused by the rules of empires and war. He wrote about the "fear of war" that permeated humanity and argued that the concept of modern fear included "an important and typical component of our time: the fear of losing one's roots." What he meant by that was "the fear of being blown off the ground. The fear of starting everything, literally everything, over and over again. That is, if new ground is found. But what if it isn't?"

These were not abstract considerations for Shevelov: they were personally meaningful to him, indeed existential. He was talking about himself and the situation in which many immigrants from different countries found themselves after World War II—in total, there were more than a million displaced persons in Germany and Austria at that time. Today we might disagree with Shevelov about whether migration always means uprooting and is always accompanied by fear, because we now have the concept of "existential migration", which no longer implies fear of losing one's roots, but rather satisfaction at finding a place in the world that best suits us personally. We live in an era of transnational migration where migration is becoming voluntary, even desirable, and rootlessness itself is a symbol of a global outlook. In this context, Shevelov's ideas seem outdated and easily identifiable as modernist and typical of the first half of the twentieth century.

But it's more complex than that, especially when you go from being a philosopher and an observer to a living person who has been displaced from their homeland by another war—this time the Russo-Ukrainian one. We tend to discuss immigrants as displaced persons, rather than focusing on their existence from within their own experience. But it is there—in the very essence of a person as an immigrant, in an existence reduced to alienation and displacement—that fear and rootlessness reside. Post-war Germany came to understand this unique ontological state of being in the world, and Shevelov felt it and documented it based on his own experience, from within his own being.

The fear of forced resettlement is real, and I felt it acutely. That is why the overlap of the two time periods resonated with me—an imaginary repetition of that status of ripped-out existence, uprooting, and suspension between being and non-being that I had read about in Shevelov's intellectual essays and the works of Yuri Kosach and Viktor Petrov. So, finding myself in Munich, I tried to catch traces of the past and relive it. I wanted to understand—no, I wanted to learn—how to live in this world of suspension and falling out of existence and time, that is, in that state of transit I had spent so much time thinking and writing about. I often told my friends that I had fallen out of time, that it was flowing somewhere outside of me, and I couldn't feel it. Only the green waters of the Isar River rolled on and seemed to be the linchpin of all existence.

My vision was split: I was looking for traces of the past, but they intersected with the present. It was all provoked by being in Munich, where the Ukrainian Free University opened in 1945 and where Yuri Shevelov defended his second dissertation (the first was in Kharkiv), where Viktor Petrov, Volodymyr Derzhavin, and a large group of Ukrainian professors and scholars taught, and where Kosach wrote a German-language history of twentieth-century Ukrainian literature; Munich, which came to life in the pages of the greatest émigré novel of the time—Kosach's *Aeneas and the Lives of Others*, which for me is the immigrant gospel of the 1940s, the Ukrainian version of Joyce's *Ulysses*, transplanted to the mid-twentieth century and the center of post-war Europe.

I tried to guess what those people from the 1940s would have felt and seen around them. I'd catch myself looking closely at buildings and wondering whether they would have been there back then and whether they would have looked the same. Often, while walking in the English Garden, I would stop to look at the old trees, especially the war-scarred ones, picturing them growing in this park even then, and reflecting that Petrov, Kosach, Shevelov, and Kostiuk would have walked beneath them. Seeing strong, beautiful young men and women swimming in the Isar reminded me of Shevelov's story about the German scouts on a lake in Bavaria. I imagined the atmosphere of Munich mornings back then—the "music of a morning in Munich," as Shevelov described it: "the wooden rhythm of blinds being raised" in people's homes. Blinds remain a distinctive feature of Munich to this day.

They say you can never step into the same river twice, and today's immigrants are vastly different from those who fled World War II. Yet there is a common thread—the subjective experience, what Shevelov called being uprooted, losing your sense of place. I would call it being rooted out, as if your roots are suspended in the air. This idea is captured in Jacques Hnizdovsky's illustration for V. Domontovych's novel *Doctor Seraphicus*, another tale of rootlessness.

My book is about how trauma affects us across years and distances, and how literature and culture manifest trauma and respond to it. It is about conflicts and ruptures, resentment and intergenerational post-memory. I wrote it before 2013, but I am rewriting it in the fall of 2023, from within the war and within forced displacement. I write about the symbolic wounds caused by historical traumas, but in the war that is raging in Ukraine, imaginary and chronic traumas have become all too real and tangible. In short, we live in a transit world after Bucha.

October 2023

Bibliography

1. Agamben, Giorgio. "Svidetel [The witness]." *Sinii Divan*, no. 4 (2004): 177–204. http://krotov.info/library/01_a/aga/mben.htm.
2. Adorno, Theodor W. "Posle Osventsima [After Auschwitz]." In *Negativnaia dialektika* [Negative dialectics], 332–335. Translated by Petrenko, E. Moscow: Nauchnyi mir, 2003.
3. Ak47_416. "Maidan eto samyi bol'shoi performans za vsiu istoriiu ili byli bol'she?" *Otvet.mail.ru* (blog). 2014. Accessed August 19, 2025. https://otvet.mail.ru/question/165153241.
4. Aleksiievych, Svitlana. "Vy rozghornete tsiu knyzhku i ne zmozhete zakryty . . . [You will open this book and will not be able to close it . . .]" In *Litopys samovydtsiv. Deviat misiatsiv ukrainskoho sprotyvu* [Chronicle of eyewitnesses. Nine months of Ukrainian resistance], 3–4. Kyiv: Komora, 2014.
5. "Andrei Danilko: 'Serdiuchka'—simvol potentsii!" *NEWSmuz.com*. Last modified March 17, 2008. http://www.newsmusic.ru/news_3_10126.htm.
6. Andrukhovych, Yurii. "1984. 2014?" In *Yevromaidan. Khronika vidchuttiv* [Euromaidan. Chronicle of feelings], 20–22. Brusturiv: Dyskursus, 2014.
7. Andrukhovych, Yurii. "Erts-herts-perts." In *DezOriientatsiia na mistsevosti* [Disorientation on the ground], 5–14. Ivano-Frankivsk: Lileia-NV, 1999.
8. Andrukhovych, Yurii. "Chas i mistse, abo Moia ostannia terytoriia [Time and place, or My last territory]." In *DezOriientatsiia na mistsevosti* [Disorientation on the ground], 118–19. Ivano-Frankivsk: Lileia-NV, 1999.
9. Andrukhovych, Yurii. "Inodi ya sumuiu za Maidanom [Sometimes I miss the Maidan]." *Zbruch*. Last modified November 21, 2021. https://zbruc.eu/node/108848.
10. Andrukhovych, Yurii, and Andrzej Stasiuk. "Tsentralno-skhidna reviziia [Central-eastern revision]." In *Moia Yevropa. Dva esei pro naidyvnishu chastynu svitu* [My Europe. Two essays about the most wondrous part of the world], 69-127. Lviv: Klasyka, 2001.
11. Arendt, Hannah. *The Origins of Totalitarianism*. San Diego: Harcourt Brace Jovanovich, 1973.
12. Assmann, Aleida. *Cultural Memory and Western Civilization: Functions, Media, Archives*. Cambridge: Cambridge University Press, 2011.
13. Assmann, Jan. *Kul'turnaia pamiat'. Pis'mo, pamiat' o proshlom i politicheskaia identichnost' v vysokikh kul'turakh drevnosti* [Cultural memory. Writing, memory of the past and political identity in the high cultures of antiquity]. Translated by Mariya Sokol'skaya. Moscow: IASK, 2004.

14. Bazhal, Alina. "Mykhailo Brynykh, 'Elektronnyi plastylin', vydavnytstvo 'Fakt.'" *Dzerkalo tyzhnia*, no. 13 (692) (April 2008). https://zn.ua/ukr/ART/mihay-lo_brinih,_elektronniy_plastilin,_vidavnitstvo_fakt.htm.
15. Batenko, Taras. "Bunt i my. Nasha epokha [Revolt and us. Our epoch]." *Postup*, n.d. Accessed August 19, 2025. http://postup.brama.com/001005/164_1_1.html.
16. Bakhtin, Mikhail. "Dopolneniia i izmeneniia k 'Rable' [Additions and changes to 'Rabelais']." *Voprosy filosofii*, no. 1 (1992): 135–168[.
17. Belei, Les. "Khymernyi sotsrealizm Serhiia Zhadana [The whimsical socialist realism of Serhii Zhadan]." *Litaktsent*. Last modified October 29, 2010. http://litakcent.com/2010/09/27/dvi-recenziji-na-voroshylovhrad/.
18. Benjamin, Walter. "Mystetskyi tvir u dobu svoiei tekhnichnoi vidtvoriuvanosti [The work of art in the age of mechanical reproduction]." In *Valter Beniamin. Vybrane* [Walter Benjamin. Selected works], 53-98. Translated by Yurii Rybachuk. Lviv: Litopys, 2002.
19. Burke, Edmund. *A Philosophical Enquiry into the Origin of Our Ideas of the Sublime and Beautiful*. London: Routledge and Kegan Paul, 1958.
20. Biehlov, Volodymyr. "Chy mozhna pyshatysia Serdiuchkoiu? [Can one be proud of Serdiuchka?]" *JeyArt*, n.d. Accessed August 19, 2025. http://jeyart.com.ua/people/sub158.
21. Binswanger, Ludwig. "Ekstravagantnost [Extravagance]." In *Bytie v mire. Vvedenie v ekzistentsialnuiu psikhiatriiu* [Being in the world. Introduction to existential psychiatry], 293-98. Translated by E. Surpina. Moscow: KSP+Iuventa, 1999.
22. Bilozir, Oksana. "Virka Serdiuchka—tse ne dukh nashoho narodu." ForUm. Last modified March 15, 2007. http://ua.for-ua.com/interview/2007/03/15/090549.html.
23. Baudrillard, Jean. *The Transparency of Evil: Essays on Extreme Phenomena*. Brooklyn: Verso, 1993.
24. Bodriiar, Zhan. "Kytaiskyi syndrom [Chinese syndrome]." In *Symuliakry i symuliatsiia* [Simulacra and simulation], 79-87. Translated by V. Khovkhun. Kyiv: Osnovy, 2004.
25. Bodriiar, Zhan. "Pro nihilizm [On nihilism]." In *Symuliakry i symuliatsiia* [Simulacra and simulation], [page range]. Translated by V. Khovkhun. Kyiv: Osnovy, 2004.
26. Bondar, Ihor. "Zhyttia v ZhZh." *Chetver*, no. 28 (November 2007). http://chetNver.com.ua/n28/01.html.
27. Bondar-Tereshchenko, Ihor. "Oksamyt Ukrainy." *Yi*, no. 34 (2004). http://www.ji.lviv.ua/n34texts/ibt.htm.
28. Brynykh, Mykhailo. *Elektronnyi plastylin*. Kyiv: Fakt, 2007.
29. Volnova, Svitlana. "Maidan sobral intelligentnykh romantikov." Viva! Last modified December 20, 2013. http://viva.ua/lifestar/news/24730-svetlana-voljnowva-maydan-sobral-intelligentnih-romantikov.html.
30. Wolff, Larry. *Inventing Eastern Europe: The Map of Civilization on the Mind of the Enlightenment*. Redwood City: Stanford University Press, 1994.

31. Honchar, Oles. "Vytiaz molodoi ukrainskoi poezii [Knight of young Ukrainian poetry]." In *Vasyl Symonenko. Poezii* [Vasyl Symonenko. Poetry], p. 3-8. Kyiv: Radianskyi pysmennyk, 1984.
32. Horbachov, Mykhailo. "Chornobylskyi perelom [The Chernobyl turning point]." *Den*, no. 65 (April 2006).
33. Gordon, Dmitrii. "Esli by Pugacheva predlozhila mne, kak Galkinu: 'Davai v reklamnykh tseliakh razduem istoriiu', ia by v etom ne uchastvoval, ne smog. Ia ne takoi, mne stydno! [If Pugacheva had offered me, like to Galkin: 'Let's blow up a story for advertising purposes', I would not have participated, I could not. I'm not like that, I'm ashamed!]" *Gordon: Geroi smutnogo vremeni* [Gordon: Heroes of troubled times]. Last modified 2002. https://www.gordon.com.ua/books/heroes/danilko/.
34. Hrabovych, Hryhorii. *Shevchenko yak mifotvorets. Semantyka symvoliv u tvorchosti poeta* [Shevchenko as myth-maker. Semantics of symbols in the poet's work]. Kyiv: Radianskyi pysmennyk, 1991.
35. Hrabovskyi, Serhii. "'Skysle moloko' Andriia Danylka ['Sour milk' of Andrii Danylko]." *Detektor media*. Last modified May 15, 2007. https://detector.media/kritika/article/8871/2007-05-15-skysle-moloko-andriya-danylka/.
36. Hrytsak, Yaroslav. "Revoliutsiia tsinnostei [Revolution of values]." *Ukrainska pravda*. Last modified November 7, 2014. http://life.pravda.com.ua/socie4 ty/2014/11/7/183467/.
37. Hrytsak, Yaroslav. "Shcho zalyshylosia pislia Pomaranchevoi revoliutsii? [What remained after the Orange Revolution?]" *Istorychna pravda*. Last modified October 18, 2010. https://www.istpravda.com.ua/articles/2010/10/18/559/.
38. Hrytsenko, Oleksandr. "Vierka Serdiuchka yak dzerkalo kulturnoi transformatsii [Vierka Serdiuchka as a mirror of cultural transformation]." *Izbornyk*. n.d. http://litopys.org.ua/heroes/hero15.htm.
39. Hundorova, Tamara. "'Kotliarevshchyna': kolonialnyi kitch ['Kotliarevshchyna': colonial kitsch]." In *Kitch i literatura. Travestii* [Kitsch and literature. Travesties], 92–122. Kyiv: Fakt, 2008.
40. Hundorova, Tamara. *Femina melancholica. Stat i kultura v gendernii utopii Olhy Kobylianskoi* [Femina melancholica. Gender and culture in the gender utopia of Olha Kobylianska]. Kyiv: Krytyka, 2002.
41. Hundorova, Tamara. *Lesia Ukrainka. Knyhy Syvilly* [Lesia Ukrainka. Books of the Sibyl]. Kharkiv: Vivat, 2023.
42. Hundorova, Tamara. *Pisliachornobylska biblioteka: Ukrainskyi literaturnyi postmodernizm. Rozvidka z komentariamy iz "kintsia postmodernu"* [Post-Chernobyl library: Ukrainian literary postmodernism. An exploration with commentary from "the end of postmodernism"]. Kyiv: Krytyka, 2013.
43. Hutsuliak, M. "Chornobylska trahediia—navichno v pamiati narodu [The Chernobyl tragedy—forever in the memory of the people]." *Kosiv*. Last modified December 25, 2008. http://kosivart.if.ua/2008/12/25/821.

44. "Danilko Andrii Mykhailovych." *Internet-vydannia "Poltavshchyna"*. Last modified November 3, 2010. https://poltava.to/dossier/31/.
45. Danilko, Andrii. "'V detstve ia khotel byt vrachom ili sviashchennikom' ['In childhood I wanted to be a doctor or a priest']." *Internet-vydannia "Poltavshchyna"*. Last modified December 13, 2009. http://www.poltava.pl.ua/news/236.
46. "Danylko: Serdiuchka ne maie analohiv [Danylko: Serdiuchka has no analogues]." *Tabloid*. Last modified January 16, 2012. https://tabloid.pravda.com.ua/news/4f13fb152d96d/.
47. Datsiuk, Serhii. "Chto takoe Maidan? [What is Maidan?]" *Ukrainska pravda*. Last modified February 20, 2014. http://blogs.pravda.com.ua/authors/dat-suk/5305cb8896062.
48. Deineka, Artemii. "Radykalna utopiia Dony Harvei: vid kiborhiv do khtonichnykh mohutnostei [Donna Haraway's radical utopia: from cyborgs to chthonic powers]." *Svoie*. n.d. https://svoye.wordpress.com/2016/10/30/%D1%80%D0%B0%D0%B4%D0%B8%D0%BA%D0%B0%D0%BB%D1%8C%D0%BD%D0%B0-%D1%83%D1%82%D0%BE%D0%BF%D1%96%D1%8F-%D0%B4%D0%BE%D0%B-D%D0%B8-%D0%B3%D0%B0%D1%80%D0%B2%D0%B5%D0%B9/.
49. Deresh, Liubko. *Kult*. Lviv: Kalvariia, 2004.
50. Dzhud. "O gore, radosti i razumnykh liudiakh [About grief, joy and reasonable people]." *S.T.A.L.K.E.R. Shadow of Chernobyl*. Last modified July 27, 2007. http://stalker-portal.ru/page.php?al=alias2274.
51. Dolgoprudnyĭ. "Moskva—Kyiv—Chornobyl—Pripiat—Moskva." n.d. http://pripyat.com/people-and-fates/dolgoprudnyi-moskva-kiev-chernobyl-pripyat-moskva.html.
52. Donii, Oles. *Pokolinnia oksamytovoi revoliutsii*. Kyiv: Smoloskyp, 1999.
53. Donii, Oles. "Smert shistdesiatnykiv." *Postup*. n.d. http://postup.brama.com/010209/23_2_3.html.
54. Donchenko, O., O. Zlobina, and V. Tykhonovych. "Chornobylskyi syndrom: sotsialno-psykholohichnyi analiz." *Sotsialni naslidky Chornobylskoi katastrofy: Rezult. sotsioloh. doslidzhen 1986–1995 rr*, 1996.
55. Dorozhkina, Polina. "Serdiuchka storonitsia Rossii." *Ytro.ru*. Last modified May 25, 2018. https://utro.ru/showbiz/2018/05/25/1361959.shtml.
56. Dorosh, Maryna. "Taras Liutyi: Yakshcho my ne osmyslymo radiansku epokhu, istoriia dali ne rukhatymetsia." detektor media. Last modified November 18, 2014. http://osvita.mediasapiens.ua/trends/1411978127/taras_lyutiy_yakscho_mi_ne_osmislimo_ radyansku_epokhu_istoriya_dali_ne_rukhatimetsya.
57. Arker, M. "Ekstremist z Yevromaidanu dorvavsia do pianino." *YouTube*. January 26, 2014. https://www.youtube.com/ watch?v=1JBjOe7B27k.
58. Yehorova, Viktoriia. "Andrii Danylko vidmovyvsia vid premii YUNA." tochka.net. Last modified January 16, 2012. https://glamurchik.tochka.net/ua/201426-andrey-danilko-otkazalsya-ot- premii-yuna/.

59. Serhy Yekelchyk, "What Is Ukrainian about Ukraine's Pop Culture?: The Strange Case of Verka Serduchka," *Canadian–American Slavic Studies* 44 (2010): 217–232.
60. Yermolenko, Volodymyr. "Pro te, shcho nasha stsena—tsilyi svit [About the fact that our stage is the whole world]." *Krytyka*. Last modified November 2013. http://krytyka.com/ua/community/blogs/pro-te-shcho-nasha-stsena-tsilyy-svit.
61. Zhadan, Serhii. *Anarchy in the Ukr.* Kharkiv: Folio, 2008.
62. Zhadan, Serhii. "Immigrant Song." *Krytyka* 14, no. 9–10 (September 2010): 35–39. https://krytyka.com/ua/articles/immigrant-song.
63. Zhadan, Serhii. *Big Mak*. Kyiv: Krytyka, 2003.
64. Zhadan, Serhii. *Voroshilovgrad*. Translated by Reilly Costigan-Humes and Isaac Stackhouse Wheeler. Dallas: Deep Vellum Publishing, 2016. E-book.
65. Zhadan, Serhii. *Depeche Mode*. Translated by Reilly Costigan-Humes and Isaac Stackhouse Wheeler. London: Glagoslav Publications, 2018. E-book.
66. Zhadan, Serhii. "Pro spilne mizh riznymy Zakhodom ta Skhodom [About what is common between the different West and East]." In *Yevromaidan. Khronika vidchuttiv* [Euromaidan. Chronicle of feelings], 100-102. Brusturiv: Dyskursus, 2014.
67. Zhezhera, Vitalii. "'Dvotysiachnyky' miriaiut poeziiu kilohramamy ['Two-thousanders' measure poetry in kilograms]." *Hazeta po-ukrainsky*. Last modified February 19, 2008. http://gazeta.ua/index.php?id=209675&eid=555.
68. Zherebkin, Serhii. "'Mogut li ugnetennye?..', ili Ukrainskii postkolonialnyi feminizm mezhdu Zh.-P. Sartrom i F. Fanonom ['Can the oppressed speak?..', or Ukrainian postcolonial feminism between J.-P. Sartre and F. Fanon]." *Gendernye issledovaniia* [Gender studies], no. 17 (January 2008): 149–169. http://kcgs.net.ua/gurnal/17/14.pdf.
69. Žižek, Slavoj. *Vozvyshennyi ob"ekt ideologii* [The sublime object of ideology]. Translated by Vladyslav Sofronov. Moscow: Khudozhestvennyi zhurnal, 1999.
70. Zabuzhko, Oksana. *Kazka pro kalynovu sopilku* [The tale of the guelder rose pipe]. Kyiv: Fakt, 2000.
71. Zabuzhko, Oksana S. *The Museum of Abandoned Secrets*. Translated by Nina Shevchuk-Murray. Seattle: Amazon Crossing, 2012. Kindle edition.
72. Zabuzhko, Oksana S. *Fieldwork in Ukrainian Sex*. Translated by Halyna Hryn. Seattle: Amazon Crossing, 2011. Kindle edition.
73. Zahakailo, Oksana. "Poeziia i proza Yevromaidanu [Poetry and prose of Euromaidan]." *Dzerkalo tyzhnia*. Last modified December 6, 2013. https://zn.ua/ukr/ART/poeziya-i-proza-yevromaydanu-_.html.
74. Zemlianska, Alina, and O. Strilets. "Trahichnyi obraz ukrainskoi molodi u romani S. Zhadana 'Voroshylovhrad' [The tragic image of Ukrainian youth in S. Zhadan's novel 'Voroshylovhrad']." *Naukovi zapysky Kharkivskoho natsionalnoho pedahohichnoho universytetu imeni H. S. Skovorody. Literaturoznavstvo* [Scientific notes of H. S. Skovoroda Kharkiv National Pedagogical University.

Literary studies] 1, no. 95 (2020): 114–116. https://www.researchgate.net/pub2lication/321779934_Tragicnij_obraz_ukrainskoi_molodi_u_romani_S_Zadana_Vorosilovgrad.

75. Ivanova, V. A., and V. N. Shubkin. "Struktura strakhov i trevog v Rossii i na Ukraine [Structure of fears and anxieties in Russia and Ukraine]." *Mir Rossii* [The world of Russia], no. 1–2 (1998): 151–166. http://ecsocman.hse.ru/data/532/989/1219/1999_n1x2c2_p151-166.pdf.

76. Izdryk. *Votstsek & votstsekurhiia*. Lviv: Kalvariia, 2002.

77. "Interaktyvnyi vystavkovyi proekt 'TVORCHIST SVOBODY: (r)evoliutsiina kultura Maidanu' [Interactive exhibition project 'CREATIVITY OF FREEDOM: (r)evolutionary culture of Maidan']." *Muzei Ivana Honchara*. n.d. https://old.honchar.org.ua/events/interaktyvnyj-vystavkovyj-proekt-tvorchist-svobody-revolyutsijna-kultura-majdanu/.

78. Kamysh, Markiian. *Oformliandiia, abo Prohulianka v Zonu* [Stalkerland, or A walk in the Zone]. Kyiv: Nora-Druk, 2015.

79. Kamysh, Markiian. "Plavannia sered chornobylskykh bolit bulo chymos na zrazok kolumbovoi mandrivky [Swimming among Chernobyl swamps was something like Columbus's journey]." *Vikna*, December 2015. http://vikna.if.ua/news/category/culture/2015/12/21/46336/view.

80. Camus, Albert. "Buntivna liudyna [The rebel]." In *Alber Kamiu. Vybrani tvory: u 3 t* [Albert Camus. Selected works: in 3 volumes], 133–144. Translated by Oleh Zhypansky. Kharkiv: Folio, 1997.

81. Karpa, Irena. *50 khvylyn travy [50 minutes of grass]* [*Koly pomre tvoia krasa* (When your beauty dies)]. Kharkiv: Folio, 2007.

82. Kirshbaum, Genrikh. "Konferentsiia 'Vnutrenniaia kolonizatsiia v Rossii' [Conference 'Internal colonization in Russia']." *Zhurnalnyi zal*. n.d. http://magazines.russ.ru/nlo/2010/105/ge46.html.

83. Klymenko, Valentyna. "Hirkyi 'mykolaichyk' vid Liny Kostenko [Bitter 'little Nicholas' from Lina Kostenko]." *Ukraina moloda*, no. 238 (December 2010). http://www.umoloda.kiev.ua/number/1805/164/64070/.

84. "Klip uchastnika (Obraz) [Participant clip (Image)]." n.d. http://pripyat.com/video.

85. Kononenko, Yevheniia. *Bez muzhyka* [Without a man]. Lviv: Kalvariia, 2005.

86. Conrad, Joseph. "Geografiia i nekotorye issledovateli [Geography and some explorers]." In *Izbrannoe: v 2 t* [Selected works: in 2 volumes], 652–670. Translated by Alexandra Krivtsova. Moscow: GIKHL, 1959.

87. Kostenko, Lina. *Zapysky ukrainskoho samashedsheho* [Notes of a Ukrainian madman]. Kyiv: A-ba-ba-ha-la-ma-ha, 2010.

88. Kostenko, Lina. "Ukraina yak zhertva i chynnyk hlobalizatsii katastrof [Ukraine as victim and factor of globalization of catastrophes]." *Den*, no. 76 (April 2003). http://ukrlife.org/main/evshan/kostenko_l.htm.

89. Kostiuk, Vasyl. "Dyskurs nenavysti v obolontsi pornohlamuru [Discourse of hatred in the shell of pornoglamour]." *Krytyka* 14, no. 9–10 (September 2010): 42-43. https://krytyka.com/ua/articles/dyskurs-nenavysty-v-obolontsi-port noglamuru.
90. Kotyk-Chubinska, Mariia. "Dorozhni znaky do Voroshylovhrada [Road signs to Voroshylovhrad]." *Litaktsent*. Last modified September 27, 2010. http://litakfi cent.com/2010/09/27/dvi-recenziji-na-voroshylovhrad.
91. Kotsarev, Oleh. "Voroshylovhrad: 'livyi roman'? Ale liubymo my yoho ne za tse! [Voroshylovhrad: 'left novel'? But we love it not for that!]" *Texty.org*. Last modified April 20, 2011. https://texty.org.ua/articles/28530/Voroshylovgrad_ livyj_roman_Ale_lubymo_my_jogo-28530/.
92. Kraliuk, Petro. "Bez 'kulturnykh kompleksiv' [Without 'cultural complexes']." *Den*, no. 16 (2004).
93. "Kultura tsyhan [Roma culture]." n.d. http://4ua.co.ua/moscow/yb3ad68a4d 43b89521206c37_1.html.
94. Kuryk, Mykhailo. "Chornobyl dushi nashoi. Ukraintsiam potribna ekolohiia svidomosti [Chernobyl of our soul. Ukrainians need an ecology of consciousness]." *Den*, no. 75 (April 2009). http://www.day.kiev.ua/273696/.
95. Lauda, Liera. "'Irena Karpa—literaturoiu navit ne pakhne...' ['Irena Karpa— doesn't even smell like literature...']" *Khai Vei*. Last modified December 23, 2005. http://h.ua/content/about/.
96. Lemarshand, Frederik. *Topos Chornobylia* [Topos of Chernobyl]. Kyiv: Dukh i Litera, 2001.
97. Lyotard, Jean-François. "Zametka o smyslakh 'post' [Note on the meanings of 'post']." *Inostrannaia literatura* [Foreign literature], no. 1 (1994): 54–66.
98. Lipovetsky, Mark, and Aleksandr Etkind. "Novoe literaturnoe obozrenie [New literary review]." *NLO* [*Novoe literaturnoe obozrenie*], no. 4 (2008): 291–300. http://magazines.russ.ru/nlo/2008/94/li17.html.
99. Minakov, Mykhailo. "Maidan stav chastynoiu suchasnoi politychnoi kultury Ukrainy [Maidan became part of contemporary political culture of Ukraine]." Interview by Yevheniia Syzontova. *Dialog.ua*. Last modified February 28, 2014. http://dialogs.org.ua/ru/dialog/page160-2477.html.
100. Malaniuk, Yevhen. *Poezii v odnomu tomi* [Poetry in one volume]. New York: NTSh and UVAN, 1954.
101. Slavinska, Iryna. "Tania Maliarchuk: 'Ia peretvoriuiusia na fanatku luzeriv' [Tania Maliarchuk: 'I am turning into a fan of losers']." *Ukrainska pravda*. Last modified September 8, 2008. https://life.pravda.com.ua/society/2008/09/08/7802/.
102. Afric_Dymon. "Manifest anty-Vierka Serdiuchka [Manifesto anti-Vierka Serdiuchka]." *LiveJournal*. Last modified March 20, 2007. http://afric-dymon. livejournal.com/28455.html?thread=35623.

103. Makhun, Serhii. "Lina Kostenko: 'Poidte tudy, de vmerla Ukraina' [Lina Kostenko: 'Go there where Ukraine died']." *Dzerkalo tyzhnia*, no. 44 (2005). http://dt.ua/SOCIETY/lina_kostenko_poyidte_tudi,_de_vmerla_ukrayina-45094.htm.
104. Menninghaus, Winfried. "Mezhdu podchineniem i soprotivleniem: Sila i nasilie v teoriiakh vozvyshennogo [Between submission and resistance: Force and violence in theories of the sublime]." In *Nemetskoe filosofskoe literaturovedenie nashikh dnei. Antologiia* [German philosophical literary studies of our days. Anthology], 268–290. Translated by Marina Bobrik. St. Petersburg: Izdatelstvo S.-Peterburskogo universiteta, 2001.
105. Mimandusova, G. I., Iu. A. Privalov, and Iu. I. Saenko. "Sotsialnyi monitoring postchernobylskoi situatsii [Social monitoring of the post-Chernobyl situation]." *Sotsiologiia katastrof* [Sociology of catastrophes], 1999: 201–214. http://ecsocman.hse.ru/data/414/669/1216/015_Sotsiologiya_katastrof.pdf.
106. Mykhailovych, Dragoslav. *Koly tsvily harbuzy* [When watermelons bloomed]. Kyiv: Fakt, 2008.
107. Muzychenko, Yaroslava. "Volodymyr Viatrovych: maidan stav antyradianskym povstanniam [Volodymyr Viatrovych: Maidan became an anti-Soviet uprising]." *Ukraina moloda*, April 2014. http://www.umoloda.kiev.ua/numd ber/2445/222/86888/.
108. Naumenko, Oleksandr-Nestor. "Vozvrashchenie v ad. Chernobyl: kinodokumenty epokhi glazami rezhissera i operatora [Return to hell. Chernobyl: film documents of the era through the eyes of director and cameraman]." *Zerkalo nedeli* [Mirror of the week], no. 15 (April 2009). http://zn.ua/SOCIETY/vozvraschenie_v_ad__chernobyl_kinodokumenty_epohi_glazami_rezhissera_i_operatora-56740.html.
109. Nikonov, Hryhorii. "Teatr boiovykh dii [Theater of military operations]." *Komentari: Cholovichi ihry* [Comments: Men's games] 3, no. 387 (2014): 4-5.
110. Nietzsche, Friedrich. *On the Genealogy of Morals*. London: Penguin UK, 2013.
111. Pahutiak, Halyna. *Zapysky Biloho Ptashka* [Notes of the White Bird]. Kyiv: Ukrainskyi pysmennyk, 1999.
112. Podoroga, Valerii. *Fenomenologiia tela. Vvedenie v filosofskuiu antropologiiu: materialy lektsionnykh kursov 1992–1994 gg* [Phenomenology of the body. Introduction to philosophical anthropology: materials of lecture courses 1992–1994]. Moscow: Ad Marginem, 1995.
113. Potapenko, Ya. "Spryiniattia Yevromaidanu v suchasnomu ukrainskomu informatsiinomu prostori [Perception of Euromaidan in contemporary Ukrainian information space]." *Visnyk Pereiaslavshchyny* [Herald of Pereiaslav region], November 2015. http://visnik-press.com.ua/?p=44064.
114. *Programma sovmestnoi deiatelnosti po provedeniiu posledstvii chernobylskoi katastrofy v ramkakh Soiuznogo gosudarstva na 2006–2010 gody* [Program of joint activities to address the consequences of the Chernobyl disaster within the framework of the Union State for 2006–2010]. Minsk, 2007.

115. Prokhasko, Taras. "Kozhnomu svoie [To each his own]." In *Yevromaidan. Khronika vidchuttiv* [Euromaidan. Chronicle of feelings], 19-21. Brusturiv: Dyskursus, 2014.
116. Prokhasko, Taras. "Oznaky zrilosti [Signs of maturity]." In *Yevromaidan. Khronika vidchuttiv* [Euromaidan. Chronicle of feelings], 13-14. Brusturiv: Dyskursus, 2014.
117. Prokhasko, Taras. "Svitlo i tin [Light and shadow]." In *Yevromaidan. Khronika vidchuttiv* [Euromaidan. Chronicle of feelings], 21-23. Brusturiv: Dyskursus, 2014.
118. Pukivskyi, Yurii. "Illia Riepin 'Zaporozhtsi pyshut lysta turetskomu sultanovi' [Ilya Repin 'Cossacks writing a letter to the Turkish Sultan']." *Lokalna istoriia* [Local history]. Last modified April 13, 2021. https://localhistory.org.ua/rubrics/painting/illia-riepin-zaporozhtsi-pishut-lista-turetskomu-sultanovi/.
119. "Radioaktivnyi ogon'. Pochemu opyt Chernobylia stavit pod somnenie nashu kartinu mira [Radioactive fire. Why the Chernobyl experience calls into question our picture of the world]." *Lettre international*, no. 60 (2003). https://alexievich.info/wp-content/uploads/articlesDialog.pdf.
120. Rakhmanin, Serhii. "Vona superzirka, ale yoho malo khto znaie. Providnytsia Vierka Serdiuchka maizhe zatmaruje sutnist samoho avtora. Khto vin naspravdi? [She is a superstar, but few people know him. The leading lady Vierka Serdiuchka almost overshadows the essence of the author himself. Who is he really?]" *Radio Svoboda*. Last modified June 23, 2007. http://www.radiosvoboda.org/content/article/965700.html.
121. Roy, Arundhati. *Boh dribnits* [The God of Small Things]. Translated by Andrii Masliukh. Lviv: Vydavnytstvo Staroho Leva, 2018.
122. Rüsen, Jörn. *Novi shliakhy istorychnoho myslennia* [New paths of historical thinking]. Translated by Volodymyr Kamianets. Lviv: Litopys, 2010.
123. Riabchuk, Mykola. "Za ogozheiu Metternikhovoho sadu [Behind the fence of Metternich's garden]." *Ji: Journal of the Institute*. https://www.ji.lviv.ua/n13texts/riabchuk.htm.
124. Saienko, Yurii. "Sotsialno-psykholohichnyi slid Chornobylia [Social-psychological trace of Chernobyl]." In *Sotsialni naslidky Chornobylskoi katastrofy. Rezultaty sotsiolohichnykh doslidzhen 1986–1995 rr* [Social consequences of the Chernobyl disaster. Results of sociological research 1986–1995], 87-93. Kharkiv: Folio, 1996.
125. Saienko, Yurii, and Yurii Privalov. "Zhyttievi tsinnosti naselennia, poterpiloho vid avarii na ChAES, ta otsinka shansiv yikh realizatsii u postchornobylskyi period [Life values of the population affected by the ChNPP accident and assessment of chances for their realization in the post-Chernobyl period]." In *Sotsialni naslidky Chornobylskoi katastrofy. Rezultaty sotsiolohichnykh doslidzhen 1986–1995 rr* [Social consequences of the Chernobyl disaster. Results of sociological research 1986–1995], [PAGE RANGE]. Kharkiv: Folio, 1996.
126. Said, Edward. *Kultura y imperializm* [Culture and imperialism]. Translated by [translator name]. Kyiv: Krytyka, 2007.

127. Sarna, Oleksandr. "Katastrofa kak zrelishche: reprezentatsiia sobytii 11 sentiabria 2001 g. v diskurse telenov estei [Catastrophe as spectacle: representation of the events of September 11, 2001 in television news discourse]." In *Vizual'noe (kak) nasilie* [Visual (as) violence], 331–346. Vilnius: EGU, 2007.
128. "Serhii Zhadan: 'Voroshylovhrad' ne rypadie do dushi tym, khto upodobav 'Depesh Mod' [Serhii Zhadan: 'Voroshylovhrad' will not appeal to those who liked 'Depeche Mode']." *Hrechka*. Last modified September 23, 2010. https://gre4ka.info/kultura/111-68serhii-zhadan-voroshylovohrad-roman-pro-zakhyst-svoikh-pryntsypiv-vid-zovnishnoho-tysku/.
129. "Sytuatsiia postmodernizmu v Ukraini. Kruhlyi stil [The situation of postmodernism in Ukraine. Round table]." n.d. http://www.ktm.ukma.kiev.ua/2001/6/postmodern.html.
130. *Sled chornogo vetru. Vachima dziatsei* [Trail of the black wind. Through children's eyes]. Minsk: Beloruski sotsial'no-ekologichny soiuz "Charnobyl'", 1996.
131. Sorokin, P. A. *Chelovek. Tsivilizatsiia. Obshchestvo* [Man. Civilization. Society]. General editor, compiler and preface by A. Yu. Soiumonov. Translated from English. Moscow: Politizdat, 1992.
132. Sosland, Aleksandr. "Udovol'stvie ot apokalipsisa [Pleasure from the apocalypse]." http://www.ruthenia.ru/logos/number/2000_3/07.htm.
133. Stasiuk, Andrzej. "Korabelnyi shchodennyk [Ship's diary]." In *Moia Yevropa. Dva esei pro naidyvnishu chastynu svitu* [My Europe. Two essays about the most wondrous part of the world], by Andrzej Stasiuk and Yurii Andrukhovych, 7-67. Lviv: Klasyka, 2001.
134. Stasiuk, Andrzej. "Pered zapravkoiu [Before refueling]." In *Fado*, 82-87. Kyiv: Hrani-T, 2009.
135. Stepanets, Kirill. *Zapiski Chernobyl'skogo Nelegala* [Notes of a Chernobyl illegal]. Kyiv, 2014.
136. Stekh, Pavlo. "Skhid Serhiia Zhadana: pysmennyk rozmirkovuie pro dytynstvo v Starobilsku ta identychnist rehionu [Serhii Zhadan's East: the writer reflects on childhood in Starobilsk and regional identity]." *Svoi.City*. Last modified July 9, 2019. https://svoi.city/articles/36462/shid-sergiya-zhadana-pismennik-rozemirkovue-pro-ditinstvo-v-starobilsku-ta-identichnist-regionu.
137. Tarnavskyi, Yurii. "U ra na (tysiacha rokiv samotnosti) [U ra na (a thousand years of loneliness)]." In *Yikh nemaie. Poezii 1970–1999* [They are not there. Poetry 1970–1999], 220-30. Kyiv: Rodovid, 1999.
138. Tytorova, Aleksandra. "Aktory i muzykanty, zvychaino, potribni Maidanu, ale tse ne naiholovnishe, vpevnenyi Andrukhovych [Actors and musicians are certainly needed by Maidan, but that's not the most important thing, Andrukhovych is convinced]." *Dzerkalo tyzhnia*. Last modified December 28, 2013. https://dt.ua/UKRAINE/andruhovich-zasterig-maydan-vid-peretvorennya-na-karnaval-134809_.html.

139. Toper, Pavel. "Tragicheskoe v iskusstve XX veka [The tragic in twentieth-century art]." *Voprosy literatury* [Questions of literature], no. 2 (2000). http://magazines.russ.ru/voplit/2000/2/toper.html.
140. Trofymenko, Tetiana. "'Voroshylovhrad' zemnyi i nebesnyi ['Voroshylovhrad' earthly and heavenly]." *Zaxid.net*. n.d. http://zaxid.net/home/showSingleNews.do?voroshilovgrad_zemniy_i_nebesniy&objectId=1113793.
141. Tulupenko, Liliia. "Maidan yak kultura protestu [Maidan as a culture of protest]." *24 Kanal*. Last modified February 25, 2014. https://24tv.ua/maydan_yak_kul0 tura_protestu_n413494.
142. "Ukraintsy ne strashchatsya ustanovleniia diktatury i opasaiutsia bezrabotitsy [Ukrainians are not afraid of the establishment of dictatorship and fear unemployment]." *Podrobnosti* [Details]. Last modified August 19, 2011. http://podrobnosti.ua/society/2011/08/19/786773.html.
143. "Ukraintsy obespokoeny rabotoi AES [Ukrainians are concerned about the operation of nuclear power plants]." http://www.novostimira.com.ua/news_4843.html.
144. *Ukrainska dramaturhiia pershoi polovyny XIX st.: Malovidomi piesy* [Ukrainian drama of the first half of the 19th century: Little-known plays]. Kyiv: Derzhavne vydavnytstvo khudozhnoi literatury, 1958.
145. Ushkalov, Sashko. *BZhD. Crazynovel*. 2nd ed. Kyiv: Fakt, 2008.
146. Fanon, Frantz. *Hnani i holodni* [The wretched of the earth]. Translated by [translator name]. Kyiv: Vpered, 2016.
147. Fonda, P., and E. Iogan. "Razvitie psikhoanaliza v poslednie desiatiletiia [Development of psychoanalysis in recent decades]." In *Psikhoanaliz v razvitii* [Psychoanalysis in development], p. 128. Ekaterinburg: Delovaia kniga, 1998.
148. Franko, Ivan. "Batkivshchyna [Fatherland]." In *Zibrani tvory: u 50 t* [Collected works: in 50 volumes], vol. 21, *Opovidannia (1898–1904)* [Stories (1898–1904)], p. 391–423. Kyiv: Naukova dumka, 1979.
149. Freud, Sigmund. "Zhutkoe [The uncanny]." In *Khudozhnik i fantazirovanie* [The artist and fantasy], 265–281[. Translated by G. Baryshnikova and E. Smirnova. Moscow: Respublika, 1995.
150. Fukuyama, Francis. *Nashe postchelovecheskoe budushchee. Posledstviia biotekhnologicheskoi revoliutsii* [Our posthuman future. Consequences of the biotechnological revolution]. Translated by M. B. Levin. Moscow: AST, LIUKS, 2004. http://alt-future.narod.ru/Future/Fnpb/fukunpb.htm.
151. Khapaeva, D. R. "Tsena zabveniia: Rossiiskoe goticheskoe obshchestvo [The price of oblivion: Russian gothic society]." *Fond imeni D. S. Likhacheva* [D. S. Likhachev Foundation]. http://lfond.spb.ru/programs/likhachev/100/stenogrammi/hapaeva.html.
152. Hayles, N. Katherine. *Yak my staly postliudstvom. Virtualni tila v kibernetytsi, literaturi ta informatytsi* [How we became posthuman. Virtual bodies in cybernetics, literature and informatics]. Translated by E. Maricheva. Kyiv: Nika-Tsentr, 2002.

153. Khoma, N. M. "Sotsializuiuchyi vplyv aktsionizmu: mystetsko-politychnyi syntez v proektsii modeliuvannia politychnoi povedinky [Socializing influence of actionism: artistic-political synthesis in the projection of modeling political behavior]." *Aktualni problemy polityky* [Current problems of politics], no. 53 (2014): 366–373.
154. Khofman, T. *Literaturnye etnografii Ukrainy: proza posle 1991 goda* [Literary ethnographies of Ukraine: prose after 1991]. St. Petersburg: Aleteiia, 2016.
155. Tsyperdiuk, Ivan. "Vira [Faith]." In *Yevromaidan. Khronika vidchuttiv* [Euromaidan. Chronicle of feelings], by Taras Prokhasko, Ivan Tsyperdiuk, Yurii Andrukhovych, Serhii Zhadan, and Yurii Vynnychuk, 44. Brusturiv: Dyskursus, 2014.
156. Tsyperdiuk, Ivan. "Kulminatsiia [Culmination]." In *Yevromaidan. Khronika vidchuttiv* [Euromaidan. Chronicle of feelings], by Taras Prokhasko, Ivan Tsyperdiuk, Yurii Andrukhovych, Serhii Zhadan, and Yurii Vynnychuk, 49. Brusturiv: Dyskursus, 2014.
157. "Chego boiatsia ukraintsy? Rosta tsen, bezrabotitsy, zadolzhennosti [What are Ukrainians afraid of? Rising prices, unemployment, debt]." http://www.trust.ua/news/48801.html.
158. "'Chornobuildorf': startuvav novyi mizhnarodnyi opernyi proekt ['Chornobuildorf': a new international opera project has started]." https://artarsenal.in.ua/povidomlennya/chornobyldorf-startuvav-novyj-mizhnarodnyjopernyj-proyekt/.
159. *Chornobyl: rana i bil planety (Do 20-richchia avarii na Chornobylskii AES). Veb-bibliohrafichnyi pokazhchyk* [Chernobyl: the wound and pain of the planet (On the 20th anniversary of the Chernobyl NPP accident). Web-bibliographic index]. http://webcache.googleusercontent.com.
160. Scheler, Max. *Resentiment v strukture moralei* [Ressentiment in the structure of morals]. Translated from German by A. N. Malinkina. St. Petersburg: Universitetskaia kniga, 1999.
161. Shekhovtsov, Anton. "Ukrainska revoliutsiia ye yevropeiskoiu i natsionalnoiu [Ukrainian revolution is European and national]." *Radio Svoboda*. http://www.radiosvoboda.org/a/25203341.html.
162. Spengler, Oswald. *Zakat Evropy. Ocherki morfologii mirovoi istorii: v 2 t* [The decline of the West. Essays on the morphology of world history: in 2 volumes]. Vol. 1, *Geshtal't i deistvitel'nost'* [Form and actuality]. Translated by [translator name]. Moscow: Mysl', 1993.
163. Schulz, Bruno. "Tsynamonovi kramnyti [Cinnamon shops]." In *Tsynamonovi kramnyti. Sanatorii Pid Klepsydroiu* [Cinnamon shops. Sanatorium under the sign of the hourglass], 13–14. Translated by Andrii Pavlushynsky and Andrii Shkrabiuk. Lviv: Forum vydavtsiv, 2004.
164. Shuman, Efim. "Nemetskie kritiki o vostochnoukrainskom vesterne Sergeia Zhadana [German critics about Sergei Zhadan's Eastern Ukrainian western]." *Deutsche Welle*. Last modified February 14, 2013. https://p.dw.com/p/17Z9w.

165. Epshtein, Mikhail. "Zhutkoe i strannoe: O teoreticheskoi vstreche Z. Freida i V. Shklovskogo [The uncanny and the strange: On the theoretical meeting of Z. Freud and V. Shklovsky]." *Russkii Zhurnal* [Russian Journal], 2003. http://old.russ.ru/krug/razbor/20030314_ep.html.

166. Etkind, Aleksandr. "Russkaia literatura, XIX vek: Roman vnutrennei kolonizatsii [Russian literature, 19th century: A novel of internal colonization]." *Zhurnal'nyi zal* [Journal hall]. https://magazines.gorky.media/nlo/2003/1/russkaya-literatura-xix-vek-roman-vnutrennej-kolonizaczii.html.

167. Etkind, Aleksandr. "Fuko i tezis vnutrennei kolonizatsii: postkolonial'nyi vzgliad na sovetskoe proshloe [Foucault and the thesis of internal colonization: a postcolonial view of the Soviet past]." *Zhurnal'nyi zal* [Journal hall]. https://magazines.gorky.media/nlo/2001/3/fuko-i-tezis-vnutrennej-kolonizaczii.html.

168. "Ia duzhe zakompleksovana liudyna [I am a very complexed person]." *TSN*. Last modified July 20, 2011. https://tsn.ua/analitika/ya-duzhe-zakompleksovana-lyudina.html.

169. Ianchuk, Mykola. "Po yarmarku. Ukrainskyi vodevil na odnu diiu [At the fair. Ukrainian vaudeville in one act]." In *Ukrainskyi vodevil. XIX st* [Ukrainian vaudeville. 19th century], 135–150. Kyiv: Mystetstvo, 1965.

170. Iaroshinskaia, Alla. *Prestuplenie bez nakazaniia. Chernobyl' 20 let spustia* [Crime without punishment. Chernobyl 20 years later]. Moscow: Vremia, 2006.

171. Abrams, M. H. "Apocalypse: Theme and Variations." In *The Apocalypse in English Renaissance Thought and Literature: Patterns, Antecedents and Repercussions*, edited by C. A. Patrides and J. Wittreich, 342–368. Manchester: Manchester University Press, 1984.

172. Agamben, Giorgio. *Remnants of Auschwitz: The Witness and the Archive*. New York: Zone Books, 1999.

173. Alexander, Jeffrey C. "Cultural Pragmatics: Social Performance between Ritual and Strategy." In *Social Performance: Symbolic Action, Cultural Pragmatics and Ritual*, edited by J. Alexander, B. Giesen, and J. Mast, 29-97. London: Cambridge University Press, 2006.

174. Alexander, Jeffrey C. "From the Depths of Despair: Performance, Counterperformance, and 'September 11.'" In *Social Performance: Symbolic Action, Cultural Pragmatics and Ritual*, edited by J. Alexander, B. Giesen, and J. Mast, 375-430. London: Cambridge University Press, 2006.

175. Alexievich, Svetlana. *Voices from Chernobyl: The Oral History of a Nuclear Disaster*. Translated by Keith Gessen. New York: Picador, 2006.

176. Anderson, Mark D. *Disaster Writing: The Cultural Politics of Catastrophe in Latin America*. Charlottesville: University of Virginia Press, 2011.

177. Ankersmit, F. R. *Sublime Historical Experience*. Stanford: Stanford University Press, 2005.

178. Artaud, Antonin. *Selected Writings*. Edited by Susan Sontag. Translated by Helen Weaver. Berkeley: University of California Press, 1988.

179. Auslander, Philip. "The Performativity of Performance Documentation." *PAJ: A Journal of Performance and Art* 28, no. 3 (2006): 1–10.
180. Baudrillard, Jean. *The Illusion of the End*. Translated by Chris Turner. Stanford: Stanford University Press, 1994.
181. Bial, Henry, and Sara Brady, eds. *The Performance Studies Reader*. 3rd ed. London: Routledge, 2016.
182. Bilaniuk, Lada. *Contested Tongues: Language Politics and Cultural Correction in Ukraine*. Ithaca, NY: Cornell University Press, 2005.
183. Binswanger, Ludwig. "Extravagance, Perverseness, Manneristic Behaviour and Schizophrenia." In *The Clinical Roots of the Schizophrenia Concept*, translated by J. Cutting, edited by J. Cutting and M. Shephard, 83–88. Cambridge: Cambridge University Press, 1987.
184. Bourdieu, Pierre. *Photography: A Middle-Brow Art*. Stanford: Stanford University Press, 1990.
185. Bousher, Georgie, and Sarah French. "Postfeminist Pleasure and Politics: Moira Finucane and The Burlesque Hour." *Australasian Drama Studies* 58 (2011): 193–211.
186. Braidotti, Rosi. *The Posthuman*. Cambridge: Polity Press, 2013.
187. Brummond, J. "Liquidators, Chornobylets, and the Masonic Ekologists: Ukrainian Environmental Identities." *Oral History*, no. 61 (Spring 2000): 53–65.
188. Bushkovitch, Paul. "What is Russia? Russian National Identity and the State, 1500–1917." In *Culture, Nation and Identity: The Ukrainian-Russian Encounter, 1600–1945*, edited by A. Kappeler, Z. Kohut, F. Sysyn, and M. von Hagen, 9–24. Edmonton: CIUS, 2003.
189. Childs, Peter. *Modernism and Post-Colonial Literature and Empire, 1885–1930*. London: Continuum, 2007.
190. Curran, Angela. "Brecht's Criticisms of Aristotle's Aesthetics of Tragedy." *Journal of Aesthetics & Art Criticism* 59, no. 2 (2001): 167–184.
191. Debord, Guy. *The Society of the Spectacle*. Translated by Donald Nicholson-Smith. New York: Zone Books, 1995.
192. Derrida, Jacques. *The Ears of the Other: Otobiography, Transference, Translation*. Lincoln: University of Nebraska Press, 1988.
193. Drakulic, Slavenka. "Bosnia, or What Europe Means to Us." In *Café Europa: Life after Communism*, 107-113. New York: Penguin Books, 1996.
194. Fanon, Frantz. *A Dying Colonialism*. Translated by Haakon Chevalier. Introduction by Adolfo Gilly. New York: Grove Press, 1965.
195. Fanon, Frantz. "On National Culture." In *Literature in the Modern World: Critical Essays and Documents*, edited by Dennis Walden, 231–235. Oxford: Oxford University Press, 1990.
196. Ferguson, Frances. "Nuclear Sublime." *Diacritics* 14, no. 2 (1984): 4–10.
197. Fukuyama, Francis. *The End of History and the Last Man*. New York: Harper Perennial, 2006.

198. Gikandi, Simon. *Maps of Englishness: Writing Identity in the Culture of Colonialism.* New York: Columbia University Press, 1996.
199. Griesinger, Wilhelm. "Hypochondriasis and Melancholia." In *The Nature of Melancholy: From Aristotle to Kristeva*, edited by Jennifer Radden, 227–234. New York: Oxford University Press, 2000.
200. Haraway, Donna. "The Biopolitics of Postmodern Bodies: Determinations of Self in Immune System Discourse." In *Feminist Theory and the Body: A Reader*, edited by Janet Price and Margrit Shildrick, 203–214. New York: Routledge, 1999.
201. Hinnant, Charles H. "Schiller and the Political Sublime: Two Perspectives." *Criticism* 44, no. 2 (2002): 121–139.
202. Hirsch, Marianne. *The Generation of Postmemory: Writing and Visual Culture After the Holocaust.* New York: Columbia University Press, 2012.
203. Ian, Marcia. *Remembering the Phallic Mother: Psychoanalysis, Modernism, and the Fetish.* Ithaca: Cornell University Press, 1993.
204. Jameson, Fredric. "Modernism and Imperialism." In *Nationalism, Colonialism, and Literature*, edited by Terry Eagleton, Fredric Jameson, and Edward Said, [PAGE RANGE NEEDED]. Minneapolis: University of Minnesota Press, 1990.
205. Kappeler, Andreas. "Mazepintsy, Malorossy, Khokhly: Ukrainians in the Ethnic Hierarchy of the Russian Empire." In *Culture, Nation and Identity: The Ukrainian-Russian Encounters, 1600–1945*, edited by A. Kappeler, Z. Kohut, F. Sysyn, and M. von Hagen, 135-159. Edmonton: CIUS, 2003.
206. Kazanova, Yuliya. "'The Instinct of Resistance to Evil': Postmemory and the Ukrainian National Imaginary in Oksana Zabuzhko's Novel *The Museum of Abandoned Secrets*." *Memory Studies* 15, no. 2 (2021). https://journals.sagepub.com/doi/full/10.1177/17506980211044710.
207. Keats, Jonathon. "Apocalypse Made Easy." http://dir.salon.com/story/books/feature/2002/02/07/doomsday/index.html.
208. Kellner, Douglas. *Jean Baudrillard: From Marxism to Postmodernism and Beyond.* Stanford: Stanford University Press, 1989.
209. Kermode, Frank. *The Sense of an Ending: Studies in the Theory of Fiction.* Oxford: Oxford University Press, 1968.
210. Khineyko, Ilya. "The Little Russian: Verka Serduchka." http://ukraineanalysis.wordpress.com/2007/05/22/the-little-russian-verka-serduchka.
211. Kristeva, Julia. *Black Sun: Depression and Melancholia.* Translated by Leon S. Roudiez. New York: Columbia University Press, 1989.
212. Kroker, Arthur. *Hacking the Future: Stories for the Flesh-Eating 90s.* New York: St. Martin's Press, 1996.
213. Mannheim, Karl. "The Problem of Generations." In *Essays on the Sociology of Knowledge*, edited by Paul Kecskemeti, 276–320. London: Routledge, 1952.
214. marisa_t. "Maidan yak performans [Maidan as performance]." *LiveJournal*. Last modified December 17, 2013. https://marisa-t.livejournal.com/480580.html.

215. Matsunaga, Kyoko. *Post-Apocalyptic Vision and Survivance: Nuclear Writings in Native America and Japan*. Lincoln: University of Nebraska Press, 2006.
216. McAvinchey, Caoimhe, ed. *Performance and Community: Commentary and Case Studies*. London: Bloomsbury Methuen Drama, 2014.
217. McClintock, Anne. *Imperial Leather: Race, Gender and Sexuality in the Colonial Contest*. New York: Routledge, 1995.
218. "Michael Jackson: Kitsch Art." http://www.traffictetris.com/michael-jackson-kitsch-art/.
219. Nancy, Jean-Luc. "The Sublime Offering." In *Of the Sublime: Presence in Question*, translated by Jeffrey S. Librett, vii–x. Albany: State University of New York Press, 1993.
220. Norris, Christopher. "Versions of Apocalypse: Kant, Derrida, Foucault." In *Apocalypse Theory and the Ends of the World*, edited by Malcolm Bull, 227–249. Oxford: Blackwell, 1995.
221. Parker, Andrew, and Eve Kosofsky Sedgwick, eds. *Performativity and Performance*. New York: Routledge, 1995.
222. Polese, Abel, and Donnacha Ó Beacháin. "The Color Revolution Virus and Authoritarian Antidotes: Political Protest and Regime Counterattacks in Post-Communist Spaces." *Demokratizatsiya*, no. 2 (2011): 111–131.
223. Ricoeur, Paul. *Memory, History, Forgetting*. Translated by Kathleen Blamey and David Pellauer. Chicago: University of Chicago Press, 2004.
224. Rothe, Anne. *Popular Trauma Culture: Selling the Pain of Others in the Mass Media*. New Brunswick, NJ: Rutgers University Press, 2011.
225. Rushdie, Salman. *The Moor's Last Sigh*. New York: Vintage Books, 1997.
226. Schechner, Richard. *Performance Theory*. Revised and expanded ed. New York: Routledge, 2003.
227. Sharpe, Jenny. "Figures of Colonial Resistance." In *The Postcolonial Studies Reader*, edited by Bill Ashcroft, Gareth Griffiths, and Helen Tiffin, 99–103. London: Routledge, 1995.
228. Shcherbak, Iurii. *Chernobyl: A Documentary Story*. Translated by Ian Press. Edmonton: CIUS, 1989.
229. Myroslav Shkandrij, "The Shifting Object of Desire: The Poetry of Oleksandr Irvanets," *Canadian-American Slavic Studies* 44, no. 1–2 (2010): 67–81.
230. Shore, Marci. "The Bard of Eastern Ukraine, Where Things Are Falling Apart." *The New Yorker*. Last modified November 26, 2016. https://www.newyorker.com/books/page-turner/the-bard-of-eastern-ukraine-where-things-are-falling-apart.
231. Slemon, Stephen. "Unsettling the Empire: Resistance Theory for the Second World." In *The Postcolonial Studies Reader*, edited by Bill Ashcroft, Gareth Griffiths, and Helen Tiffin, 104–110. London: Routledge, 1995.
232. Snow, Peter. "Performing Society." *Thesis Eleven* 103, no. 1 (2010): 78–87.

233. Stephensen, Helene, and Mads Gram Henriksen. "Not Being Oneself: A Critical Perspective on 'Inauthenticity' in Schizophrenia." *Journal of Phenomenological Psychology* 8, no. 1 (2017): 63–82. https://www.researchgate.net/publication/317006094.
234. Strauss, William, and Neil Howe. *13th Gen: Abort, Retry, Ignore, Fail?* New York: Vintage Books, 1993.
235. Strauss, William, and Neil Howe. *Generations: The History of America's Future, 1584 to 2069.* New York: William Morrow, 1991.
236. Strauss, William, and Neil Howe. *Millennials Rising: The Next Great Generation.* New York: Vintage Books, 2000.
237. Strauss, William, and Neil Howe. *The Fourth Turning: An American Prophecy.* New York: Crown, 1997.
238. Tenbusch, Lynne G. "Resentment as a Defense against Skillful Vulnerability." *Other/Wise.* https://ifpe.wordpress.com/2017/03/30/resentment-as-a-defense-against-skillful-vulnerability/.
239. Turner, Victor W. *The Anthropology of Performance.* New York: PAJ Publications, 1986.
240. Weart, Spencer R. *Nuclear Fear: A History of Images.* Cambridge: Harvard University Press, 1988.
241. Weart, Spencer R. "Nuclear Fear 1987–2007: Has Anything Changed? Has Everything Changed?" In *Filling the Hole in the Nuclear Future: Art and Popular Culture Respond to the Bomb,* edited by Robert Jacobs, 229-65. Lanham, MD: Lexington Books, 2010.
242. Weibel, Peter, ed. *The Vienna Group: A Moment of Modernity 1954–1960: The Visual Works and Actions.* New York: Springer, 1997.
243. Widrich, Mechtild. "The Informative Public of Performance: A Study in Viennese Actionism." *TDR: The Drama Review* 57, no. 1 (2013): 137–151.
244. Žižek, Slavoj. *In Defense of Lost Causes.* London: Verso, 2008.

www.ingramcontent.com/pod-product-compliance
Lightning Source LLC
Chambersburg PA
CBHW071819230426
43670CB00013B/2507